YELLOW

PAINT

YELLOW PAINT

PAINT

LEARNING TO LIVE AGAIN

KAREN GOSLIN MSW

Copyright Notice

Yellow Paint: Learning to Live Again

For permission requests, write to the publisher:
Karen Goslin MSW, RSW
Social Worker and Psychotherapist
Karen Goslin & Associates
Toronto, ON M6C 2Y8
www.karenrsw.com
www.karengoslinspeaks.com

Library and Archives Canada Cataloguing in Publication
Goslin, Karen
Yellow Paint: Learning to Live Again / Karen Goslin.

ISBN:
978-1-0690684-5-3 Paperback
978-1-0690684-4-6 Hardcover
978-1-0690684-1-5 Electronic
978-1-0690684-0-8 Audio

1. Self-help books. 2. Personal growth. 3. Recovery from trauma.
Published by Karen Goslin & Associates
Printed in Canada

ACKNOWLEDGMENTS

I want to start by telling you that there would not even be Yellow Paint without the love, dedication, and commitment of my parents, Dwain and Sophie Goslin (Baba and Papa). The only reason Yellow Paint exists in the first place is because of them. You'll understand more about that later.

I also want to recognize that anonymously written within these pages are the brave, vulnerable clients I am honored to sit with every day, who share their pains and reach their triumphs. They prove that the resilience of the human spirit is possible, that there truly are ways of finding opportunity within crisis and banking strength from weakness.

I wish to thank those who agreed to be interviewed for this book and who shared heartfelt memories, including my parents, my brother Rick, my Uncle Larry, my cousin Jerry, my best friends, Donna and Susan, and my beautiful daughter Madeline. Their contributions filled in important details that helped pull the story together. The interviews were also a good reminder to me of how everyone has a story worth understanding and sharing. My Uncle Larry even concluded at the end of his interview, "Maybe, I should write a book, too!" Yes, indeed, he should!

I appreciate Beth Parker for her expertise and patience as she introduced me to the wild world of writing and editing. I am incredibly grateful for the collaboration of the entire 'Yellow Paint Team'. Angela McKenna of Omera Press, Neal Burstyn of NTB Creative, Judy Basso of Judy Basso Events, and Melanie Harvard of Harvard Ink. The final product reflects the deep commitment of what *Yellow Paint* means to all of us.

Finally, I acknowledge the boots on the ground, including Dr. Deborah Sinclair, Dr. Audrey Karlinsky, and Dr. Alison Bested, who over many years, provided me with life-changing guidance and direction. Honestly, I would not be anywhere near where I am today without them.

I dedicate this book to those of you who find yourselves in deafening, defeating darkness when giving up seems like the only choice. I couldn't write this book if I hadn't been there and found *my* way through. This book is your invitation to consider the way through for *you*—and a way *up* to a life that's been waiting for you the whole time, a life that is only found on the other side of darkness.

That's what this book is about.

I also dedicate this book to my daughter Madeline, whose idea it was to write this book in the first place. My true gift is that the legacy unveiled in these pages will paint her life forever and be passed onto her own children someday.

Finally, this book is dedicated to my grandma, whose sweet rose scent I can still smell, whose giggles I can still hear, whose love is still felt.

She would love this book.

PREFACE

This book is a **230-page** invitation.

Read these pages as an open invitation to you.

As humans, we share a common experience.

We get ourselves so twisted up in all kinds of trouble. So easily. Too easily.

Some of us figure it out.

I figured it out.

I thought that was worth sharing with you.

I thought it was worth inviting you to join a party where inspiration, strength, courage, healing, and glorious success were being served.

Where the music once played noisy lyrics of shame and loss and betrayal,

and then somehow raised its frequency to success and joy.

You see, I deeply believe in the human capacity for growth and change.

I know we get better when things are better.

But I believe we change even more when things are going badly.

That's what happened to me.

That's what happens to those I meet in therapy rooms.

In fact, I've become fierce with that knowledge, and it inspires me every day.

So, accept this invitation.

Get prepared to figure it out.

Own your journey.

Roll up your sleeves.

And get ready to paint!

CONTENTS

CHAPTER 1
YELLOW PAINT:
HITTING ROCK BOTTOM

I look inside myself

And see my heart is black

I see my red door

I must have it painted black

Maybe then, I'll fade away

And not have to face the facts

It's not easy facing up

When your whole world is black

(The Rolling Stones - Paint It Black, 1966)

I invite you to think about times you hit the bottom and how you dug yourself out.

The Bitch Is Back

I had become a complete bitch to live with. I was angry. I hated everything and everyone. I had spent years, literally years, telling everyone and anyone who made eye contact with me how angry I was. Then one day, I couldn't stand the sound of my own voice anymore. Like Forrest Gump, who ran down his driveway, then down the road, across the state, across the country, and back again—running until he left all his pain behind. And then, on a quiet, desolate road in the desert, he stopped, turned around, and walked himself home. I finally stopped running too. In the midst of agonizing despair, on a hot Friday afternoon in June, I stood on an empty driveway, alone. And everything changed.

How had I lost everything that mattered to me? How the hell did I get here? For what felt like the first time in my life, I didn't know where to go or what to do.

It felt like I'd been pulled down into some deep, black pool of quicksand made from blame and shame that seemed unbearable, and I was panicking. But of course, the more you scramble, the deeper you sink. And there was no doubt, *I was drowning*.

The fact is, my quicksand had been deepening for years, based on a seemingly unsuccessful search to find a place to belong. Don't get me wrong, I had grown up knowing I was safe and knowing my parents were dedicated to me. But they could be strict and struggled with the emotional communication I was yearning for. In addition, my brothers were close in age and frankly, didn't want anything to do with me. I struggled to fit in, so I felt alone for a long time. Even more importantly, my aloneness made me feel deeply unworthy, and insecure. Acting out from that place had created a bit of a train wreck in my life over many years. So, I was completely unprepared for what had faced me that day…

A bit of a backstory:

Thirteen years earlier, in May of 1989 at the age of 25, I wrongly concluded that I had singularly fucked up what would come to be my most meaningful relationship. I had been dating someone who brought everything to the table: looks, intelligence, ambition, family, humour, social life. He really was the true love of my life—a love I still dream about. Despite stability growing up, my deeper insecurities and unworthiness intersected with his need for control. We were both too young, unaware, and immature to figure it out so our relationship burned out from endless clashes. Although relieved when it was finally over, and finding ways to push through, the breakup had devastated me.

I remember crashing at my parents' home that spring, literally collapsing with uncontrollable tears onto their kitchen table. My dad, sitting across from me, was obviously worried, but mostly perplexed about what to do with me. The fact is, my parents loved me with acts of service and those *would* serve me for many years to come, some in the most profound ways possible. But in that particular moment I felt alone. I just needed a good hug. Without a blink of an eye, he spread out multiple paint strips of the new 1990 exterior car tints, coming out later in the year, across the table in front of me. I was expected to choose a color for the next Chrysler vehicle he was going to lease me. I couldn't believe how he shifted gears so quickly. I remember slowing my tears and focusing on the choices. Maybe a red car would be fun?

During that time, and quite unusually for me, I compartmentalized my heavy emotions, just like my father did. This was probably due to the fact that I was embarking on a new chapter in my career that was extremely important to me. I had just been accepted into the Master of Social Work program at the University of Toronto. I pushed the devastation down and away from me. Instead, I dove into the hard work of my studies, locking myself for ten months into my 300-square-foot bachelor apartment at the then epicentre of Toronto's "young and eligible" neighbourhood at Yonge and Eglinton. We called the building *Friendship Towers*. There were no less than half a dozen of us friends living at any one time in the ten-floor, budget high-rise, which was a lot of fun! I pumped out essay after essay on the electronic typewriter my parents had given me, graduated in the top one percent of my class, and was immediately invited into the doctorate program at the University of Toronto, which I never accepted.

When the intense focus of my studies ended the following summer of 1990, that compartment of pain blasted open. I plunged deeply into shame, dating bad boys and sleeping around *a lot*, all to confirm how unworthy I was. After all, what I thought would be my forever relationship had failed. It was pure luck that during the high-risk lifestyle I led for several months, I was never assaulted, at least not physically or sexually. I actually consider that time in my life more as a *self*-assault, as I punished myself for not feeling deserving of his commitment. When I ran out of steam, I decided to take my recent academic achievement and work on my career, which would come to pay off in ways I never imagined back then.

I tried therapy. The counselling gave me a place to tell my story, which I badly needed. But it did not offer the structured grief therapy which, many years later, I would come to learn about, and offer my own clients. This approach goes beyond listening, beyond letting go. It moves you from the loss toward identifying and healing deeper wounds, ultimately breaking dating patterns for the future. Repairing what you couldn't while in the relationship, but is still possible after the relationship ends. And that is power.

After many more years, and heartbreaks, I eventually completed my own grief work. That doesn't stop me from wondering how my life would have been different if I'd made a fuller emotional repair back in 1989. Why didn't I figure out how to get out of my own way faster, instead of getting increasingly more hurt in my life? Didn't I *want* to be happier, sooner? Looking back, it seemed I had more to go through, much more before that was even possible. But, why?

At some point, I began believing that we need big challenges from our *wounded self* (a concept fully explained in Chapter 10) before we change our sabotaging ways of coping. Significantly painful experiences invite us to grow. Experiences that have the potential to either damage down or level up what we believe about ourselves, others, life, and love. Key turning points that we either use to confirm our pre-existing negative beliefs from previous unresolved pain, or to discover unconditional love for ourselves, building on previous experiences of trust and worthiness. That within the problems are compelling opportunities to not only resist damage to our beliefs, but more importantly to clarify what is actually happening toward greater strength. A Chinese Proverb states: "A crisis is an opportunity that rides a dangerous wind" (Wass, 2020).

This mental and emotional clarity makes important suggestions toward more accurate important beliefs not possible before. But, the tricky parts are that 1) when the primary problems we encounter are in childhood, we lack the cognitive capacity to understand what is happening and why, 2) it's hard to recognize what is happening because we are overwhelmed, and 3) we gravitate more to what is familiar than what is different.

Yes, change really is hard. We want change, and then we get in our way of change. We attract what we need to grow and, if we're not ready, not only does growth not happen, we regress further. Consequently, the next crisis is more severe. For very good reasons, we just don't figure it out at the first opportunity. I call these repetitive worsening events *Invitations to Grow*. Growth that came with the 'wake-up' and with the clarity. Growth made possible within an accountable healing process.

When I reflected on the key experiences that helped *me*, I found seven (detailed in Appendix A). I knew that sailors believed every seventh wave in the ocean was higher (MacKinnon, 2011) and that Steiner viewed life in seven-year cycles toward psychological and spiritual growth (Monte, 2016). Perhaps there really is a universal, gravitational phenomenon bigger than our own individual moments of pain, that invites balance and restoration. Not everyone has 'seven'. Some wake up to their growth with less. They are lucky and get to reap the benefits of their growth earlier in life. Some need more to wake up. That's ok. Their life is still waiting for them to bank on a wake up toward better things. Some never do.

Can you begin to think about what the turning points in your life might be?

On My Road to the Seventh

There's always been a serious lack of men in mental health professions, so when he walked into our clinic like a Midas, a Golden God, all heads turned. He was stunning, easygoing, friendly, fun, the kind of person—I believed at the time—who would be a perfect father to my children. I overlooked his faults. I ignored his family and friends' underestimations of me. I was on a mission. In fact, at work we even had a betting pool running about whether I could 'conquer' this man. And I did.

Everything started falling into place. It was 1991, two years after that nightmare breakup. I had my master's degree, I'd landed a new job with a dynamic team, and I'd found the father of my children. I'd even won an all-expenses-paid vacation to Fiji in a Qantas airline contest on CTV. Life was pretty damn good. Six weeks into my new relationship, I left on that trip with a friend of mine. It was a trip of a lifetime, with a golden boy waiting for me back home. When I returned, he gave me a welcome home any girl would dream of—loving arms at the arrival gate and filling my apartment with all my favourite foods, flowers, and champagne. I was thrilled. Little did I know that within a week, my life would be in disarray.

I had started having pain urinating. Did I have a urinary tract infection (UTI)? Yeast infection? I tried all the usual remedies, and nothing worked. I remember it all too well.

Legs spread, feet in stirrups, Dr. Monica Pearl filling in for my regular physician, examining me. She was telling me she would have to send the sample in for testing, but from her observation I had genital herpes. Unlike my shameful past, lately I had only been sexually active with this current boyfriend, so there was no doubt that the infection had come from him.

The symptoms had gone undiagnosed for so long that that they had worsened. I couldn't easily sit up or lie down, wear underwear or pants, or urinate without major discomfort. Frankly, I wanted to rip my genitals off my body. I felt dirty, in a state of self-disgust. The room swirled around me. There is *no* cure for herpes; the virus was permanent and would never leave my body. With medications, I would be able to manage the painful symptoms. These would go on to reoccur three or four times a year for the rest of my life and have the potential of compromising future labour and delivery of any children I would bear.

I thought I was going to fall off the table.

The following moments, hours, and days were quite blurry. I remember the doctor looking at my boyfriend, explaining how much I needed him to care for me now because of how the symptoms had progressed. Little did I know that scene of a doctor advising him of the role he needed to play in supporting my health would be repeated in much more serious circumstances years later, with the same response from him. I should have paid more attention to what he didn't do next. I should have paid more attention to what *I* didn't do next. His explanation of how I contracted this from him was confusing: He knew he had 'it,' he didn't know, his doctor knew, his doctor misinformed him, he didn't understand how it was transmitted. I hated him. I hated me. I hated my body. I hated my sexuality. And then, I made myself numb.

I made a secret deal with myself. No one would know about the sexually transmitted infection (STI) except him. If I was already unwanted, which had been confirmed in my mind by being repeatedly dumped by those I dated, herpes would take me completely out of the running for anyone else, let alone someone better. I really only had one choice—convince myself that I had wanted this relationship all along, marry him, and make it work.

I never talked to anyone else about the herpes except my therapist, for almost twenty years. I went into hiding, a place that felt much more severe and completely opposite to my natural way of coping. I would later learn that although it was so foreign to do so, this shift wasn't actually that uncommon. Some of us are very consistent throughout our life in how we react when we are hurt. We can be mostly aggressive and overt with our pain, which had been my usual track. Just the opposite, others can be too passive and internalize the pain, which to my surprise, I was leaning toward. Still others can be a mixture of both and be passive aggressive (Stangor & Walinga, 2014).

I have come to liken this to the three-angled faces of the medieval sword, the epée—same core, three 'sides.' People can consciously or unconsciously experiment with these three different styles, often prompted by different depths of pain or interestingly enough, by progress. In fact, effective recovery is frequently manifested by swinging back and forth between aggression, passivity, and passive aggression under stress. It usually starts from the adapted position learned in childhood, as steadiness is mastered at the assertive empowered 'middle.'

Which side of the wound are you on?

I clearly wasn't in recovery. I was drowning in a significant sea of shame, weighed down by earlier life experiences, most recently loaded down further by the relationship ending of 1989, the sexual acting out, and now laden by the STI. This was, by that time, my *Invitation Number Five*. This uncharacteristically silenced me. I bounced from my usual 'normal' side of aggression to passivity (in this crisis) and then back to aggression later, and stayed there, without finding my middle for a long time. I unconsciously wrestled with the hurt over the years that followed.

Regardless, with the secret 'safe', and being on the path toward getting married, we were the couple others looked up to. Good-looking, adventurous, fun. Ground-breaking couple's therapist, Harville Hendrix, may have even argued that I had met my Imago match, giving us the opportunity for individual growth through the relationship (Harville and Helen, 2022).

Our contrary behavioral preferences, developed in childhood, offered complementary yet challenging opportunities with each other. What I lacked in patience, he had. What he lacked in ambition, I brought in spades. In 1994, we pulled off the big fat Ukrainian wedding, the honeymoon in Greece, and one year later we bought the house in midtown Toronto. My days at Young and Eligible were over, which satisfied some desperate need of mine at that time to belong to my growing group of married peers, even if I had to bury the sting of the STI.

The fact is, opposites *do* attract, and we were on the same collision course as any other well-matched couple. Even with the big, bad secret suppressed, we went into our marriage with hopes and dreams like everyone else. The problem was that it was an unconscious relationship, lacking self-awareness and leaving us unprepared for those invitations to progress.

So, we indulged *reactions* from our *wounded selves* rather than *responding* to each other from our *healthy selves* (labels, also explained in more detail in Chapter 10). Suffice it to say, I didn't value his patience. I had grown up in a take-charge family, so I viewed his indirect style and 'taking his time' as passive weakness. I lost respect for him and became angry. Instead of being motivated by my higher energy, he felt controlled and became passive-aggressive, fueling me further. As we repeated that aggressive anger/passive-aggressive withholding cycle multiple times, we became gridlocked at that important intersection of growth or doom. Add in his unresolved guilt about infecting me and my shame of *being* infected. We were doomed.

Over the next seven years, we completely fell apart. Therapy was tried again, but honestly, I did not find the safe, brave space that was needed to complete a deeper healing. The consequences of that were profound. The core wounds being activated in our relationship, the direct link of this to the cyclical communication breakdowns, and the herpes monster, were simply not talked about enough. Without that, we would just continue to hurt each other more. Eventually it was too late, and we disconnected.

I think we would have greatly benefitted from a therapy that was more directive with clearer interventions targeting what was truly damaging us the most and why. The reality is that the prolonged stage of disengagement we were experiencing after cumulative unresolved conflicts (both loud and quiet) was severely damaging our relationship, as it easily does with most couples. The therapy had to match and be more powerful than the momentum of that wreckage.

Good news! In 1998, our first daughter was born. She was an incredible source of joy for both of us.

Bad news! In 1999, I encountered catastrophic health problems, and I was forced to stop everything in my life. Everything. Exercising. Socializing. Working. Parenting. This was *Invitation Number Six*.

Worse news. In December 2001 (on my best friend's birthday), I miscarried our second child. I remember him standing coldly at the doorway of the bathroom while I let our unborn child pass out of me naturally. The truth was he had already let go of me, so he was relieved the pregnancy had ended. In the overwhelmed state that I was in, I blamed myself for losing focus and letting what bled out of me be flushed down the toilet. I even confessed this to a priest who tried to console me by telling me that when the remains passed, my baby was lifeless and was already in God's hands in heaven. Later, I created a memory stone in our back garden. That was an extremely dark period for me.

I was in so much pain. I had lost my health. I had lost the ability to mother in the way I had dreamt of because of my poor health. I had lost the career that had become so important to me. Now I had lost a baby. I remember belting out the Christmas hymns at Christmas Eve Mass that year, like making a plea to the heavens for some answers, some peace. I remember feeling cathartic relief from that singing, but it would be short-lived as I was later criticized for causing embarrassment.

By Good Friday 2002, while planning our annual visit to my friend's home, he sat on the bathroom counter as I bathed, and we recounted our most recent ineffective marital session. I looked into his eyes and knew he was gone (I secretly wondered why *Good* Friday was always so *bad* to me. It hadn't been the first time I'd been rejected on that day). Even God was trying to tell me to get my shit together, and He didn't even know about the invitations.

The next day, I took our three-year-old daughter and stood at the back of our overflowing church for the day-long Easter Saturday Mass, when there were no empty pews left. For over eight hours, I stood there breathing, praying, and yes, singing, as I searched for answers, now with even bigger questions; and searching for peace, now needed more than ever before. I stood there watching all of these beautiful people around us who were also praying and also singing, and in fact, singing out loud like I had on Christmas Eve. But this time they were singing with ease and love, with their families by their side who were singing too. I stood there staring all day at the glowing, stained-glass windows. As the afternoon light faded behind the panes, as the sun set, I asked myself, "What did all these people know about love that I didn't?"

The Bottom

Three months later, on Friday, June 28, 2002, it was his time with our daughter. He had rights to have her on what had been *our* annual camping weekend, a ritual we had started years earlier with my niece and nephew. He arrived and she skipped happily down the driveway to meet him. I remember looking up at his face. He was lighter. He was happier. I guess he was free. She was happy too. And then, they just left. My family just left and in that moment all I had ever wanted was gone.

I stood on that driveway.

For a long, long time, I just stood on that driveway in the heat. The worst part of it by far was that I stood alone.

Everything seemed to crash down on me that day. It was as if everything I had done wrong in my entire life had landed me on that hard, cracked asphalt. That driveway became a dead end for me, proving how bad a human being I was.

The pathway of painful invitations can often lead you to this point.

The overwhelming loneliness of my life that I had so vehemently been running from had overtaken me. It was as if standing alone that day was my final punishment for being so wrong and so bad for so long. I was immobilized. I came to a grinding halt.

I had been running and numbing and hiding and working and fighting and pushing to be happy for a long time. And all that ever got me was losing a marriage, losing my health, losing my career, and losing a baby. It felt like I was losing all that was left—my only child, my daughter. I *was* alone, now more than ever.

I opened the garage door and searched for the orange electrical extension cord I knew was hanging on the hook. I carried it down to the basement, to the laundry room where I knew there were gas and water pipes, big pipes that could hold my weight. This was my answer. Working hadn't worked. Sex hadn't worked. Hiding hadn't worked. Raging hadn't worked. Therapy hadn't worked. Numbing hadn't worked. Even God hadn't helped. This was my only way out.

I stood on the chair. I started going through the list of what was in my calendar. I literally ran through my entire schedule for the coming week in my head to make sure it was all covered. All was clear. All was, except for *one thing.*

The tenant from the basement apartment I rented in our home had given notice and moved out early. A new person wasn't moving in until July first, in three days. My ever-reliable dad had decided the space needed a fresh coat of paint while it sat unusually empty. I then remembered in my fog that my parents were due *first* thing in the morning to come and help paint that fucking apartment!

We had decided to brighten the space with a yellow. A soft, lemony yellow. Honestly, I had been running on adrenaline in the previous months and had just agreed. I didn't care about the walls. I didn't even like yellow. I guess if they couldn't cry with me or hug me, they could paint. One friggin' thing they could do was paint those friggin' walls! What was I going to do?

I pictured my parents arriving in the morning with paint and brushes and ladders to discover my lifeless body in the basement.

I dropped the cord.

I stepped down from the chair.

I honestly don't know what happened between midnight and 9:00 a.m. But I do remember standing on that very same driveway the next morning, welcoming them, carrying in the brushes and ladders, drop cloths and cans, and getting down to work.

But, this time, instead of stopping there, instead of reverting back to compartmentalizing, instead of fighting, instead of hiding, I finally dug deep to do the unfinished *emotional* work that had been screaming at me for years and just like Forrest Gump, I found my way home.

To the home within me.

To the home that had been waiting for me the whole time.

I had just landed on the good side of **Invitation Number Seven.**

Think about this:

1. When did you feel like giving up in your life? What did you learn when you didn't?
2. How many significant experiences or turning points do you think you have had in your life?
3. What have been the common themes of those events? What were they ultimately inviting you to do differently?
4. How could using those invitations change the direction of your life?
5. Where would you find your yellow paint; the external resources and internal strengths that could help you find a healthier path?

This chapter is dedicated to Debbie and all others who could not find their yellow paint and lost their way in the blackness.

CHAPTER 2
GRIT & GUTS: A FAMILY LEGACY OF HARD WORK AND COURAGE

(Eminem - Lose Yourself, 2002, aka the year of the yellow paint)

I love the hard-hitting sound of "Lose Yourself" for this chapter. Some may think this is an odd choice as it relates to my Baba and Gigi. But what I am inspired by is the powerful lyrics about determination and about seizing over losing opportunities.

I invite you to think about: What your family legacy is, and how that serves you.

Consider thinking about where hard work and courage has mattered the very most to you.

Eighty Years Earlier... (Baba and Gigi's Grit and Guts)

In 1922, Ukraine's brief post-WWI independence, granted through a treaty, was lost with the creation of the Ukrainian Socialist Soviet Republic (part of the USSR), placing Ukrainian identity under threat. It would take another sixty-nine years for Ukraine to regain independence with the dissolution of the USSR in 1991. During that time:

As many as five million Ukrainians would be killed in one single year (1932), a year known as the Holodomor (the Ukrainian word for 'killing through starvation'). The Holodomor was a devastating chapter of the larger Soviet-engineered famine, aimed at seizing Ukraine's abundant wheat and grain to fund industrialization projects while crushing Ukrainian independence movements. Ultimately, it was a catastrophic failure with unimaginable human costs. During World War II, many Ukrainians were deceived into welcoming the Nazi occupation, hoping to collaborate with the Germans to regain independence. However, instead of liberation, 1.5 million Jewish Ukrainians were killed, and millions of non-Jewish Ukrainians were sent to labor camps. Communist powers would continue to oppress Ukrainians, forcing them into lives of extreme hardship and social control, maintained through systemic corruption by political and economic powers.

President Volodymyr Zelensky was elected in 2019. He challenged Soviet interference and successfully integrated his country into the European Union and NATO, achieving EU status for Ukraine in 2022. It was the same year Putin invaded the country and began the war against Ukraine—a direct and deliberate invasion.

At the time of the writing of this book, the Office of the United Nations High Commissioner for Human Rights (OHCHR) verified a total of 30,457 civilian casualties, including children, during Russia's invasion of Ukraine as of February 15, 2024 (Statista Research Department, 2022).

My grandfather, Theodore (Fred) was born in Ukraine in 1905, the oldest of three sons. Known always to me as Gigi, he was born in a village later destroyed by the Russians in the 1940s. There is little to no current information available about his village. The family grew vegetables in a life of chronic poverty and oppression. When Gigi was twenty-two, he married Anna (my Baba), who was twenty, the fourth of six siblings and the eldest daughter.

In 1928, Anna's older brother Pete immigrated to Canada, which at the time was attracting immigrants to clear and farm the land. He settled in Southwestern Ontario where the soil was well suited for growing vegetables they had experience with from their homeland. Uncle Pete was always described to me as flamboyant, energetic, and passionate about his politics. He died in his early sixties while volunteering at a campaign office trying to improve the lives of Canadians.

Gigi was also ambitious and bright and wanted a better life for his family. So in May 1930, when his first-born, a son, was only two months old, he likewise made the voyage across the Atlantic to join Pete. The plan was to earn a living as farmers in Canada, then return to Ukraine with the fruits of their labour to provide for their families. Little did they know that their plan would never come to be. As communism spread across the USSR, those who had emigrated were prohibited from ever returning to their original home villages back in Ukraine.

During the 1930s, seven hundred-feet-long ocean liners left ports in France to make the seven-to-ten-day-long journey across the Atlantic. The liners carried nearly three thousand passengers. Ukrainians were considered fourth class, crammed into the bottom of these large vessels, battling sea sickness and worse.

Gigi was designated by the government to settle and grow wheat in Manitoba. He had another plan. After making the treacherous voyage across the Atlantic and arriving in Montreal, he boarded the cross-country train in Quebec City meant to transport him two provinces west. During a scheduled stop in Sudbury, Ontario, he got off as many passengers did, to use the washroom facilities. Before the rail cars departed, monitors checked the bottom openings of the bathroom stalls to ensure all passengers had, in fact, reboarded the train for their assigned voyages. Gigi stood on the toilet seat quietly to go undetected. After the train left, with all of his belongings on it, he continued his journey, sticking to his plan. With 25 dollars in his pocket, he made his way down to Leamington Ontario, seven hundred km away, to begin farming with Pete, who was expecting him.

Over the next four years, Gigi earned money that he sent back to Anna and the family. He also sent them kerchiefs, easily purchased in Canada, which they could sell on the black market as another means to survive. In the letters Gigi wrote home about his life in Canada. He talked about the place where 'sidewalks were paved in gold' just as advertised abroad to entice the immigrants, and hoped this would encourage his wife. However, Canada, in need of aid for clearing and farming the land, was also in the midst of the Great Depression. Many dreams were hardened by the reality of the economic crash of the times. None of this dampened Gigi's persistence. He kept farming. He kept writing Anna. He kept insisting she come. In 1934, he sent one last packet of money in a letter, letting her know it would be the final package and her last chance to join him.

Many wives didn't come. They could not find the courage to leave everything they knew behind, regardless of the deplorable living conditions and hopeless futures in Ukraine. But Anna came with my uncle, by that time a four-year-old boy. Without the capacity to read, write, or speak any other language, she somehow rode the railways from Ukraine to France, boarded the ocean liner, and arrived at Pier 21 in Halifax. From there, she traveled across Canada to Windsor, stepping off the train into mud puddles, not golden sidewalks. There, she waited for several days in the empty station until Fred and Pete received a telegram sent to a local convenience store announcing her arrival. The two men then apparently loaded up their truck and filled the side running board with potatoes as a gift to greet her. Three years later my mother was born.

In Leamington, the Ukrainian community developed in a marsh area with rich soil, well-suited for growing vegetables. It was there that my grandparents, my parents, my aunt and uncle, my Baba's brother Pete and his wife, along with many other Ukrainian families, would successfully plant, grow, harvest, and sell onions. Initially, Baba and Gigi worked as sharecroppers for others, and then they succeeded in purchasing their own five-acre lot. For some years, they lived in a modest home they built on that land, without any electricity or running water.

Over time, however, their success grew, and the dreams of a better life came to fruition. They acquired an additional five-acre lot, taking their property to the next road over, and then another five acres beside the initial plot. Eventually, Gigi purchased eight acres in a nearby township to expand his farming further. By 1961, he had purchased sixty additional acres closer to the town of Leamington, where he would diversify, growing tomatoes, tobacco, and soya beans. A new family home was later built on this parcel of land, where my grandparents lived until they died. Gigi had been a very methodical and determined business owner and his efforts were evident.

He developed *BG Farms* the same year he purchased the sixty-acre plot, named after the two surnames of his children, his birth name used by his son, Beniuk, and Goslin, my mother's new surname after marrying my father. He structured shares in the company and divided them equally among his children, with one extra for himself so that he could retain control as the third shareholder.

Unfortunately, tragedy struck in 1983 when Baba and Gigi's first-born son, my uncle, died suddenly of a heart attack at the age of fifty-three. His death had a profound impact on my grandparents, especially my Baba. She died of cardiac arrest within five years.

By 2012 *BG Farms* began selling lots on those sixty acres (by then in high demand). Gigi had intuitively bought that land close to town, an area which was rapidly growing as he had predicted. The sales from those lots would generate generous profits from a joint-venture agreement dating back to the 1980s to service the town for residential use. Eventually, 225 lots were sold in total. It was my mother's idea to name the through street 'Annfred'—the combined first names of my grandparents, as well as courts bearing the farm's name from the children's surnames. Despite desperate beginnings and personal losses, they had truly built their own golden sidewalks from the mud, with Gigi at the helm.

Gigi earned his success with discipline, vision, timing, and sheer hard work, initially toiling on his hands and knees, pulling weeds that grew on the large plots of land. Apparently, he was a stickler for accuracy about this task and to this end developed his own weeding tool in the form of a four-foot stick, with a wire at the end. He later used herbicides and analyzed wind speed to ensure that the weeds were eliminated with minimal damage to the surrounding crops. He said the best time to do this was seven in the evening, after the breezes had died down for the day, and apparently, he was usually right!

Gigi also ambitiously organized strict efforts to ensure the farm produced the first harvest in the entire marsh area, to take advantage of the best price available for the season. His only day off was Sunday, to go to church. But even then, he showed up on the land to supervise the others who were using their day off from their regular Monday-to-Friday jobs to farm. Gigi also took educated risks to purchase the additional real estate properties for investment and worked deals to his advantage to maximize profit. Unlike the other farmers in the area, he envisioned what the value of that land in town would be worth in the future and acted on that vision, despite the fact that it was located a fair distance from the familiarity and comfort of the marsh. This all led to the development, success, and value of *BG Farms*, and reflected part of a legacy I would inherit many years later.

I remember many things about Gigi. He was the smartest man I knew growing up. Despite his lack of formal education, he was knowledgeable about world geography and history. He could talk about these topics in astonishing detail and explain world events with such explicit context. He also hated being in debt and ferociously paid off mortgages with relentless determination. Understandably, Gigi distrusted government, so the chicken coop on the farm was the bank—literally where he stored his cash. When needed, he would retrieve the money from the nests, and dry it out on bed mattresses, to use for his purchases. He and Baba were part of a tight Ukrainian community. They joined friends, celebrated weddings and anniversaries with such freedom and joy, sang songs of the homeland, prayed in churches, played cards, and gathered in big halls to play bingo and dance polkas. These also made clear impressions on me.

After Gigi had worked on the farm all day, the grandchildren would line up to lay across Gigi's lap for his nightly back scratches. I remember how scruffy and hard his farm hands were and how perfect that was for calming the itches on my skin. And every night, he would lay next to Anna, with the light bulb on next to their bed, reading the Ukrainian newspaper to her—every night.

I do have some scattered yet vivid memories of the times I spent at the farm. I remember stamping the *BG* labels for the onion-bag tags. I remember jumping into the wagons drawn from the fields and gently kicking down the onions that got caught in the container's upper seams. I remember yelling out to the men in the barn when the smaller onions, redirected to one side of the farm-to-bag work lines, had filled their bags, before they overflowed. I remember watching the massive trucks arrive at the barn with huge conveyor belts to load up piles of fifty-pound bags to be sold. Everyone had a job. Everyone worked hard. I remember us seven grandchildren squeezing in front of the bathroom mirror at the end of the day, pulling out the muck that had accumulated in the corners of our eyes during the day's work to see who had the most.

Gigi lived until ninety-three, ten years after Anna passed. Although he had a detailed method and keen vision and he knew he had achieved success, he had no idea what he had truly created in his lifetime. He knew lots were approved for selling, but he wouldn't ever really know their full value, or what that represented to his family (they were only completely sold off fourteen years after his death). Years later, I came to appreciate how those deeply ingrained Ukrainian work ethics, the strong business vision, and unwavering determination would become key elements in my yellow paint, in my resilience of thriving after my divorce, and in building my *own* business.

My daughter Madeline was born the year my Gigi died. In fact, Madeline's full introduction to the extended family was at his funeral. I had been telling relatives about her colic, her relentless crying, and the struggles I was having. I'll never forget sitting in that small Ukrainian church for over an hour wondering how we would get through the ceremony of the family patriarch without disturbing everyone around us on such an important day. Madeline never cried once.

When I think back to those days, Baba never talked about her immigration. Before her departure from Ukraine, her younger sisters had been sent to labour camps in Siberia. She would never see anyone from her family again. The grief and trauma from leaving her homeland and family behind, the hardship of the voyage, and the reality of what awaited her in Canada had understandably overwhelmed her. But she would have no way to label her experience, let alone know how to heal.

My father said Baba worked as hard as any of the men on the farm, tossing those fifty-pound bags of onions across the barn floor just as strongly as the others. One of my last jobs on the farm was Baba teaching me how to sew up the bags, incorporate the tags, and create handles for their upcoming delivery. She could sew those bags up in seconds flat and move on to the next. The large barn floor was filled with those bags.

She had farmer's hands too, a demonstration of her incredible life of long days and hard work. Not only did she work in the barn; she would cook up a true Ukrainian feast every day at midday to feed the farmers' ravenous appetites. I would smell the garlic and onions coming from her kitchen before I even opened my eyes in the morning. Baba would scurry around the kitchen like Edith Bunker from the popular TV show at the time, *All in the Family*. She would have emotional outbursts of frustration and tears, emotions whose origins I couldn't understand at the time. I don't think she did either. Baba loved babies. Her entire face would light up with the biggest smile when a baby was born in our family. She also loved card playing and nightly tea parties prepared on a tray with Ukrainian pastries and sugar cubes for the tea. I suppose these small connections to family gave her some comfort and joy. After enduring famine and poverty in Ukraine, she would show her love for her family by filling your plate up repeatedly to take advantage of the plentiful food. She would squeeze your cheek so hard it hurt if she thought you were under weight and would tightly fold up twenty-dollar bills when you were leaving her home, forcefully squeezing them into your hands so you had some money.

Growing up as the youngest Ukrainian cousin in my generation, I had no idea what she had endured until many years later. I'd like to think that, despite her painful journey, she found some gratitude and happiness in the life she so bravely reached for. I also think of how challenging it must have been for her on that crowded, sickly boat for so long, leaving everything and everyone behind. Not knowing the language, with my young uncle in tow, and then realizing the realities of her new home. Later learning she would never return to her homeland.

I think about how utterly afraid she must have been getting on that boat.

I think of how she went anyway.

I think of how deeply sad she must have been leaving her family and her home.

I think of how she pushed through anyway.

I think of how strong she was to rebuild after such loss and devastation.

I think she must have really loved Gigi, and he her.

It makes me realize...

Baba is brave. Baba is strength. Baba is family.

It makes me think that the legacy I would inherit wasn't just about Gigi's determination and hard work. It was also about Baba's courage. Combined, it was about making a serious commitment toward making something better, much better, even with significant obstacles in front of you. It was about not giving up when that's all you wanted to do.

My Grit and Guts

I don't really know what made me drop the cord and step off the chair that June night. For all I know, I was just too scared to follow through. I do know I felt a responsibility for not letting my parents go through the pain of discovering me in the morning. What was particularly important was what I did *after* I stepped off. I believe that generational models of toughness and determination—of pushing through, 'rolling up sleeves', and applying 'grit and guts' in the face of hardship—played a key role in fueling my drive to take real risks, create a clear plan, and tap into a powerful strength that propelled me toward something better, something much better, even when nothing seemed possible or worth pursuing. I am not comparing my circumstance to what my grandparents endured. Not much could. But understanding what contributed to the daring resilience I found in that moment and in the hours, days, weeks, months, and years that followed was important to me.

I can tell you one thing. When I stepped off the chair, I do remember thinking that giving up would no longer be an option, even though seconds earlier that's all I thought about. In fact, I had *needed* the power of desperately wanting to give up and then *not*, to rebuild my entire life, to decide that *nothing* else would ever tear me down again. And not because I was angry. Not because I was powerless. Not because I was insecure. Because I was worth it. That's when I really rolled up my sleeves.

What I did from that deep vortex not only averted the crisis that night but launched me mentally and emotionally over the next twenty years and will probably continue to inspire me for the rest of my life. I would accomplish things in ways previously thought impossible. Not giving up ended up taking me from mere survival to unimagined levels of energy, success, fulfillment, and confidence. And trust me, there was absolutely none of that when I walked down those basement stairs.

For now, I was on the divorce path, forced by someone else, but it was a path to which I had contributed. When that choice was taken away from me, *I* made the choice to wake up and forge ahead. I found a new therapist who would help me rebuild a new kind of family for me and Madeline. I worked to understand why I chose who I married, why I added to the problems we had, and why I was stuck in repetitive rejecting relationship patterns. I faced how the herpes had really affected me and learned how to stop hiding that secret. I addressed why I got sick and figured out how to get better. I ultimately learned to move forward with less control, less insecurity, less shame, less self-sabotage, less anxiety and less anger; and more self-awareness, healthier power, and deeper worthiness.

I suppose if my husband hadn't left, there would've been a different *seventh invitation* that would have been just as serious to teach me what I needed to learn. At least, I sure hope so.

How the Family Legacy Shaped the KG Method for Accountability

I believe that my Ukrainian legacy, and how that had influenced me toward changing direction in my personal life, also shaped the kind of therapist I would become. I took risks, combining the keen vision and discipline of Gigi running a 'tight ship', with the brave commitment of Baba. I knew, as humans, we usually want and need change when we are unhappy. I also knew that we too easily revert back and get in our own way, sabotaging ourselves, and ultimately getting us further away from what we really want. If I was going to be effective, the therapy had to be diligent and disciplined, deeply brave and honest, and create commitment for the clients, the BG farm way. And from that, the spirit and success of the *KG Method* was born.

As you read further, I encourage you to think about what meaningful therapy and healing means to **you** and what specific accountability you are taking every day toward making **your** life better.

The Grit

When I interviewed my father (who also lives by a hard-work ethic) for this chapter he spoke about how *KG & Associates* had developed and why. He compared my hard work, efforts, and earnest ways to how Gigi ran the farm. That made me proud.

The therapy practice I provide offers specific programs. I draw on evidence-based treatment approaches I have studied. But I modify them to create effective treatment tools clients can use at home. The tools are customized for each client based on an initial, structured comprehensive assessment, which explains the what, the why, and the how of what they are struggling with and what to do about it. I call this the 'Emotional X-Ray' (British Vogue, 2019). Most importantly, the clear treatment plans derived from the assessments prioritize the clients' accountability to themselves, through the work.

The programs combine Self-Care Management, Self-Talk (Cognitive Behavioral Therapy), and Relapse Prevention Planning for addiction. I call this 'the brain surgery of the program' with deeper healing (Emotionally Focused Therapy), including specialized grief, shame, betrayal, and deepening of love (Imago Therapy) interventions that I call 'the heart surgery of the program (see the Glossary for more on these terms). I add in Emotional Regulation (Dialectical Behavioral Therapy) and Mindfulness Programs as the bridge between the two, to demonstrate how using clearer thinking, mindfully, mends the heart and how a healthier heart filters the brain.

These levels of the work are offered with intense exercises and experiences to ensure what is processed, learned, and practiced in session is transferrable to and user-friendly in the outside world where it counts the most. Even in the deeper, emotionally focused parts of the program, when exploring the past, clients are inevitably challenged to learn specifically what it is they will be doing differently when they wake up tomorrow morning. There is therapeutic enlightenment and relief in discovering and feeling our pain. Cathartic exercises facilitate this. But the ultimate change comes from reframing the negative inaccurate meanings we attach to the past and knowing exactly how those reframes invite us to live better now and sustainably so in the future. I call this entire approach to the work 'Accountable Therapy.'

The Self-Talk Program (the *KG* Change CBT program) is an important part of Accountable Therapy and teaches us how to go from self-sabotaging, triggered states to assertive, empowered states. It rests on the premise that to do differently, we need to feel differently. To feel differently, we need to think differently.

It has three parts:

1. Tracking the Triggers: Mapping out the situations that overwhelm in some way and lead us toward behavior that works against us. Identifying the associated negative automatic thoughts, unpleasant physical symptoms and negative behavioral reactions.

2. Analyzing: Categorizing and clustering the types of thoughts that are interfering. These are common categories of negative or unrealistic thoughts that work against us in some way when we are triggered and that need our attention:

    - **Generalized Thinking**: This involves taking a single event and magnifying it into absolutes like always/never or everybody/nobody, leading to unhelpful labels for ourselves, others, or situations. Examples include: *"Nobody will be interested in talking to me," "It's always the same, so why bother?"* or *"School is useless."*

    - **Self-Critical or Blaming Thinking**: One of the most common ways we reduce our vulnerability is through self-criticism or blaming others. While blaming may stem from a legitimate experience of wrongdoing, indulging in these thoughts often leads to being victimized twice—first by the original incident and then by the emotional weight we carry. For example: *"I'm a loser," "I'm probably overreacting," "It's all my fault,"* or *"She had no right to…"* As an extension to this, there is a play on words in Cognitive Behavioral Therapy (CBT) called "shoulding" on ourselves or others.: *"She should never have…"* or *"I should have…"* I like to call "the shoulding on", the "cousin of blame."

- **Future Worrying or Past Regretting**: This is when we mentally time-travel, jumping between the past and future while avoiding the present. While it's normal to visit the past to grieve or the future to plan, getting stuck in either can amplify depression, anger, or anxiety. Examples include: *"We'll just end up arguing like we always do,"* *"If I tell him what's bothering me, we'll probably break up,"* *"What if this completely backfires?"* *"I can't believe I didn't…"*, or *"Here we go again…"*

- **Mind Reading**: This involves projecting our insecurities onto others, assuming we know what they think, and then reorganizing our feelings and actions around those assumptions. Common thoughts include: *"They don't even like me,"* *"He doesn't believe in me,"* *"They think I'm stupid,"* or *"It's better if I don't speak up—they won't care."*

- **Stinking Thinking**: Borrowed from addiction treatment, this refers to thoughts that trick us into believing inaccurate ideas, in pursuit of immediate gratification. For addicts, this might sound like: *"I'll quit on Monday,"* *"Just one more,"* or *"I'm not hurting anyone."* However, stinking thinking also occurs in non-addiction contexts, where it tempts immediate gratification through passive, avoidant, or passive-aggressive behaviors. Examples include: *"It's never worked out for me to make friends, so why try?"* *"I'm too tired to go out,"* *"I can't do this,"* or *"Let's see how long it takes her to…"*

The most common stinky thoughts I see outside of addiction include:

- Those struggling with perfectionism and who have some version of: *"One more time, this time better."*

- Procrastination thinking, such as, *"I'll do it later"* or *"I don't have enough time now."*

- Obsessive Compulsive Disorder (OCD) - *"Let me check again to be sure."*

Interestingly enough, I often see obsessive perfectionists procrastinating when perfection is not attained. This is often due, in my opinion, to a common underlying wound of control needing repair in the emotionally focused part of the program.

3. Completing the C-H-A-N-G-E pathway that leads from a triggered state to an empowered state (see the example below and the change chart illustrated in Appendix C) and Practicing: Completing Thought-Correction Sheets to help log and improve the CHANGE practice in daily life.

Consider trying this:

Cues - Think of something recently that 'triggered' you. That is, you reacted aggressively, passively, or passive-aggressively, which ultimately worked against you in some way. See if you can identify how your brain, body, and behavior changed when you were triggered.

For example: My partner lied to me. I thought, "*He always does this. I can never trust him. We'll never work.*" (past regretting, generalized, blaming and future worrying). I got a pit in my stomach. I shut down and went to bed.

Honeymoon - Take a break and step away. None of us can easily shift in the heat of the moment. We greatly benefit from taking at least a moment to reset.

For example: I quietly got out of the bed we were sharing and left the room.

Adjust - Bring your stress about the situation under a 6/10 if you need to. Breathe. Soothe. Distract. More about that later.

For example: I took some deep breaths. I put a warm compress on my stomach.

New Thoughts – Think back to the thoughts that enabled your reaction. Take those thoughts and shift them into present, specific facts. The dwellings of the past and the worries of the future become present. The blaming or self-criticisms become facts. The generalized thinking becomes specific. We let go of mind-reading thoughts and assuming how others are thinking and/or feeling.

For example: I asked my partner why he was late, and he told me he was working late, but a friend texted me and told me she saw him getting out of an Uber at a downtown bar.

Get Honest About Your Goals - Let that inspire you to cultivate not what you want, but what *you really want*. Not what others want. Not what you want from others. *What you really want from and for yourself.*

For example: I really want to tell him what I know, how that affected me, and ask him what he is unsatisfied about in our relationship. I really want to improve our relationship and trust him more or end it.

Empower - Identify *one* thing you could say, decide, or plan that would get you one step closer to what you really want.

For example: Saying "I feel betrayed when you lie to me about where you are. I need you to come to a therapy session I have booked for us on Saturday to work on trust, satisfaction, and communication."

Watch what your partner does next and if needed go through the **C-H-A-N-G-E** cycle until you are in a place that honors your real wants.

How did you do?

Graduating KG clients practice these six steps daily in quick, five-minute Cognitive Behavioral Change Tracks. I do this as well. I don't just teach. I live the programs myself. I need to know first-hand how the tools work or not. Everyday things happen that we don't like, expect, or want. Some of those overlap with the themes of our wounded self and act as triggers. Daily brain health exercises like this are very helpful. After a month my clients don't need to look at their downloaded Change Programs. They know it like the back of their hand and get better at using it when it is needed the most.

Timing is Everything

How has timing worked for you and against you in your life?

I also finessed Gigi's clear sense of purposeful timing, which he had with the crops and real estate deals, with my clients. Timing really *is* everything in therapy and could make the difference between powerful repair and irreversible damage. Therapeutic interventions need to be carefully timed before the point of no return but not prematurely before enough strength is developed. They need to come after the 'ah-ha' moments are punctuated, but not too much later, before the fear of change sets in, regression occurs and with that, the power of the insight is lost.

I was highly dedicated to this, for obvious reasons...

For passive-aggressive people, like my ex-husband, the crisis is too quiet and needs to be effectively pulled up and out. It needs to be carefully managed sooner rather than later, without them being overwhelmed with what has surfaced. But also, before more hidden sacrifice is suffered, and before letting go, without ever knowing what the remaining work would have produced. For aggressors like me, the discontent is loud, causing damage to those we love. Immediate and straightforward talk is needed to control damage and prevent unwanted loss, but in ways that validate, so the aggressor is empowered to let go of the rage, also sooner rather than later.

In my experience our therapy didn't capitalize on that timing sharply enough to save our marriage. I was trying to take the notes provided in the sessions to soften and validate more, but it was too late for him. By the spring of 2002, my ex had given up. By Christmas of the next year, he would come to change his mind. By then, it was too late for me. The mistiming was tragic. I can still clearly see that day in my mind.

I was doing household chores. I was still quite sick at the time, but I was doing what I could to keep the home running for me and my daughter, while trying to be more mindful of my physical and mental limitations. I was folding laundry in the kitchen. The basket sat on the table while I lined up the corners of the freshly cleaned sheets. Distracted by wrestling with trying to line up the fitted sheets, I suddenly heard the regret in his voice. I did seem to know that day would come. I just didn't know it would be *that* day. I remember looking down at the floor and gently shaking my head in deep sorrow.

As it was in the early days, weeks, and months of our separation, I had stood at our kitchen window, *every* time he left our home, after visiting our daughter. He would leave and then intently walk to the bus stop at the end of the street. I stood there watching him carefully, believing that at any moment he would turn around and come back to us. I watched him until he was out of sight. He never turned around. I eventually stopped watching.

Instead, I began working actively on my grief and moved on. I don't think his change of mind was because he missed me. He had done enough work to regret his decision, but it didn't appear to me that he had any deeper understanding of why we got so stuck. I could be wrong, but I think he was mostly feeling displaced by the new relationship I had in my life by then and how close our daughter had become with my new partner's daughters. We may never know, but what I did know was that that experience thrust me into a deep commitment with the couples I work with, to carefully time my interventions to avoid tragic, unnecessary, painful endings like mine.

Timing often is everything and Gigi knew it.

The Guts

The guts of the KG Method made me a fierce therapist, bold about the agonizing edges humans face, and clear about the steps to take from those edges. The truth is, we usually know what's going wrong in our lives and why. We just don't know what to do about it.

One of my mentors once said, "You can say anything from a place of love."

That served me in my own life. That definitely serves my clients. The therapeutic conversations *are* direct but *always* from a place of love. It is about taking thoughtful, deeply respectful risks with clients—not telling them what they *want* to hear, but instead what they *need* to hear and working with that mutual raw courage toward making life-changing decisions because of the full truth that was laid out. Just like Baba had stepping onto that boat.

People value being understood *and* having a plan through the often-accumulated, confusing, devastating messes (those missed opportunities from the *invitations to growth*) toward finding healthy power and living a fulfilling life. The loving, powerful honesty runs through all of the *KG* processes, from the first phone call, through to the initial assessment, through to the brain and heart programs, through to the endings.

The Invitations Within the Legacy

What legacy did you inherit in your family?

Often, therapy involves healing from the legacies of our lives. What I learned about my family's history, and how that influenced me, sharpened my work with clients in this area. Finding empowerment from beautiful histories filled with inspirational acts of courage and determination is easy. But many generational narratives are also filled with stories of abandonment, abuse, and/or betrayals, and are understandably more complex. Unravelling the difficult lives of past generations not only to uncover the hurtful acts committed but also to connect these to the authentic human struggles behind those poor choices and judgments is compelling and freeing. This deep therapeutic analysis finds a delicate place that balances placing responsibility on those who caused harm, but with empathy. Depersonalizing and separating out what we do not own, but doing so with compassion for flaws in the humans who hurt us.

The process helps broaden the stories of the past and deepens understanding, releases resentment, soothes grief, and ultimately raises the potential for the current generation, which was not achieved by the previous ones. Within this unravelling usually lies a meaningful invitation to grow. Accepting that invitation takes guts. My job is to help people find those guts to do the work. To find balance. To find compassion. To find peace in the legacies they inherited through no choice of their own.

It is no coincidence that during our hardest times when we don't give up we discover our true worth and power. The challenge is making sure you know exactly *how* to find, and how to stay behind, that power long term.

Baba and Gigi never turned back. They forged ahead. They built an empire, one that started from deplorable darkness. They didn't just *find* gold *in* the *mud*. They *made* gold *from* the *muck*.

Sometimes… I think about the forced starvation. I think about the deaths and the invasion that is still going on in Ukraine.

Then, I think about those enormous ships and trains leaving the ports.

I think about those shaking feet on the toilet seat and the black muck in our eyes.

I think about the mud puddles.

Then, I think about the soothing back scratches and the stinky garlic.

I think about the loving late-night reading by the light bulb.

I think about those onions.

Then, I think about the grit and guts that made it all possible. This was indeed the legacy they left for me.

I forged ahead too, to find a whole new direction for myself, and for my daughter. Initially digging out of holes, and weeding out (which wasn't serving me), but then harvesting something of much greater value.

If I knew how I did that, I could teach that. And so, I did.

Welcome to the *KG Method*.

Welcome to my **Number Seven.**

Think about this:

1. Each of us inherits intergenerational legacies that shape our lives. What were the main struggles of the past generations in your family?

2. How could those struggles represent strength and resilience which inspire you in your life now?

3. How do you need to reframe the 'failures' of the past generations in your family, replacing resentments, rage, or shame with compassion, empathy, and a deep embrace of human imperfection?

4. What higher level of accountability to yourself would serve you? What would you need to do differently tomorrow to get you one step closer to what you really want?

CHAPTER 3
GIGGLES AND BUBBLES:
THE SUNSHINE OF THE HEALTHY SELF

You are my sunshine

My only sunshine

You make me happy

When skies are gray

You'll never know, dear

How much I love you

Please don't take

My sunshine away

(Jimmie Davis - You Are My Sunshine, 1939)

What were you best childhood memories and why did they mean so much to you?

Giggles and Bubbles

Toot toot! …Toot toot!

We both erupted into endless giggles.

The kind of totally free laughter that makes your face hurt and your heart explode.

She told me bedtime stories about the boats on nearby Lake Erie.

She told me stories every night, as we cuddled together in bed, about when my older brother stayed with her. They would hear the boats coming into shore at night tooting their horns and laugh.

She would recreate the sounds of those boats with me and talk in a child-like voice, mimicking my brother's surprised exclamations, so excited by the sound of the horns.

She would throw her whole face into it, eyes bulging, brows raised, silly blowing from her lips as she recreated the boats.

I could smell the gentle scent of rose from her powder puffs on her dresser.

I could feel the soft bed linens behind my head as we lay there giggling. Just Grandma and me.

I felt free. I felt sweet. Most of all, I felt loved.

I remember the small bedroom window overlooking the backyard letting in the gentle breeze, so fresh.

Her room was small, with only a double bed and a dresser. The door led to a small area filled with hooks on the wall for clothes. To the right, another doorway led up a steep stairway to the second floor. Upstairs, there were two more bedrooms and a huge attic-like storage area, which was so much fun to explore. To the left, there was a small bathroom, the kind with only floorspace for one. You could stand at the sink, stand at the toilet, and stand at the tub. All in one place.

The bathtub had one of those rubber hoses you could connect to the faucet so you could spray your body or your hair. In the corner was a box of *Mr. Bubbles*. Every night, she would fill the tub with soothing warm water and generous amounts of the powder so I could splash around, blow bubbles, and 'swim' around the tub. There was no rush. I could take all the time in the world. I could play and laugh and sing, and then be wrapped up in cushy towels that were straight out of *Downy* commercials.

Adjacent to the tiny foyer with the hanging clothes was a huge dining room where at Christmas she displayed a silver tree in the corner decorated with bright blue bulbs. The large dining table filled the room. There were no empty chairs at family dinners, and I always got to sit directly beside her.

We spent endless hours over the summers at that same table, again, just her and I. She taught me to sew. She created patterns for all my dolls: dresses with matching panties, hats, and booties; coats with hats; nightgowns with slippers; and then we sewed them together. We created over fifty outfits in every colour and pattern you could imagine (my dolls must have loved her, too).

She was patient. She was creative. She was soft.

Next to the dining room there was a small living room with a burgundy chair and couch. My parents remarked that it was the exact colour of the couch I purchased twenty-five years later for my new home, 'unaware' at the time that it was the exact same color. There was another chair and a huge grate in the floor directly above the furnace in the basement that heated the home. I was always so afraid to step on that grate for fear of falling through to the lower level or being burned by the rising heat.

Beyond these rooms was an enclosed porch that stretched the entire front width of the house. I have more memories of that porch in later years as a place where I would sit quietly without her, in deep solace.

There was a small kitchen in the back of the house. She taught me to bake there. It was so small you had to move the third chair from the table to open the fridge. I wondered how she cooked her weekly meringue pies and huge family dinners in the tiniest of kitchens. She showed me how to make triple-layer *Jello* pudding desserts, the ones with pudding on the bottom, pudding mixed with *Cool Whip* in the middle, crowned with *Cool Whip*, all topped with cherries and set in glass dishes to show the beautiful layers. So simple, and I loved it!

She had a large backyard. She would give me freshly cleaned sheets with boxes of clothespins—the extra-long old-fashioned ones. I would clip the sheets up to the wire fence that ran along the right side of her yard and bring out blankets and pillows where I built my forts. I spent hours and hours out there for days on end, sometimes inviting the girl next door to join me.

Every afternoon, she would give me five cents. She had shown me how to walk to the end of the street, turn right, and then left, which took me to the neighborhood variety store. It looked like any other house on the street, except there was a sign out front. I would go in and buy pixie sticks in grape and orange, and fruit-flavoured sweet tarts. The store owner then packaged my candy in a small paper bag that I could take back to her place, and back to my fort.

At night after my bubble bath, it was time to get into my nightgown, with slippers and a house coat. She would fill tall, turquoise-and-white plastic cups with cola, and make popcorn. If it was close to Christmas, she made popcorn balls colored red and green. Then, we would put on the TV and turn the channel to *The Lawrence Welk Show*.

We were glued to that show, dancing and singing to every talent that was presented. But…we knew in *every* show Bobby and Cissy would perform their special dance. We would wait and wait and wait (I think they purposely shuffled the sequence of performers to keep us on our toes), and as soon as Lawrence introduced them, we would jump out of our seats and shriek with joy! We watched Bobby and Cissy twirl and spin and turn. I wanted to be Cissy. I dreamt about falling in love with a 'Bobby'. We would laugh and dance and love the moment. Those are some of the best memories of my entire life, in that living room with my grandma. Afterwards, we would go to bed, where I knew the silly stories of the boats would extend the joy of the night and calm me safely into slumberland.

Many years later I was told that I had a guardian angel who had died of breast cancer.

"She is always over your left shoulder, looking over you, wanting to guide you, love you, rescue you." I sat in complete silence, nodding as tears streamed down my face.

The next choice I made was an easy one. I booked an appointment and had angel wings inked over my left shoulder. I was already having conversations with Grandma about how my life was unfolding, telling her about my triumphs and sharing my pain. In harder times, I tried to remember how much she loved me. The wings I got that day would put a stamp on this for the rest of my life.

Twenty-one years after grandma died, I delivered my daughter.

That was an easy choice, too.

Grandma's middle name was Madeline.

I will name her Madeline.

I will teach Madeline about love and cuddles, parfaits and forts, boats and roses, and bubbles and giggles.

I will also teach her about forgiveness.

And when we can, we will twirl just like Cissy.

The Birth of the Healthy Self

I invite you to think of the best versions of you and where those come from.

Take that further into thinking how the beliefs of that part of you could motivate you moving forward.

My parents were typical parents of the 1960s. They were stable, consistent, and reliable; and that rhythm helped me develop a keen sense of responsibility. But, as mentioned, they leaned more toward rules than emotion. And my brothers, for the most part, preferred to play with each other or friends in the neighborhood over me. Combined, these had made me feel somewhat powerless and mostly insecure. So, having a soft place to land at Grandma's counteracted all of that and provided an emotional sanctuary where I felt accepted. Most importantly, a place where I felt special just for being me. She didn't care if I mis-sewed a seam, spilled *Jello* on the counter, or left clothes pins hiding in the blades of grass. She just loved me. Forts and sewing, cooking and bubbles, Lawrence and boats happened every day, *no matter what*.

My father once told me I was the daughter my grandma never had. I looked just like her. We just 'clicked'. Apparently, I had become her emotional savior, her pathway out of pain, where she could shower all the love she had, love that had been interrupted by a significant loss (explained in the next chapter), so she had plenty to give. It's like she released this boundless amount of joy, gentleness, softness, and patience that needed a place. It was my luck that place was me.

My experiences with Grandma and the memories I have of her were significant because they taught me first to be loved by and to love her, and second, to love myself. The unconditional love, nurturing, and the secure attachment she formed with me mirrored back to me my own goodness and fully honored that my feelings mattered. That *I* mattered.

Many years later, as a client myself, I would make sense of just how important these experiences with Grandma were to me, breaking my self-sabotage and ultimately strengthening my capacity for growth and resilience.

My wounded self had felt powerless and insecure and had tried to protect me by generalizing that *all* others would control me, exclude me, or abandon me if I was imperfect. That if I controlled things, I could prove my good enoughness and avoid further hurt by being perfectionistic, controlling, and clingy. Conversely, my healthy self, from how my *grandma* treated me, felt worthy and accepted, and so informed me how to depersonalize the things that had hurt me the most.

I grew to understand that my experience of my parents wasn't because I was *bad*, it was because of how they were raised. They firmly believed they were teaching me how to grow up to be a successful responsible adult. I learned that it wasn't because I didn't *deserve* to belong with my siblings. It had more to do with the fact that they were the same gender and closer in age, so had more in common with each other than with me. Sounds so clear, doesn't it? So hard to understand at the time.

The fact is, I discovered a warm place to live, an unconditionally loving place where control wasn't needed to feel safe, where I didn't need to be perfect to belong. This was the healthy place my grandma had invited me to all along. From there, I could believe in myself and others more, sometimes in, especially in, situations that evoked my wounded self, where control was lost, where separateness played out. With that freedom, I would eventually go on to have healthier, more balanced relationships with my family, partners, and friends, succeed in my practice as a therapist, and take risks that fulfilled my wildest of dreams!

Even still, years later, as a therapist, I came to understand just how important unconditional love is, beyond how great it feels. I formulated that in addition to having positive experiences where we feel great pride, overcoming something challenging, or achieving something important, receiving unconditional love is often at the *root* of our healthy selves. I would use these insights to facilitate my clients' deeper emotional journeys more effectively, to ensure they *also* knew what those key events were in their lives. Even more so, that they knew how to use the *meanings* of those healthy self-events to recover from whatever suffering they were living with and give them specific tools toward building the glorious lives they deserved.

It is *through* and *from* the unconditional self-love of the healthy self, which too easily gets drowned out by the noisy weapons and secret dirty deals of the wounded self (personalizing, judging, medicating, avoiding, lying, denying, minimizing, fighting, etc.) where we do our deepest work. This is powerful. I don't have to 'tell' clients what to do to feel better, their healthy self will do that for them. My job is to create an emotionally safe space where the healthy self can become known and fully utilized in clear ways. As the wounded self repairs, it simply has less control over us, and, at the same time, the healthy self gets bigger, giving us more choices, which improves our lives. The wounded self may be masterful at tempting us with immediately gratifying, albeit short-lived, self-destructive deals that ultimately spiral us down to depression. But the healthy self, living from a place of authenticity and worthiness, creates the same vigorous momentum, but toward more sustainable freedom, spiralling up to joy (if we know how). Therapy has to be prepared to open all of this up, liberating clients with clarity *and* giving them specific meaningful daily strategies to live more from their healthy selves. Anchored by unconditional love *for* themselves.

The Wise Gut: Why I Became a Therapist

If we are living consciously, the healthy self becomes accessible to us. One way that happens is we begin listening to and trusting our gut. The healthy self actually *lives* in the gut.

I invite you to think about what your gut may be telling you.

The healthy-self experiences I had with my grandma had enough positive impact on me to believe in feelings, more importantly to believe in *my* feelings. Until I grew from **Invitation Number Seven**, many years later, I couldn't live fully free with authenticity and vulnerability. But my gut told me as early as adolescence that I wanted to go *further with feelings*. Further, in a way that made a difference.

And not just for me, for others too. In fact, Oprah calls this our calling: "I've come to believe that each of us has a personal calling that's as unique as a fingerprint—and that the best way to succeed is to discover what you love and then find a way to offer it to others in the form of service, working hard and also allowing the energy of the universe to lead you" (A Quote by Oprah Winfrey, n.d.). I knew, as young as fourteen, that I was being called to the work of psychotherapy. I recognized the calling. I knew that calling came from my gut. And the unconditional love from my grandma taught me to trust my gut.

Following that gut, while in grade nine, I searched for and found an opportunity through my oldest cousin's wife, who was a social worker. As soon as I learned about what she did, I launched into action! I asked to job shadow her child welfare work in Toronto during my March Break. Most people thought the experience would turn me off my pursuit. It didn't. In fact, it increased my interest and thrust me further into it. I threw myself into a wide variety of volunteering opportunities to learn more about serving others' emotional and mental needs. I diligently prepared my education path, receiving my bachelor's and master's degrees. And, wherever I studied and worked I always advocated strongly for my professional development. Whether it was helping female offenders' reintegration to the community; supporting hospitalized psychiatric patients; finding summer Social Work positions to research individuals and families affected by eating disorders; using three years to immerse myself in province-wide mental health programs; or taking ten years to provide individual, group, couples, and family therapy toward opening my private practice in 1998. I was determined to learn everything possible to ensure the therapy I provided made the meaningful impact both my gut instincts and my clients' gut instincts were seeking. My healthy self, living through my work as a therapist, contributed toward that part of me getting bigger, organically. Thus, creating an enormous amount of fulfillment for me over the years. After all, listening to our gut invites us to spiral up to joy, to a place we deserve, but didn't always realize.

Friends often comment on how long I have been a therapist, how hard I work, the long hours I keep, how drained I must be. The *opposite* is true. After a day of sessions, I am completely energized. I am fully alive and feel the power of the work through my clients' breakthroughs. *Being part of real conversations about real things that make a real difference!*

Something I'd been yearning for since childhood. In hearing and following my gut, I had finally found my 'place' *and* could help others find their 'place' too.

How well are you listening to your gut? Where is **your** joy?

Teaching Others How to Use Their Wise Gut: A *KG* Tool for the Healthy Self

Knowing firsthand the power of trusting my gut and how that further expanded my healthy self and my life, I knew I had to incorporate it somehow into the work I was doing with clients.

I learned that the nerve endings around our stomach are only second in complexity to our brain. When we say "I have a gut feeling" we usually do, and it's usually telling us something worth paying attention to. That *is* our healthy self, what the Buddha calls the wise gut. Our wounded self, conversely, lives in the noise of our head, and drives negative thinking, part of which I've already referred to as stinky thinking.

The clutter in our neuropathways based on what caused us pain will easily misdirect us as we react, usually impulsively, for immediate gratification, and we sabotage ourselves. Furthermore, if we indulge that noise, we either don't hear our gut, or if we do, we ignore it, argue with it, and override it. At fourteen, despite other hurts, I heard *my* gut, and I listened to it. That changed my life. That was worth learning more about and so I did.

Many years later and during Covid, when all my sessions went online, I took a closer look at the Dialectical Behavioral Therapy (DBT) program I had already been teaching (that bridge between the head and heart programs) and integrated some of the methods for a more simplified, effective practice.

DBT uses components of Self-Care and Cognitive Behavioral Therapy (CBT), but adds in other elements including mindfulness, distress tolerance, emotional regulation, and interpersonal scripting. I ended up developing a *KG* four-part, two-minute daily meditation for clients to do to build mindfulness, self-compassion, self-affirmation and...*Wise Gut* channelling. As with all other interventions, this tool would also take what we knew from theory toward specific at-home exercises clients could customize for daily brain health, and complement the CBT and deeper work we were doing in sessions.

I knew that with:

- Mindfulness: If we could find our breath easier when triggered, we would be better regulated.
- Self-Compassion: If we could be less judgmental and more compassionate with our pain ('allowing' ourselves to feel what we feel) we would be better regulated.
- Self-Affirmation: If we could remind ourselves of our goodness every day, we would be better regulated (building up resilience for when 'bad' things happen in our lives, by noticing our worth, placing ourselves in a *one-up position* every twenty-four hours). This balances the brain and invites ambiguity. It reminds us that there is goodness even within the bad. Ambiguity is one of the highest emotionally intelligent skills for good reason.

    And...

- Wise Gut: If every day we cleared that pathway between the noise and the gut, between the wounded self and the healthy self (by hearing, trusting, and acting on specific guidance from the gut) we would also be better regulated.

The meditation captures these four elements and is now a core part of the *KG* Emotional Regulation program. I was now actively practicing and teaching a part of what my fourteen-year-old self had known so long ago. I knew if it worked for me, it would work for others, and it does.

This is how it works...

Set out two minutes *every* day, ideally at the same time, each day. A lot of coaches believe this is how we should start our day to establish a positive mind set and intention (aka the 5:00 a.m. Club). I try to do it most days before my feet hit the floor. I know an eastern doctor who does it midday to refresh himself. Sometimes I love doing it at the end of my day. The important thing is to find a regular time, every day. You will be glad you do. It resets. It grounds. It nourishes the wounded self. It strengthens the healthy self. Although big moments create change through the invitations of life, it's also the little steps we take frequently which ultimately create a new neuropathway to serve ourselves better.

1) Mindfulness: The minute meditation. Find your breath. Feel it. Count it. See it. Listen to an app, video, or music. Notice the immediate five senses. Somehow, anyhow, just find it. You will get distracted. At this point, many of us get frustrated and give up. It's important to remember that the practice does not come with the expectation of not being distracted. Just the opposite. It comes with the practice of quietly noticing the distraction and reducing the effort or judgment while finding your way back to the breath. It's about making the breath

familiar. It's about knowing where to find the breath. When you need it the most. When you are triggered.

2) Self-Compassion: "It was so hard when _____ happened and made me feel _____."

3) Self-Affirmation: "But, what went well, was when _____ happened. That reminded me that I am a _____ person."

4) Wise Gut: "So, what I need from myself today is _____, by _____ing."

Try it. Do it daily. Do it daily for a month until it is a habit. Expand the layers of your negative emotions with curiosity by not repeating the same feelings for #2 in a week. Broaden the scope of your positive identity by not repeating the same descriptions of yourself in #3. Be curious about how this helps you when you are triggered, reducing the voice of your inner critic, and amplifying compassion instead; improving your self-image and clearing the way for you to take better care of yourself.

Think about this:

1. Understand your healthy self. Who has unconditionally loved you? What have you achieved that was important? What was hard that you overcame, or made you proud of yourself? How is that part of you showing up in your life now?

2. What does your healthy self believe about you that could serve you when you are in pain?

3. How are you using the breath to find intention?

CHAPTER 4
SHAME AND THE DIRTY LITTLE SECRET: REBUILDING TRUST, REPAIRING SHAME

Until you've been beside a man

You don't know what he wants

You don't know if he cries at night

You don't know if he don't

When nothin' comes easy, old nightmares are real

Until you've been beside a man

You don't how he feels

(Bob Seger & the Silver Bullet Band - Shame on the Moon, 1982)

Living with Secrets

I invite you to acknowledge the secrets you are keeping.

Ora Ford, my paternal grandmother, who I called Grandma, was the fourth of six siblings, with four brothers and a sister. She grew up in the farming community in Essex County near Leamington. She married when she was eighteen and gave birth to my father six years later. When my father was nine, she gave birth to her second son, Ronnie. Ronnie never reached his first birthday. At eight months, he died of a brain tumor. One year later, Grandma adopted a baby boy from a local hospital. My uncle. Ronnie's memory was honored when his name was given to my second brother upon his birth.

In those days, it was believed that talking about pain made things worse.

In those days, it was believed everyone was better off ignoring discomfort, burying it, and moving on. Those who could not were often institutionalized.

In those days, people suffered in silence. Children absorb the unconscious and unresolved pain of their parents. Unspoken pain complicates the pain and complicates what is absorbed.

Secrets were common. Secrets of abuse. Secrets of affairs. Secrets of unwed mothers who were sent away to give birth under false pretenses before returning to their families and communities. And secrets of adoption.

My grandma lived with the biggest grief of all—losing a child. She also lived with a secret—adopting a baby who had been born from an affair. I think the infant loss and the adoption secret were emotionally intertwined for her, in overwhelming ways. The birth mother's husband had been serving in the military overseas while his wife back home was unfaithful and became pregnant. The husband was discharged from service and arrived home the day before the baby's birth. He insisted the baby be adopted out of the family to save the marriage. Although elated following the adoption, my grandma isolated herself at home, spending most of the time at home with her new son. They lived in a small town where everyone knew everyone. She was in fear that if they were seen together in public, the secret would be revealed, and she would lose him. Grandma had already lost one baby, and she would not risk losing another.

My father, ten years old when his adopted brother joined the family, helped keep my uncle's birth history in confidence. He had grown up believing the narrative of the time— that it was better not to talk about the hard stuff. And so, he didn't. And so, they didn't. Nobody did. In his heart, my dad truly never considered his brother to be anyone else to him other than his brother. It appeared the secret was safe, and the family could move on from the loss.

Despite their efforts, my uncle would hear and see many things over the years that disturbed and confused him. Family and friends hinted about his adoption, including a cousin who once said to a blood cousin, in front of my uncle, "I can't marry you, but I can marry *you*" (and pointed *to* my uncle).

It seemed like everyone knew about his adoption but him. Even his future mother and father-in-law, who lived in another county, knew, but no one ever sat down and talked with him about it directly. When my uncle got married, my grandma hinted that there was something they should talk about, but neither followed up. Even when her health worsened years later, she affirmed to him, "No matter what anyone tells you, I am your mother." Again, there was no follow-up.

My uncle's suspicions created deep insecurity and confusion until it all blew up in front of him one random day. It had been an otherwise innocent conversation with a former co-worker of my grandpa's. My uncle was helping to sell the family vehicle once my grandpa could no longer drive, and the once co-worker expressed an interest in the purchase. During the transaction, the man unknowingly unlocked the entire drama to my uncle when he casually reminisced about how my grandpa had come to work one day, proudly boasting about picking up his *adopted* son from the hospital the day before.

Understandably, my uncle's life shattered.

How Secrets Feed the Wounded Self

I invite you to be curious about how the secrets you are keeping are working against you.

There are many painful experiences that undermine the healthy self. If significant enough, these experiences not only weaken the best versions of ourselves, they also sabotage our resilience by actually *feeding* the wounded self. Secrets are a good example of this. I often see secrets as toxic strangleholds that run insidiously in the background, creating harmful narratives of suspicion, distrust, betrayal, and passive/avoidant communication. When they surface, which they usually do at unexpected, hurtful times, secrets create drama, as was demonstrated in my own family. More damage is usually caused, more than what revealing the original secret sooner and more directly would have done. The wounded self twists us up with beliefs that we aren't good enough, or others aren't strong enough. Not enough to be honest about our fears. Not enough to be honest about the truth. The cover-up easily leads us to lie, or at the very least, omit the truth. Simply put, the wounded self muffles the voice of the healthy self.

The fact is secrets are usually kept by good people who *are* afraid. Fear that is not only absorbed inwardly but is also projected onto others. *If I can't handle the truth, neither can you.* The implicit message is that someone would be crushed by revealing the truth. When the reality is that the chronic suffering of either living dishonestly or under constant suspicions of what the truth could be, over time, crushes more.

These all-too-common projections of fear are supported in a number of ways within the human mind. One such type of negative thought pattern is the 'stinky thinking of avoidance'. This is when we trick ourselves into believing that avoiding something is better (for short-term gain) when it actually isn't because it causes long-term pain. In this case, being fooled into believing that not knowing will be better than knowing. No doubt my grandma was afraid. So was my uncle. And when his adoption was confirmed, after years of Grandma 'believing' he didn't and shouldn't know, and after years of him living while suspecting, she died. This made it impossible for them to ever work it out together once he knew, causing even more hurt. Not to mention how the secret had persistently confused and undermined family relationships for many years while my uncle grew up, long before her death.

Also, as was demonstrated by my own dirty little herpes secret, covering up also exponentially increases shame quietly from underneath. Combined, the pervasive silence and the lack of resolution of the hidden problem manifests beliefs in increasingly convincing ways of how bad we are or how bad others are. My wounded self tricked me into finding immediate relief through not working it out directly within myself or with my partner, believing that those conversations would crush me and cause me to be alone. Years later, when it was too late, I learned that the stranglehold of that suppressed pain reinforced an ugly view of myself *to* myself, contributed to persistently poorer physical and mental health for me over the years, and ultimately played a key part in the demise of our marriage. It caused me *much* more shame and isolation in the long term than if had I freed myself years earlier.

How KG Accountable Therapy Helps Rebuild Trust

The Accountable KG Therapy Method had to include the ability to help people find a way to be less afraid of uncovering the truth. And, to do it in a way that strengthened instead of crushed. That reduced shame instead of feeding it. This overlaps with the work I often do on issues of betrayal, where secrecy exists within dishonesty and lies. If trust isn't repaired, nothing else matters. I developed structured healing conversations that occur over multiple sessions with family members in different combinations. This work is incredibly powerful. I don't watch arguments. I don't chase people back to the room. We mindfully sit together—with brave, compassionate honesty—and take it carefully one step at a time.

Consider this example:

1. A teenage boy, growing up, sees differences between himself and his 'father'. He suspects the man is not his father. His younger siblings look like his father, and he doesn't. His father treats him differently than his siblings. He internalizes low self-confidence. He acts this out and gets into trouble at school. He feels worse. His father punishes him. Their arguments intensify. His mother tries, but she falls short in her mediation between the two and is caught in the middle. The boy is aggressive toward his siblings.

2. His school guidance counselor refers him to the social worker, who helps him make connections to how his actions reflect his poor sense of self and uncomfortable feelings of not belonging in the family.

3. The social worker brings in his mother one-on-one and learns that when the boy was very young, his birth father abandoned the family; she remarried and had two more children. She felt telling her son the truth would hurt him too much, and believed acting as though the second husband was his biological father would be better for him over knowing that his birth father abandoned him.

4. The social worker empowers the boy to ask good questions of his mother about his background, why he feels like he doesn't belong, and, upon learning the truth, asking about his birth father, about why she never told him the truth. The mother learns how to reveal the truth with compassion and honesty and fills in the gaps.

The boy is supported to explain the full impact of the secret. The mother validates his experience without justifying. The boy expresses what he needs differently to the mother (how she can support him better in the current family) and the mother follows through.

5.   The truth sets them free. Additionally, a strong precedent is set for the wounded self who learns that happiness comes from letting go of the acting out, the arguing, and the avoiding. More power is delivered to the healthy self through direct expression and communication.

6.   The mother is more effective in supporting a better relationship between her firstborn and stepfather and gets out of the middle. The boy is freed up to work through his anger, poor self-image, and abandonment by the birth father. The stepfather and boy are freed up to develop a new relationship together. The siblings, age appropriately, become part of the honest discussions, so better sibling relationships develop over time.

I am especially proud of these parts of the therapy. In particular when there are serious, heart-wrenching ruptures of betrayal, impeding connections, and fueling of destructive rage (internal or external) that would have otherwise gone on for years, if not forever. Clients are able to finally find *their* way home. I sometimes think about how tools such as this could have helped my uncle have a happier life, my grandma a more peaceful death, and helped my marriage get out from under the shame of the STI.

I invite you to think about:

- The questions you need answers to **or** answers you have that might help someone else's questions.
- The impact secrets have on you and how you're seeking validation of those or how you're validating how your secrets affected someone else.
   And…
- What you need to move on, to rebuild trust or what you can offer to regain someone else's trust.

Living with Shame: Invitation Number Two, Imperfect Endings

I invite you to think about what your experiences of 'endings' have been and how these impacted you.

In March 1977, I was thirteen and, on a plane, back from Tampa, Florida, with my parents. My dad had received a call that Grandma had died, and we were on an emergency flight home for the funeral. He had seen her before we left on our annual trip down south. She had been declining and only worsened while we were away. I guess that was his goodbye. My uncle had gone to see her too, sensing that she had been aching to tell him something on her death bed. He later realized those final moments would be her last attempt to share the details of his birth and the delicate decisions she had made. It would also be *his* last chance to express to her what his experiences of the secret had been. But she lost courage and so did he, and she passed away without the two ever exchanging those intimate stories together.

I fell into a deep sleep while on that plane and had a nightmare which shook me awake. I started screaming and crying uncontrollably in the cabin, making everyone around uncomfortable. After we returned, I remember sitting with our friends, laughing inappropriately for the somber tone of the conversation. I honestly could not make sense of, or process, the flood of emotions that I was feeling. They were surfacing with a weird mix of nightmare numbness and deflective humor, and I didn't know what was happening.

What was more confusing to me had to do with the last time I saw her. We had gone to see her in the hospital. She was dying of breast cancer. We walked down the long hallway and when we approached her room I stopped. I stood outside in the hallway. I looked over. Grandma was in a double room to my left. Her bed was the closest one to the door. She was leaning up in her bed, motioning for me to come in.

Suddenly, I resisted.

I froze.

And I froze in fear.

She knew she was dying. She had wanted to say goodbye to me. But I stood immobilized in that hallway while she spread her arms out open wide for me to come in. She wanted to cuddle with me, as we had so many times before. But I just stood there. And then, I walked away.

For a long time, that day in the hallway caused me enormous guilt and shame and created this thick impenetrable block of nausea—and frankly—disgust within myself. And, as I got older and learned more about her story, the death of her second child, and my uncle's adoption, honestly, I felt worse. I knew I had let her down. I knew I had let myself down. I felt she lost me that day in ways that she had been fearful of her entire life. That I had diminished all that we had shared together. All that she had given me. All that she had meant to me. And I couldn't do the one thing that she needed. And I would never get that chance again. The blanket of shame suffocated me.

How KG Accountable Therapy Repairs Shame

Why do smart people make 'dumb' decisions that then haunt them for years to come? How on earth could I ever forgive myself for what I didn't do? Sometimes, I honestly don't know how to think about 'forgiveness', but I do know about the freedom we discover from deep 'acceptance'. I understand how anchoring into the full facts of the history, we can accept how the past could not have been any different. I believe even more that our power rests in living from the associated invitations of that acceptance to benefit our future.

The answer lays in unlocking the attached shame—period. This is where it gets real. There was no way I would ever be free if I carried *my* version of that hospital day with me.

Researcher and author Brené Brown encourages us to deeply embrace the human experience of imperfection, to free ourselves from shame in order to live fully with healthy vulnerability. Brown believes this helps us connect more authentically to others because in essence, we are more authentically connected to ourselves. Otherwise, if we shame, we blame. If we blame, we shame. This would be critical for me. And it had to start with what I believed was the biggest mistake I had made that day in the hospital. As long as I shamed myself, I would try harder to be perfect. As long as I expected to be perfect and failed, I would turn the shame of that failure inside out and blame others if they weren't perfect. With that paradigm, others would frequently let me down. Of course, they would. They were imperfect just like me. But how could I take the concepts Brené was telling us about and turn the theory into useable practice for me and for my clients?

I developed a 3-step shame tool to use with clients. Listed below is the tool with my example:

As you read this, I invite you to think about what shame you are carrying around with you. Apply these three steps and see what you discover.

1. **Normalize – identify how anyone else who experienced everything that you had up until that moment you are ashamed of, may have, in fact likely would have reacted the exact same way as you.**

    As you read this, you will read common sense. Common sense that I couldn't see, for a long time. Shame easily robs us of the ability to rationalize, or invites us to over-rationalize. Both blind us.

    These were my experiences that normalized my reaction.
    - Losing someone as important as Grandma was to me, makes most people afraid.
    - I was only thirteen years old, and my body was going through major hormonal changes, naturally disrupting emotional stability as it does for most adolescents.
    - Although I had significant love from my grandma, I had not had enough emotional conversations in my life up until that point to understand my

feelings, let alone put my feelings into words under that amount of pressure and fear. I had been rewarded more for suppressing emotions.

Others in a similar place would have reacted the same. That was worth reminding myself.

2. **Precipitate – identify the specific stressors present at the very moment you are ashamed of, relevant to explaining your reaction.** The factual thinking promoted in the Cognitive Behavioral Change Program helps us anchor to specific truths instead of sinking into the depths of generalized, self-critical shame. The facts were:

   - The complete shock and fear of what was happening paralyzed me. I was in complete shock in that sterile, ugly, stinky hallway.
   - I was unprepared for what I was facing. We had never really talked as a family about what was happening and how *any* of us were feeling.
   - When she sat up in bed it became the 'goodbye' I never wanted. If I had stepped closer and we cuddled, it would be our last cuddle and that was unbearable for me to face. No more bedtime stories. No more bubble baths. No more Cissy.

   In my massive ball of fear, I was imperfect and couldn't give us the perfect goodbye. The immediate facts spoke for themselves.

3. **Benefit – identify what would you benefit from doing differently when faced with a similar situation in the future.** As much as we'd frequently like to, we can't turn back time. What we can do, however, is make our future better because of the past. This is powerful and possible because laying within the lesson of our past regret is the message of what to do better in the future. **This is Regret Without Shame.**

   I would benefit from:

   - Empowering myself with facts instead of criticizing myself for imperfections and increasing my sense of self-compassion to normalize my fears. Instead of compassion, I had developed a strong internal critic. I would be too hard on myself and that would only increase fear and shame and lead to more regrettable moments in my life.
   - Learning how to face endings with radical acceptance and ground grief (explained later). As part of the missed second invitation in my life, losing my grandma and avoiding the goodbye to my favorite person, I went on to avoid endings. I concluded that I couldn't face endings, so they should be avoided at all costs. That meant I stayed in unhealthy relationships too long.

How did you do?

If I had been my kind of therapist to myself, I would have taught myself:

- The Cognitive Behavioral Change Program to silence my inner critical voice and to empower myself with a direct expression of negative emotions, even if, especially if, it meant ending a relationship.
- The four-part meditation tool to a) increase my self-compassion to allow myself the freedom to be fearful without judgment, and b) to increase my self-affirmation, reminding myself of my worthiness, to advocate for my needs more effectively.
- The three-step shame tool to normalize my fears and let go of the shame of the non-goodbye.
- How the shame of the ending was in essence an invitation to recover my good enoughness that had been damaged previously and was piggybacking on my regret of the non-goodbye.

Living Without Secrets

Long after Grandma died, my uncle began picking up the shattered pieces of his life. He found his birth family living in California, and finally learned the full circumstances of his birth. His birth mother had continued to struggle throughout her life. The couple's marriage had ended despite him being sent away from the family. It turned out his adoption had not been the solution after all. The biological father died before ever meeting him. But with the truth now out in the open, my uncle could begin a journey toward freedom, not possible before.

Living Without Shame

Finally, after accepting the seventh invitation that came with my divorce, I learned how to communicate my emotions more effectively, set better boundaries in relationships, and live with less shame and much more confidence, compassion, and healthy power. Part of that was possible because I had worked through the unworthiness of my childhood and let go of the shame of my STIs and my imperfect ending with Grandma. I finally recovered a part of myself that had been begging to come out for a long time.

One autumn day, when the chill in the air was somehow softened by the amber leaves on the ground, I sat at Grandma's grave. However, I did not sit there alone. I sat with my daughter, Madeline. Beside Grandma lay my grandfather. Beside her also lay her second-born infant son, Ronnie. I introduced Grandma to Madeline. I introduced Madeline to Grandma. I happily told my beautiful daughter the stories of the giggles and bubbles. We laughed. We cried. Now, she understood her namesake and what she meant to me. Now, she understood where my deep capacity for love came from. Now, *we* could love each other more. Now we could laugh and play more together, just like Grandma and I once did.

Think about this:

1. What are the unspoken questions or unexpressed feelings you have never discussed with a significant someone who broke your trust?

2. What are the secrets in your life that are holding you emotional hostage or creating unnecessary shame for you?

3. Understand your wounded self. What experiences harmed you growing up and negatively changed what you believed about yourself, others, life, and love? How do these overshadow your healthy self and cause you to act in ways that get you further away from what you really want in your life?

4. What might you still be carrying shame about?

5. How could you accept your imperfection about what happened?

6. What do you need to think, do, or say as evidence that you have let go of that shame?

CHAPTER 5
CAN YOU SEE ME?:
SEEING YOURSELF

I am sailing, I am sailing

Home again, 'cross the sea

I am sailing stormy waters

To be near you, to be free

I am flying, I am flying

Like a bird cross the sky

I am flying, passing high clouds

To be with you, to be free

Can you hear me? Can you hear me?

Through the dark night, far away

I am dying, forever crying

To be with you, who can say?

(Rod Stewart - Sailing, 1975)

It's the middle of the night. All is quiet. Everyone is sleeping.

There's a hum that gets increasingly louder as it approaches.

And then…*The Flash of Light*. It streams through the huge living-room windows, completely lighting up the room. The entire room is exposed to the outside—the couch, the tables, the walls…everything.

He can see everything, and so there is no guesswork about how he would come into the home and take everything. Break into the home to take *me*.

I am awakened by the light. I scramble out of bed, run to the door, and begin what feels like a marathon to get to safety across the entire width of the house to the opposite hallway leading to the other bedrooms where my parents and brothers are.

I stumble, I get lost in the dark; my direction is confused, and I stumble again.

I am running out of time.

He finds me. I am captured by the bad guy. The boogeyman gets me.

And then I wake up.

This was my childhood nightmare. I had that dream over and over, countless times through the years. It was the same every time, usually marked by the flash of light in the window which sent me unsuccessfully tripping across the dark to get to my family.

This dream may seem like an old, silly dream to you. To me, it was anything but. To me, it was about separateness and difference. Don't get me wrong. My home was safe. My parents loved me, and I knew it. They were deeply committed and dedicated to me in many ways, but there was this element of being *different* that had an impact on me. Understanding how, at a deeper level, my loss of control and sense of unworthiness developed from this, and how I found my way out, became a big part of my life.

Separation

I invite you to think about what 'got in your way' growing up.

Did you experience separateness?

Growing up, 'separation' for me took on a variety of forms.

The house I was born into had that huge living room with the window in the middle (from my dream), where my parents would host fun house parties in the sixties and seventies; parties with silly games like hockey using orange-filled pantyhose tied around your hips as the sticks, and wieners strung to your waist that you had to stick into slim-necked pop bottles for points. The family room ran adjacent to the living room and led into the kitchen. Off the kitchen, at the front of the house, was my very tiny bedroom, apparently the original dining room? On the complete opposite side of the house—past the kitchen, past the family room, past the living room—was my parents' bedroom, the washroom, and a bedroom shared by my two brothers. For some people, having a private place away from everything may have been quiet in an appealing way, even special. But to me, it felt like everyone was so far away (from me), especially as I lay awake in my bed alone, and I hated it.

I was also separated by age (five-to-seven years younger than my two brothers). I hated being the youngest. All I knew was that I wasn't included where I deeply wanted to be. This *is* important because our sibling relationships are our first chance with peers to achieve a healthy sense of interdependence through reciprocal interactions. These times in our lives are also a chance to develop our self-worth as positive responses from others that reflect our goodness back to us. If there is rejection or exclusion, dependent insecurity rather than interdependent worthiness is internalized. I think that's what happened to me.

The sibling gap in age also meant, in my rather strict home, that my bedtime was significantly earlier than everyone else's, and because my bedroom was near the family room, I could hear all the family fun that carried on without me from my room. I would obediently go to bed on time. There was no choice. But I was not happy about it. I would lay awake for a long time, then quietly creep (or so I thought) along the kitchen cupboards to peek into the family room to be a part of what was going on, if only at a distance. That only got me into trouble.

My bedroom was also at the front of the house beside the driveway where kids gathered, so I could hear all the older neighborhood friends playing with my brothers long after I had been sent to bed. Extended daylight hours in the summer months meant that kids seemed to play for *hours* without me, and I felt I was missing out; all made more dramatic because I was bored and alone in bed.

One random incident didn't help. While we were still young, my brother was giving horseback rides to kids around the house, and, to my surprise, he invited me to be a part of it. But on my first round up the driveway to the finish line, I fell over his shoulders and landed on the pavement, mouth first, knocking out all of my front teeth. What a scene that was. I paid the price (so did my parents) of getting my teeth fixed over the next decade. But what was far more disappointing to me than my teeth was that my chance to be included had ended before it had hardly started, and it had ended badly.

On another day, that also didn't end well, I found myself huddled away from the rain in our large garage with all the neighborhood kids. It was completely out of the ordinary for me to be involved, and I was thrilled. I decided I should throw a few swear words into the conversation to fit in. The problem came when my mom overheard me, and I was in big trouble again. The only way I thought to save myself from the consequences was to blame my brothers for teaching me those words. She took the story hook, line, and sinker. I watched at the bathroom door while their mouths were literally being washed out with soap, short-sightedly relieved that it wasn't me.

I never came 'clean' to my mother and of course that only widened the gap between me and my brothers. Initially it felt cool, swearing like the others to be 'one of the group'. I also felt a sense of control by avoiding the immediate punishment from my mom. But, in the end, I actually felt less connected to the people I was trying to win over and less in control of the situation. The swearing and then lying caused me to be *more* separated from my siblings, who were now in trouble because of me, and they knew it. I was also more separated from my new 'friends' who actually *didn't* think it was cool to throw others under the bus the way I had done.

I also felt separateness because of *gender*. Being the only daughter was more than just having different stereotypical play preferences to my brothers. In a conservative household, it also meant stricter rules and expectations for me, which never really made sense to me. In fact, I remember as a teen speaking out about this (alone, with no sisters to ally with me). I actually became the butt end of everyone's joke one night at dinner, like I was the crazy one for even thinking that I should be parented the same as them. The fact that I could get pregnant as a teen (which I never did) when my brothers couldn't, that this somehow justified much tighter controls on me, and me being the odd one out in thinking that was weird, just disconnected me further.

I also seemed to be separated emotionally. The rest of the family seemed 'fine' focusing on tasks and chores. I remember being confused, *a lot*, by the strong feelings I was having of joy, enthusiasm, creativity, but also loneliness, frustration, and sadness; which no one else seemed to be talking about. I think they tolerated me, but they didn't really *get* me. I would spend hours making homemade cards for family members' birthdays and anniversaries and other events and leave them on their pillows to surprise them. I would dream up special meals to make for my family that in my imagination were over-the-top gourmet. I would dress up and perform dances. But I would never get back an amount of excitement that came anywhere close to mine, so I would be regularly disappointed. They loved me, they just operated on a different frequency. This experience of difference started to take on a deeper meaning to me and I consequently concluded that something was wrong with *me, not them*. This is the egocentricity of the child's brain, that too easily internalizes personalization when things go wrong.

For a short while, I found a place where I did fit in better. Our family moved to the Maritimes when I was in about grade two. Here I found the people to be friendly, open, and expressive! I loved their warm energy, and I found my place. Once back in the GTA, where I spent most of my growing-up years, I continued to desperately look for that same level of connection and purpose. Life had somehow become a search for belonging.

It seemed that when my brothers became teenagers, I placed them on an even higher pedestal, and the gap between how I saw them vs. how I saw myself widened. I would try to learn their music (usually leading me to recklessly scratching their vinyl records). So, that backfired. I would also awkwardly drink and smoke to fit in with them when they hosted their house parties. That backfired, too… again trying too hard and ending up with less, not more, control and less, not more, acceptance. I think my mom could see what was happening and would come to my defense, just like the day of the soap, but as much as she tried, it just made things worse, and I came to be seen as the favoured one.

When my own teenage years arrived, I was a stand-out studious nerd and going about things all the wrong way. My mom (bless her heart for trying) slipped a pink pamphlet about sex under my door and left me on my own, shocked as I read its content. I can only imagine how that subject had been tackled—or not—in her home! Now, I *really* needed someone to address my emotions, with sex, drugs, and rock and roll on the table. So, I adopted two surrogate mothers. One was the passionate mother of my first boyfriend introduced in the next chapter, who was full of emotional energy like me and who I leaned on a lot. The other was Carol, who lived across the street, and who I'd babysat for. She was younger, more emotional, more open, and she thought I was adorable, kinda like Grandma had. No coincidence. I was drawn to her.

With Carol, we navigated through what seemed at the time to be overwhelming and important decisions I was facing. I brought my friends to her home too so as a group we could sort out our adolescence. I practically lived at Carol's, going there anytime I could. I think that hurt my mother, and I regret not having clearer conversations with her about that at the time. I just didn't have the maturity or awareness of what I was doing and why. I just knew I needed genuine conversation about real struggles and real feelings.

Family Dynamics and The Invitations

The families and communities we grow up in heavily influence how the parts of self and related belief systems develop.

I invite you to think about the narratives and roles present in your family while growing up, and how those shaped your beliefs and the patterns in your life.

My parents were very dedicated to our family, and I think because of the times and their upbringing, it was 'normal' for them to be strict and more focused on chores and school than emotions. That wasn't all bad and did wonders for me in terms of becoming disciplined, hardworking, and academically strong. My mother was a homemaker most of our growing up years, immersed in working hard in the house, which she did very well. What else could I expect from her, growing-up with the demands of an onion farm? My father worked hard too and traveled a lot. When he was home, he was also very task-driven, which I know was his way of providing. Although not living on a farm, he had been raised by parents who did grow up on farms, so hard work was also highly valued. I also think the innocent, albeit tight rein on his brother's birth history must have planted a seed of emotional avoidance. A sign of the times, and nothing to do with the love the brothers felt for each other. But the overall emotional suppression in my home went against my instincts.

I learned that I was what is called the 'emotional barometer' (Bram Levinson, 2022) of the family, expressing the unexpressed, which feels natural to do and balances the family system but is a tough role to take as it sets you apart and sets you up to be disappointed. I didn't know anything about that growing up. To me, I just felt different.

The truth was, when personality, strictness, distance, age gap, birth order, gender, and task-focused family scripts collided, there became a clear divide between me and my siblings, and I felt extremely alone. More importantly, I inaccurately attached my experience of separateness to conclusions of powerlessness and unworthiness, believing I wasn't good enough, others would reject me, and life was lonely. These are examples of the negative core beliefs I unconsciously internalized during that phase in my life. While the healthy self develops positive beliefs about self, others, life, and love (aka my grandma's unconditional love), the wounded self becomes entrenched in negative beliefs in the same categories. When the negative experiences that change core beliefs are powerful enough, they form those invitations of growth.

If you're interested in understanding more about the healthy and wounded self and commonly held core beliefs, detailed explanations of these are available in Appendix B as they relate to key developmental life stages.

The early separateness was my life's **Invitation Number One**. Not understanding the invitation however, meant that I carried core wounds of powerlessness and unworthiness with me that led me astray, as it does for all of us. Without knowing how to feel and think differently, I would be set up for **Invitations Two Through Six**, which spotlighted these same hurts in different circumstances with different people. Ignoring or being confused by the wound ultimately limits and downgrades our choices. For me, those were particularly important in my relationships and especially in relationships when I wasn't easily accepted, until I woke up. That's just how core wounds and beliefs work.

The real wake-up came for me at **Invitation Number Seven**, after my divorce many years later, when the deeper wounds of control and unworthiness resurfaced in one of the most severe ways. Finally, I dug deep to discover and correct the incorrect core beliefs I had internalized about myself that had been misdirecting and undermining me my whole life. As a result, I made a much fuller recovery at that point, not just helping me survive the divorce, but launching me into places of pure sustainable joy not possible before.

To achieve this, I had to clarify and accept two key beliefs:

1) That my parents' overcontrol was more about their legacies of strict hard work and the associated emotional suppression derived from those legacies, than about me deserving to be punished and silenced.

2) That my brothers' exclusion of me had nothing to do with me not deserving to belong, but had more to do with their close age and common gender. This was at a time when conservative, stereotypic gender roles were mainstream (boys will be boys and girls will be girls) which naturally connected them more to each than to me.

So clearly defined here, yet so twisted up in my mind and heart for so long. But why?

Because it is common for us humans to seek congruence in our brains to make sense of our lives. But what is also common is that when we face painful events which create the uncomfortable dissonance, we are usually in confused, overwhelmed emotional states. The dysregulation of this significantly reduces the required cognitive and emotional energies we need for clarity. Therefore, we too easily make sense in ways that are inaccurate. This may help us 'get through', but the problem is that we take those inaccuracies with us, contaminating those deeper core beliefs we develop of self, others, life, and love. In turn, this causes generalizations and projections which put us at risk of making future similar events fit in the same way, also incorrectly. Even worse, this puts us at risk of provoking future similar events happen, confirming those beliefs, creating a self-fulfilling prophecy.

Take the example of someone bullied as a teen for their different clothes or hair. They are overpowered and they begin dressing like the others to fit in, wrongly concluding that they are not good enough as they are and that others are better. The normal, healthy process of exploring their unique identity at that stage in their life is disrupted. As they move into young adulthood, they are at risk of losing themselves further by engaging in pleasing, accommodating behaviors with friends and partners; *or* riding the aggressive side of the wound and becoming bullies themselves, creating bigger, deeper problems in the next developmental stage of achieving intimacy. The wounded self insidiously takes full control before we even know what is happening. The good news is that these events are repeated, and in essence, are the very opportunities we *need* to master the wounds. We arrive at the ever-important invitations until we figure it out.

As we got older, the gap between me and one of my siblings changed for the better. At my wedding, my oldest brother proclaimed in his speech (voice cracking) 'how he never really knew me.' As much as it hurt to hear that, and slightly embarrassing as it was being advertised to our guests, I knew it was the truth, and I completely appreciated his vulnerability. When that same brother went through a divorce and other family issues years later, he reached to me for support and expert advice. I immediately flew out to his home in western Canada and helped him more than once. It meant the world to me that he sought and respected my opinion. Finally, I wasn't separate anymore and that helped restore a sense of control and value. We are still close. We have more fun together now, as adults than we ever had as children. And, interestingly, he has become an incredible business coach, so we have collaborated professionally, even doing a podcast together. It drew my biggest audience to date. My middle brother, not so much. The ruptures have been irreparable.

It took my father and I until I was almost fifty to build the emotional side of our relationship. Don't get me wrong, we spent time together, and I could call on him for anything that needed fixing, moving, and calculating; and of course, he had provided lifesaving support during my divorce. But into his seventies, he softened emotionally, and that meant so much more. By that time, so did my mother. Finally, we all talked about the real things that I had been wanting to talk to them about my whole life—fears, hopes, love, secrets, betrayal, loss, conflict—and I loved it! I know they did too. The journey between my father and uncle would also evolve and I was lucky to be a part of that as well. I watched my parents completely unwrap. In doing so, I discovered their hearts which had been previously hidden, and they discovered mine. I could thank them for all their efforts with me, and they could declare their pride in my hard work and success.

Birth Order

A few further points I'd like to make about the birth-order effect (Paulhus et al., 1999).

I invite you to think about the birth order effect in your family.

Generally speaking, the typical birth order 'roles' usually relate to a competition for parents' attention include (Leman, 2015):

1. The oldest is usually the responsible one, often precious as the firstborn, and can be at risk for internalizing or pleasing behaviors as they are rewarded with the attention.
2. The second born, differentiating from the oldest to ensure they are noticed separately from their older sibling, generally acts out more and is prone to over-externalizing.
3. The middle child usually feels forgotten or invisible between the more obvious identities of the older and younger ones and commonly exhibits sensitivity to being overlooked.
4. The last born acts in ways to stand out that can be experienced as attention-seeking behaviors.
5. Twins exhibit an interesting birth-order effect, either creating high degrees of enmeshment or disengagement in their relationships, as they work out the often-complicated boundaries.
6. Only children, explained in more detail in later chapters, tend to be indulged, similar to the first-born but even more so. They can show tendencies of self-centeredness and pseudo-maturity, are often more comfortable with adults over peers, and have enmeshed boundaries with parents leading to struggles to individuate from the family.
7. Gender and culture add an extra layer of complexity. For example, the oldest-born daughter often taking on the responsibility role that the oldest child would typically take.
8. Pregnancy loss, fertility issues, or health problems can interrupt the spacing and number of children, and commonly creates legacies of loss and grief that alter the parenting scripts and the roles that the born children play (admin, n.d.).

In addition, the degree to which birth order matters is heavily influenced by the nature and degree of compounding family problems including:

- Parental relationship conflicts
- Divorce

- Stepparents/stepsiblings/half siblings
- Parental health including:
  - medical problems
  - mental health
  - trauma
  - addiction issues
- Sibling health including:
  - Medical issues
  - Emotional
  - Social
  - Mental
  - Academic problems

The challenge for parents is in managing the natural rivalry without over- or under-giving to any one child. How equipped (or not) they are to deal with this, determined by their own states of health and histories, is important. Intergenerational patterns are common. How the internalized birth order narrative is transferred into the real world at school age, building friendships with peers outside the family, is equally important. Finally, it can be relevant to identify the degree to which the birth order experience plays out over time, during the various life stages of the family through births, deaths, leaving home, marriages, divorce, illnesses, losses, etc. And this relates to and reinforces the wounded or the healthy self (Howe et al., 2023).

How KG Accountable Therapy Addresses Birth Order

In conjunction with my own therapy, the birth-order effect provides a useful framework for not only understanding and depersonalizing my own journey but directly informs the work I do with clients. The sibling 'line-up' became a clear consideration in the assessment and formulation process of the *KG Method*. This ultimately shapes the recommended treatment plans.

If significant, birth order can shed light on the meaning behind trigger situations and informs the cognitive behavioral programs, with the goal to clear up negative thinking when the past shows up in the present. For example, why I would be extra sensitive to being the third wheel with two friends who knew each other better than me. From CBT, I would learn to anchor to the facts of who simply knew who better, rather than indulge self-critical thoughts that I didn't belong (again). This gave me better choices and helped preserve friendships.

If relevant, birth order also shows up in the mapping out of the wounded and healthy self to clarify needed focus for the deeper work phase of therapy. Take the example of the youngest daughter who has much older male siblings, and is triangulated into her parents' dysfunctional marriage. She unconsciously resists moving on with her life as a young adult, fearing what will happen to her parents' relationship if she leaves the home, believing that she is the glue that is keeping them together. The Emotionally Focused Program identifies how becoming responsible for 'helping' her parents, magnified after her siblings successfully moved out to carry on with their own lives, led to her failure to launch in life. This interrupts her natural pathway toward healthy individuation and enables the parents' unhealthy relationship, actually avoiding the crisis they need to either repair or separate.

It is important for the daughter to:

1. Clear out the emotions of responsibility, fear, and guilt.
2. Reframe what could otherwise appear to be random self-sabotaging actions of not launching her life, are *really* about.
3. Use the wisdom of the healthy self to carve out a different direction.

This ensures clients understand the connections between their past and present and learn what to do about it. The number of children does matter. Age gap does matter. The gender differences or lack thereof do matter.

The theory and my own experiences propelled me to the important work I do, not just with individual clients, but also with young families with children, as well as with adult siblings when older. The unresolved competition, as with many core wounds, lasts a lifetime if we let it. I could help others become more aware, more forgiving, more communicative, and closer to the people who, although at one time were their conscious or unconscious daily 'competitors', were also people who still mattered to them. For obvious reasons, the fulfilling albeit challenging work I do with adult sibling conflict is invigorating to me. I pour extra effort into that work, knowing firsthand what it means when it is resolved and what it means when it isn't.

Often, as it was with me and my older brother, what wasn't possible to repair when younger is made possible when we are older. I capitalize on this. I tell clients, "It's never too late." And I believe it. In fact, I love working with clients who are giving up the idea that things could ever be better and then discover that they can. I also love working with seniors—when they come to me so it's *not* too late—so that they can die being part of a loving ending, and creating a peaceful legacy for themselves and for their loved ones that didn't seem possible before.

While I tell my older clients to "never say never," on the other side of age demographics, I tell young twenty-something clients "don't wait" to take important chances to create their best lives now. The twenties are no longer viewed as the throwaway decade. It is recognized as *the* decade that sets us up for education, career, love, and money. It's always the right time to wake up.

My parents, who have had the good fortune of aging, are now in their late eighties and are embracing these opportunities. With their hard work behind them, they have taken time to poignantly reflect on their lives and reclaim the emotional pieces that had been left behind. This has been incredibly beautiful to watch for their sake, and to be a part of, for mine. As they share their reflections with me, it creates the intimacy I (and they) had always been seeking, and I can finally see myself more realistically—no longer from that place of lost control or unworthiness, no longer the lonely girl; now, the valuable, powerful woman.

Think about this:

1. How has birth order shaped your life?
2. What would you benefit from understanding, to close any emotional gaps with your siblings?
3. Where have you felt unseen in your life? What beliefs do you need to change to see yourself more clearly?
4. What are your next steps toward correcting any internalized, inaccurate beliefs of self, others, life, and love?

CHAPTER 6
PICKLEMEN AND AUTHORS:
THE DANCE OF INTIMACY

(Leonard Cohen - Ain't No Cure for Love, 1988)

Dating Authors

I invite you to think about whether you choose Authors or Pickle men/Pickle women to date and why.

In New York City, there's a street named Delancey. It's a main thoroughfare on the Lower East Side, which, until the late 2000s, was predominately Jewish. The street was named for a politician who originally owned farmland in the area. This part of the city was traditionally known for its bargain and discount clothing stores, and its pickle stores…yes, pickle stores! The most famous one was "Guss' Pickles."

In 1988, when Leonard Cohen was writing ballads to help people make sense of the complexity of love, Isabelle (played by Amy Irving) was fighting off Sam, the Pickle Man (introduced to the audience when he was literally combing through stinky pickle vats with his bare hands). The film was *Crossing Delancey*. Sam was genuine and honest, the man her Bubbah had picked for her to marry. But Isabelle chose instead to indulge her fantasies of Anton, the sexy, superficial Author. We were all obsessed with this film, pulling for Sam, and knowing all too well the mistakes Issy was making by chasing Anton instead. The plot of that movie helped us single girls in the eighties create our dating mantra and we would grill each other on our choices: "Is he a Pickle Man, or is he an Author?"

Like Issy, my own dating experiences were mostly with Authors and also, like her, they inevitably led to heartbreak. I know I missed opportunities from the pickle men in my midst. I was completely unaware of that unworthiness wound I was carrying, so I was really only left with two 'bad' options: turn it inward and hide or act it out. By now you know, I more often rode the aggressive side of the wound. This was visible in the overt, unhealthy decisions I continued to make, including how I dated. In doing so, I chose Authors again and again and again. Each time I would be surprised that the relationships failed. I ended up feeling more unworthy and then of course, from that wounded place, I kept repeating this by dating more Authors.

Two years before Leonard and Amy were writing and acting about twisted-up love, I had thrust myself away from the strict limits of home into the wild world of the university campus. We lived close by McMaster University, but I knew I needed to explore, so I worked hard at my summer jobs and raised the needed fees for residence. Amazing. On move-in day, we saw the large warning signs on the highway close to our exit: "Say Goodbye to your Daughters!" This intrigued me. Seeing the reasons for the signs in person was even more thrilling! It was ten in the morning when we made our way across 'the notorious quad.' This was the courtyard, the party space, smack dab between the then all-girls' and all-boys' residences. The gender-separated residences have since been replaced by all co-ed dorms to quell the 'debauchery' of the all-male residences. In fact, there was even a rumor, later proven to be false, that the popular *Animal House* film starring John Belushi, released in 1978, was based on one of those all-male McMaster dorms.

All of us girls were pushing heavy carts of brightly coloured eighties clothing from the cars in the parking lots to our building (luckily on pathways that went directly past the boys dorm). Because of my love for music, I was also moving my significant vinyl record collection and huge stereo equipment (the biggest items I was moving by far). At the same time, boys were drunkenly hanging out of their windows from their dorm yelling, "we want your daughters!"

This was going to be terrific, I thought. Although I couldn't care less at the time, I often wondered, after becoming a mother myself, how my parents got back in that car to drive home after dropping me off at that scene. That night, the quad party was in full swing. I immediately and desperately started scanning the crowd to find my Author.

And there *he* was, on top of a huge mound of dirt, probably twenty-feet high, wearing super-cool shades and of course, a piano tie. He was Party Marty. He *was* an Author—just like Anton.

Marty was good looking. Marty was bold. Marty knew how to dress. Marty was smart. Marty was a lot of fun. And deep down, I knew Marty wanted and needed to be loved. He had a huge influence on building up my world of music, and he was more than happy to do that for me. Authors have that in them. They stay on the cutting edge of pop culture or anything that is new and different, to bolster their charm. It's part of what makes them so interesting and vibrant. It's also why their behavior seduces the deep insecurities of those around them who know they are not on that same cutting edge; aka Marty meet Karen. What Anton did in *Crossing Delancey* by captivating his female audience by public readings and book signings of his published works, Marty did with fashion and music. He beamed when showing me *his* world, and I guess the reflection of *his* beam cast a light on *me*—a light I was seeking from within my own refractions.

When I first met Marty, I had fully embraced seventies rock tunes, trying to be cool like my older brothers. But I suppose to somehow impress me, he made frisbees and ashtrays out of those old vinyls of mine and introduced me to new wave music. "You won't be needing those," he confidently proclaimed. It was shocking to see my once cherished records swerving in the air down the dorm hallways, only to crash into the corners and break, but I quickly (too quickly) turned my focus to what had become 'cooler', riding Marty's coat tails.

If that wasn't more than enough, the timing of all of this wasn't ideal. That September, I had won a contest at Q107 (the best local *rock* station at the time), to host my own DJ show on the top floor of one of the downtown city skyscrapers for one Saturday night. I was thrilled. The 'Q' certainly did not have copies of the eighties singles Marty had recently introduced to me, so I had to switch back, even if only for one night, to my original love. Family and friends across the GTA, including my new tribe at the university, tuned into the program while I spoke passionately in between tracks about the meanings of my carefully thought-out selections, dedicating songs as I went. I was riding high. Everyone listened to my show except Marty. He took advantage of being in the city to visit the local strip club instead.

Despite Marty's behavior, I found the energy of the extended dance plays in the new music era electric, and I felt free away from home to really explore more exciting parts of myself. We began seeing all the new bands live. Before long, us girls started to dress like Madonna, recently popularized in the exciting new release of her music video *Like a Virgin*. We were amazed watching it at the campus bar *The Downstairs' John* where Marty worked as a bouncer and got me a waitressing job (a very far cry from my first job as a Miracle Food Mart cashier). As my new sense of self flourished, I took risks and wore red pantyhose, miniskirts with big wide belts, laced ankle socks, stilettos, and dyed my asymmetrically shaved hair. I was making up for lost time during my less confident adolescence, with Marty as my ambassador to this new world. But he was still just like any other Author.

Marty cheated on me multiple times over the next two years, and everybody knew it. I even caught him red-handed. It didn't matter. Although I was badly hurt, I was more captivated by his charm and attention, albeit divided. My deep insecurities made it too easy to be manipulated by his apologies, too desperate for attachment. Nowadays we call it 'love bombing' by the 'narcissist.'

After the two long years of heartache, I finally smartened up and ended the relationship with him, only to directly go on to date the guy introduced in chapter 1 which ended with devastating heartache. By that time poet Leonard Cohen had released his song about the impossible cures to love. I should have taken note and cured myself from my own romance aches and pains.

Several years later, post-graduation, the university gang reunited at the old CNE concert grounds in Toronto to watch one of our favourite eighties bands, *Depeche Mode*. Marty was a no-show. We learned the next day that he had suffered a breakdown the day of the concert, was hospitalized, diagnosed with a major mental health disorder, and prescribed medication. As I understand it, that health crisis turned out to be the turning point in his life (hopefully his final ***invitation***). He finally got the help he deserved, went on to live a better life for himself and others, and eventually married.

You see, Marty had a secret too. He had shared it with me while we were dating. One afternoon while in high school, he came home and, alone, discovered his mother dead on the kitchen floor from a brain aneurysm. She'd died instantly, and the trauma had been deeply disruptive to Marty's emotional development. This likely resulted in severe wounds of control at the sheer panic of what he had walked into completely unexpectedly and being unsuccessful at reviving her. This event probably caused a cascading, undermining effect on his ability to master subsequent developmental stages of interdependence, worthiness, and identity. It ultimately and significantly lowered his capacity for intimacy. Because he had no idea of how to cope with the trauma of losing his mother that way, he likely *fixed* his cognitive dissonance incorrectly. From this, he aggressively sabotaged anyone who tried to get close to him, especially females, including me. I remember feeling such deep sorrow for him that day after the concert, knowing it must have all come to a head for him. I realized how scared he must have been that day, and honestly, how scared he had probably been for a long time. Likely he was wrestling with deep despair, grief, guilt and shame. In fact, the shame likely complicated his grief process. Complicated grief, if unregulated long enough, becomes depression (Mayo Clinic, 2022).

Male depression is often different from female depression. In fact, Terrence Real coined the term: 'male covert depression' (Real, 2003). Real's research highlighted how traditional socialization of boys, rewards internalizing vulnerability, which is replaced with false displays of strength. Authentic feelings of sadness and despondence are masked but over time surface through overt behaviors not conventionally associated with depression. These include alcoholism, drug abuse, love bombing, gaslighting, cheating, and other narcissistic actions. Marty checked off all the boxes. Most narcissism, in particular covert narcissism, actually originates from a place of deep inferiority, not superiority (*5 Ways Narcissists Compensate for Their Inferiority*, 2018). This inferiority is usually predisposed by weakening experiences of childhood abuse, neglect, parental conflict and infidelity, parental addiction, trauma, and abandonment. And, in Marty's case, shame and depression from complicated grief.

Not all depressed males are aggressive. Not all abusive males are depressed, but a lot of depressed males act out, and innocent partners are victimized.

They can be the ones dragged into therapy by those who are responsible for them and/or have been hurt by them. Either way, my job is to get underneath the armour to the mis-expressed pain. Honestly, some of my favourite therapeutic breakthroughs have been with males, using the safe space of therapy to take off their masks, reveal their deeper pain, make the link of this to the relationships they have destroyed, and make major shifts. This happens through acceptance, *healthy* self-love, and enhanced vulnerability with those they love.

I invite you to think about whether the presence of covert depression exists anywhere in your life.

Trail of Broken Dreams

What have your negative dating patterns been inviting you to grow from?

Authors had come before Marty. In fact, my first Author relationship would be my **Invitation Number Three**, which piggybacked onto how I had felt unworthy with my siblings and ashamed of my unfinished ending with Grandma. My first important love connection came, as with most in that era, during a last-dance ballad—was it *Hey Jude* or *Stairway to Heaven*? The Catholic Youth Organization (CYO) dances were epic in Burlington (seems strange, I know, but ask anyone who was there, and they will concur). It all took place in the basement of the same church where we attended upstairs as a family every Sunday. To my complete surprise, *he* asked me for that last dance and at that moment, my sexual awakening bloomed. I felt feelings I never knew existed! *That* had not been covered in the pink booklet from my mom!

After that, I regularly snuck out of my house for late-night humping escapades in his bedroom, although both of us stayed virgins like good Catholics. But Gary two-timed me with two different girls over the next two-and-a-half years, a shock every time I discovered his lies (the first one happening on Good Friday). I had become used to being disappointed and distanced by males, but these betrayals hit me hard. With even less confidence now, I begged and pleaded with him to keep me. He lost complete interest. We ended. Eventually, Gary directed the charming energy of his macho high school persona into a very successful motivational speaking career. He also married and raised a beautiful family. We connected many years later in 2020 to collaborate on a professional project. During the writing of this book in 2023, Gary died suddenly of a massive heart attack in the back of a car enroute to one of his speaking events. He was only sixty.

I think that because he was my *first* romantic love, that because this was the first time I encountered meaningful rejection *outside* of my family; that because I was so shocked by what he did (twice), this relationship betrayal qualified as an invitation. It just seemed to confirm to me that I would never be chosen and without repairing that wound, I would continue to live a trail of broken dreams until I found my way.

Enter Bob, the golfer. He was a gorgeous model, a golf pro, and new to the city from Vancouver. His parents were going through an ugly divorce, so he was couch-surfing at the homes of every new acquaintance looking for a place to stay. Captivated by his good looks and charm, even at eighteen, I played my 'baby of the family' card and convinced my parents to let him move into a temporary apartment we set up for him in our basement.

I lost my virginity to Bob in a car on my prom night. It was unremarkable. Behind my back, Bob cheated on me too, with girls I had naively introduced him to while helping him integrate into his new community. Boyfriends of co-workers at my cashier job knew all of Bob's secrets. He broke up with me on Good Friday. Once again, I was completely humiliated, and honestly, heartbroken. Bob later moved out to live with a guy I had gone to school with since grade school. I never heard what happened to him.

For years I had done what many do from the core wound. We unconsciously organize relationships and experiences as self-fulfilling prophecies to confirm the core beliefs of the wounded self. This is a key ingredient in repeating poor dating choices, management of the intimacy, and endings. I believed I was unworthy, and others would leave me. I continued to mismanage my romances, reaching all-time lows during those Yonge and Eligible days. Although I had found success at school and in my career, my wounded self was doing my dating and that would never work.

The fact is, stumbling with intimacy is common because earlier emotional stages of trust, control, interdependence, self-worth and identity are usually impaired to some extent or the other. Going back to repair the impairment is powerful. We all want to love and be loved. Love makes the world go round. Until it doesn't. And when it doesn't, it's an invitation.

Healthy Self Dating

What have been your positive dating patterns?

How did your healthy self help you with that?

As I reentered the dating world post-divorce, I leveraged the significant growth I had made and learned ways to give my healthy self more airtime by regulating more moderated levels of control in decision making, advocating for healthy boundaries of what was and wasn't acceptable to me, and reducing my fear of endings by bravely calling the end when it was warranted.

However, the recovery trajectory is never a straight upward line. There is progress and there are setbacks. This pathway of recovery zigzags because triggers never completely dissolve.

This happens for two big reasons:

1. Our historical pain never *completely* evaporates even when we repair, so what specifically pains us will continue (the Achilles' heel).

2. The imperfections in our day of what we didn't want, expect or like, no matter how big or small, are sometimes thematically similar to our original wound which also has the potential for regression.

But, when we do our work, the U-turn between the trigger and recovery gets shorter, and less damage is caused and felt.

This allowed me to make better (not perfect) decisions when loss of control and unworthiness reared their ugly heads in my love life, sooner rather than later. The idea is to keep going, knowing how complex and imperfect the journey is. Those who succeed do indeed keep going.

So, I kept going. So, I kept growing.

Right out of the gate, I chose a Pickle Man—a total nerd, socially awkward and completely misunderstood by others (which would have really bothered me before), and at the same time, deeply romantic and thoughtful. Every Thursday afternoon at about 4:00 pm, the Pickle Man would call me to present special dating plans for the upcoming weekend, having usually researched the latest best new band that was coming to town, and made reservations at a cool restaurant. Craig had two amazing daughters who got along beautifully with my own growing daughter. They were like the three musketeers, virtually inseparable. Although I still secretly dreamt of having more children, that never happened, so like my daughter I felt I truly had a second chance for a full family with this new grouping of five.

However, even Pickle Men are wounded. But this time, I had more courage to act on red flags earlier. I became aware of the severity of Craig's alcoholism immediately after he moved into my home. My wounded self-recovery made space for my healthy self to show up with clear communication and advocacy with him about the problem. We received solid clinical support for ourselves and the relationship this time. All combined, this helped him achieve sobriety. It looked as though I had locked in a healthier relationship. The unfortunate game changer occurred however, from a relapse when his abstinence plan failed. This was triggered from the overwhelming experiences of selling his family home, having his best friend (his dog) die, and adapting to going from a part-time family of three in his home to a full-time family of five in mine. I set a boundary.

He pushed back—literally. I initiated a police investigation—a level of drama I never thought I would experience, and the relationship ended.

The way it ended was understandably difficult. I knew I had done the right thing. I teetered with confusion and guilt, but overall, I was proud of how I was beginning to break my patterns by initiating and tolerating an undesirable ending sooner with less overall damage. The greatest loss in the end, I think, was my daughter losing her stepsisters, especially because they had become so close. This was made worse by the fact that, with the ending of that relationship, close sibling relationships were not going to be possible for her ever again; no future pregnancies for me, and hurtful relationships with her father's new partner's children. This was particularly painful for me. The fact is, that our children's experiences mirror our own, and feeling so alone with my own siblings made seeing her alone as an only child difficult. I made extra efforts to keep her close with her cousins and worked hard to facilitate an active social life of play dates for her so at least she could have close peers.

Then, completely unexpectedly, I fell in love with a woman. I dove into that relationship wholeheartedly, feeling a thrill and excitement I had not always felt with men. I felt free but also confused. So, I started to research what was happening. Interestingly, Oprah had recently done a telecast about how otherwise heterosexual women in their forties were having homosexual affairs. It had turned out, surprising to some, that in 1948, Dr. Alfred Kinsey had already recognized this in his ground-breaking research on the fluidity of human sexuality. The Heterosexual-Homosexual Rating Scale (Kinsey, 1948)—more commonly known as The Kinsey Scale, identified how people did not fit into exclusive heterosexual or homosexual categories (Kinsey Institute, 2009).

We had a long way to go before Kinsey's research and other findings would inform the main culture. The associated mental health issues caused by fear and ignorance in the meantime would be alarming. We made some progress: the sexual revolution of the sixties; the decriminalisation of homosexuality in 1969 (Human Dignity Trust, 2022); and the declassifications of homosexuality as a mental disorder in the Psychiatric Diagnostic and Statistical Manual (DSM) in 1973; and gender identity disorder in 2013 (amended to gender dysphoria) (American Psychiatric Association, 2017).

It is indeed encouraging to witness millennials' strong advocacies for nonbinary orientation and transgender identity in modern times, and I was glad to be a part of those cultural shifts, both personally and professionally, by honoring my own personal fluidity and bringing knowledge and experience into my private practice, directly helping clients and their families embrace their own healthy sexuality.

For me, the journey allowed me the freedom to explore this new relationship, while facing some internal confusion and external pressures, and in doing so, I furthered my capacity for self-love.

The relationship failed for multiple reasons, none of which had to do with sexuality, and although teetering again as I struggled with the painful experience of letting go of something I had high hopes for, I continued to grow from this breakup as well. I learned even more about where and how to set a boundary, how to end love, and how to face being alone without being lonely. I forced myself to be single for an entire year, to do more work in therapy on myself to ensure I would continue to reduce the residual pieces still floating around that weren't serving me. I declared that I would 'date Tony Soprano' that year. So instead of being typically out, after a day full of sessions, I went grocery shopping, then came home to Tony—every Saturday night. This was a great idea. Sometimes, it indeed takes a big change, a big break from normalcy to really punctuate that you want something different. This is worth advertising to yourself, but it often raises accountability even further to advertise things like this to others in your life.

I would carry this emotional growth with me as I embarked on my next foray into relationships—the world of internet dating.

By the time I got to online dating, which started with telephones as the only mode (no video or even pictures), my efforts were noticeably paying off and I had evolved into a stronger, more independent woman, mother, therapist, daughter, friend, and business owner. I was dedicated to the process, and there was *no* way now that I would set myself up for more bad Good Fridays or any of the other 364 days of the year. If I was to be in a relationship again, it would be because my partner would make my life better, not worse! Obvious I know, but not always obvious to me, let alone enforceable by me for many years.

The good news about internet dating is that it opens you up to meeting people you wouldn't otherwise meet. The bad news is it opens you up to meeting people you don't *want* to meet. This is partly based on how easy it is to create profiles, sometimes under false pretenses. The anonymity of online dating invites a lot of individuals who are not really emotionally available to date. Married people, addicts, financial dependants, financial scammers, emotionally regressed individuals—all have a platform to 'date.' Although disappointed by these kinds of online trials and tribulations, I was not bitter. In fact, I was feeling more alive and stronger than ever before, and I had gained momentum exponentially by saying no in many situations that I knew were unhealthy, not only bearing an ending, but finding and then using the strength to call it myself.

I still deeply believe in love. I deeply believe in romance. And as I write this, I am single—happily single—in fact, I've never been happier and more fulfilled. Apparently, I'm not alone. Recent studies by consumer analyst Mintel identifies strong societal shifts toward greater independence and singledom for women, with 61 percent being happier single than in relationships (*How Brands Do Communication with Female Consumers*, 2024). I don't think this is about the failure of love. I think it's about feminism, liberation, changing societal norms, destigmatizing mental health and therapy, and higher levels of self-awareness. It's about a sharper focus on education, careers, solo travel and self-improvement, fertility options, and healthier 'not settling' if your partner is not ready to accept the invitation of a deeply intimate love. When true self-love is achieved, it *is* enough. Self-love is the cake on your plate; love with *another* is the icing, but often, the cake is tasty enough, sometimes *even better without* the icing, especially if the icing is too runny, too sweet, or overpowers the cake.

The Complex Dance of Intimacy

I invite you to think about what your intimacy 'dance steps' have been.

The best definition of intimacy:

> *"Intimacy: the ability to openly share fears, needs, and joys without being crushed or causing crushing to the other."*
> – Unknown

This definition of intimacy places the focus of pushing the emotional envelope toward co-creating spaces of authenticity with another who has earned our vulnerability, without negative consequences. Adults need this space, even if introverted, to feel a level of fulfillment in their lives.

I use this definition almost daily with clients looking for a more meaningful life, pushing *them* to find ways to be *real* in their relationships with family, friends, and lovers in ways that maximizes the connections. This just makes people happier.

Brené Brown says humans are hardwired for these connections (Brene Brown, 2012) and, as discussed in chapter 4, she discovered that people who are more deeply connected can be vulnerable with others due to the absence of *shame*. Basically, in order to feel connected, we need to be vulnerable. In order to be vulnerable, we need to reveal ourselves, and in order to reveal ourselves, we need to fully accept and love ourselves, with the knowledge of our own imperfection. One might, in fact, say that the imperfection is *needed* for connection. We are free to reveal our true selves to *others* because we accept *ourselves* for who we are, without having to change, edit, cover, or fake. This invites a closeness to and from the other, thereby contributing to an overall deepening of the relationship.

Unfortunately, to avoid crushing and being crushed, and to show up with vulnerability instead of shame, requires a certain degree of mastery of those developmental stages discussed. It requires the ability to be and stay empathic, flexible, co-operative, confident, and communicative in difficult times. But inherently, our imperfections as humans come from the fact that we have been unable to master those stages perfectly. As such, our resilience is most precarious when the vulnerabilities of trust, control, independence, self-worth, and identity are at their peak, at that inevitable stage of conflict in our relationships where differences appear.

The fact is, our wounded self (originating from the imperfect development) sometimes shows up at work, usually shows up with friends, but *always* shows with lovers where the emotional stakes are at their highest. It's where our healthy self is needed the most. But it's *the* exact same place where the wounded self shows up instead and shows up in ways that overprotect, misprotect, and trip us, our partner (and the relationship) up.

Therefore, what so easily occurs is that the inevitable necessary differences between partners are misunderstood, misused, and mismanaged. Negative reactions worsen over time, weakening the connection. Trust is stolen. Vulnerability is misdirected and overcontrolled. Partners begin to see the other as the enemy and the projection of this plays out in how communication or lack thereof is not only unproductive but compounds the problems. Couples have repetitive arguments, silent tensions, or displaced irritabilities. This causes increased frustration and exhaustion, easily resulting in 'Kitchen sinking'—throwing in the accumulated unresolved topics of past arguments into the current conflict. Focus is distracted onto trivial issues and symptoms rather than where it is needed, on the deeper patterns and root causes. When prolonged, one or both partners exit the intimacy altogether through conflict avoidance, over-attention to work or friends, overuse of alcohol or other compulsions, or extramarital affairs.

So, *if...*

We desire a more conscious relationship where the wounded self is healed, and intimacy is achieved, the following is required:

1. Understanding the troubled or missing pieces in our developmental histories.
2. Knowing how those struggles contributed to the wounded self we brought with us into the relationship with negative core beliefs and attachment styles.
3. Seeing how these elements are manifesting toward unhealthy conflict reactions undermining intimacy.
4. Having the tools to correct those reactions, close developmental gaps, and repair our wounded self, *within* the love of the relationship.

But...

Most of us have stumbled over those stages. Most of us have wounded selves that are very convincing but out of control, taking us off track of what we really want. Most of us don't completely understand why we do what we do with the person we love the most. Most of us don't have the tools.

Then...

Most of us will stumble over the intimacy. It is the dance of intimacy where we trip over our own feet, and usually trip our partner in the process.

...Some even fall.

How we have stumbled has changed over the years. There was a time when divorce rates were much lower, in part because marriage partners *stayed* together for better or worse. This underlined a good commitment to *stay* married, but too often with low levels of intimacy so the unresolved conflicts *also* stayed unresolved. They ended up with parallel relationships like platonic roommates and parents, co-running homes and families like business partners rather than lovers.

Divorce

My generation witnessed a major change where couples were generally no longer satisfied staying in unfulfilling marriages. We saw divorce rates dramatically rise when divorce was legalized in Canada 1968, updated in 1985, which effectively permitted no-fault divorce (*Divorce Law in Canada* (96-3e), n.d.). Divorce was now 'made easy' and couples only had to wait a year as a separated couple to end the marriage in divorce. The most recent *Divorce Act* of 2021 (Canada, 2021) declared needed improvements in promoting children's interests, updated parenting planning and terminology, challenged parental alienation, and held obvious payers for child support and spousal amounts accountable sooner and more easily. It upheld the needs of children to have good relationships with both parents in the absence of abuse and addiction and promoted mental health supports. All of this was encouraging and, indeed, helped many to use their divorce as their final *invitation*, to grow in ways not previously taken toward a more simplified, mature, and collaborative process. If the work of carrying the marriage from the stages of conflict to deeper intimacy wasn't going to happen, then striving toward a conscious divorce would benefit everyone.

But there is nothing easy about divorce. The fall is real. In fact, the psychiatric community has deemed it as the second most stressful life event, only less than death of a child (*Life Changes Stress Test*, n.d.).

Why is that? It is the sheer magnitude of the mental, emotional, social, and financial losses, magnifying pre-existing developmental ruptures, combined with ungrounded grief of the separation. A collapse of the individual's fragile developmental achievements occurs, and regression happens, often creating major emotional breakdowns of anxiety, depression, and anger. Individuals display problematic reactions, usually similar to their preferred adaptations to childhood stressors, but heightened, and the ungrounded grief often manifests in extreme expressions of blame or shame, also representative of earlier struggles. In addition, once the stakes change, when the chance of reconciling is no longer, all bets are off. Any efforts that could have otherwise helped save the relationship are washed away, and motivations are skewed. The clinical belief at this stage is that it can be harder to have a good divorce than a good marriage. The challenge is real.

With that in mind, divorcing couples easily get further entrenched in negativity, resulting in wasteful, prolonged, expensive, and painful battles. Aggressive or passive reactions of the wounded self are indulged and unresolved grief is weaponized for usually short-lived insignificant wins, causing damage to the mental health of all family members. Not only is the upheaval, pain, and expense *not* worth it, it usually causes more emotional harm to themselves, their ex-partner, and most importantly, to the children and teens whose neuropathways are developing in the midst of the turbulence. Children are triangulated in toxic ways which can have profound effects on their development. Without effective resolve, opportunities to correct reactions get buried. Chances to heal get lost. Patterns are repeated or are offset by opposite reactions, indicative of overcompensation, in the next relationship *and* in the next generation.

I believe most divorces are preventable. More often than not, we do pick each other *right*. It *is* possible to track how:

1. The differences that once seemed attractive have now become increasingly frustrating and hurtful.
2. These differences actually reflect deeper, unmet needs that existed even before the relationship began.
3. This often leads to regressive, ineffective reactions, causing harm to the relationship.

Good couple therapy directly tackles all three levels.

Consider the man who attracts powerful women into his life to master a deeper wound of not speaking up to a father who was emotionally abusive to him and abandoned him. Unprepared, the man feels disempowered by his partner, and cheats on her to sabotage the relationship and leaves (just like his father).

The woman who finds a man addicted to alcohol to master a deeper wound of having a mother whose alcoholism made her feel unimportant. She is too insecure to advocate for her needs and instead enables the overdrinking. The relationship disintegrates.

Despite tried or untried interventions, sometimes separation is imminent. Marriages typically end when one or both partners cannot commit to the needed change, so nothing changes.

Common obstacles occur when:

- One partner stays too 'big' forcing their needs onto the other who stays too 'small', suppressing their needs.
- The decision making power or social plans don't achieve a healthy balance of 'I' and 'We' and either:

    a) Has too much 'I' with couples too disengaged from each other and there is too much independence, or...

    b) Too much 'We' and it is enmeshed or codependent where partners are over entangled and not separate enough.
- Betrayals and dishonesty continue.
- Abuse continues.
- Dysfunctional roles become entrenched such as:

    a) The parent/child dance (one partner adopts the caregiver responsibility function while the other partner underachieves, under-performs), or...

    b) The pursuer/retreater dance (one partner chases, forcing engagement while the other partner avoids, or over-distances).

Separation counselling, often underutilized for obvious reasons, is quite impactful, and works through:

- The gifts from the relationship despite its ending.

- The irreconcilable differences and tipping point of the end. And...
- The future relationship boundaries.

Co-parenting counselling, however, is essential and a powerful invitation to mature, if not through the relationship, through the deep desire to be good parents.

Failed couple counselling shifts my role from building intimacy for the couple toward ensuring the individual partners use their healthy selves to separate. The clinical work supports growth from the loss, as a viable 'second choice'. Improved responses to stressors are learned. Grief is grounded. Deeper healing is provided.

Good grief therapy teaches us to grow from what we couldn't or didn't while still in the relationship.

Grief Therapy

I went into therapy for the first time in my life after my devastating breakup in 1989. It gave me a place to tell my story, which I badly needed to do. But, looking back now, with experienced therapist's eyes, I think there were some key things missing. The process just didn't go deep enough, powerfully enough to help me grieve the ending, enough to make a needed difference in where I would go next in my dating. The fact is grief therapy from a relationship breakdown is not just about getting over the loss. That's not enough. It's not just about working through feelings of wishing the person back. Often, we actually don't *want* the person back, yet we're still suffering. So, that's usually not enough either. It's not only about working through the feelings of letting go. There is more that is needed. Grief therapy needs to expand and broaden the loss experience and then go deeper, a lot deeper, to identify a key takeaway of how to do differently, if it is going to be truly helpful.

When you read this next part, I invite you to deeply think about why a significant relationship **really** ended for you? Can you begin to identify where the key clashes came from for each of you and how that got you stuck instead of growing?

As discussed, when we pick each other 'right' (when our wounds 'match') at usually between one and three years into the relationship we will face an important emotional intersection that starts to drown out the romantic love felt at the beginning. The once attractions become frustrations. It is here that the noise of critically unresolved past issues (usually based on intrusions of key developmental stages of (re)trust, control, dependence, worthiness, and/or identity) echo into present interactions (Lewis, 2023). This creates conflict (overtly or covertly) giving us challenging opportunities to grow. In fact, we have unconsciously invited these conflicts into our life, to give us an opportunity to master a specific wound of the past. These act as reenactments of what is unresolved. Painful reenactments that are at their essence, invitations. At this point, we either consciously heal this wound through the love, or unconsciously indulge it and the wound is not only not healed, it is reinforced.

It's too easy to give into our wounds at this stage because we usually regress to familiar dysfunctional ways of managing those frustrations and conflicts and the relationship prematurely ends one way or another. Not because we didn't care or love, because we didn't know how to grow through the conflict. Even more problematic is when we let *the internal self-critic* conclude the ultimate reason for the ending. It's this shame and blame of 'who did what wrong' that may have the immediate gratification of bringing some emotional conclusion to the ending, and protecting our vulnerability, but long-term eats us alive and puts us at higher risk of repeating a self-defeating relationship pattern.

Reframing this regressed judgmental narrative to include how each partner's wounds created opportunities to grow in the relationship but weren't utilized becomes a story about how two good people came into the relationship, but instead of loving deeper, hurt each other beyond repair. It literally flips the conflict narrative on its back and invites the couple to grow instead of separate.

For example, it would have helped me to understand that my boyfriend from that 1989 break up likely carried a control wound from an overbearing mother and that this contributed to him stubbornly resisting making a full commitment to me from a fear of (re)engulfment. It would have also helped me to understand my own control and unworthiness wounds. Wounds originating from my parents and brothers, a previous breakup, and shame I was carrying from an unresolved ending with my grandma were unknowingly contributing to me pushing back too hard when he disengaged. I felt too threatened by the distance. My pushing evoked the very fears he had of being engulfed and undoubtedly, he disengaged more, and we fell apart. The ultimate invitation for me would have been to calm my insecurities in the face of the separateness he (re)created for me with his stubbornness, recognizing how much he cared. The ultimate invitation for him would have been to find a way to engage when I moved in to be close to him, without any intention of consuming him. We didn't know how to do that while we were still together and the therapy never laid this out clearly enough for me to grow from, after it dissolved.

I developed a grief program that formulates how:

1. **Attractions make it appear the relationship would be successful.**

   For example, the husband who was initially attracted to his wife's flexibility, which was so much more open than what he had growing up with parents who could be overtly rigid and critical and to whom he acted out against. She had parents who were more flexible but almost to the point they avoided conflict.

2. **Unmet developmental needs act as invitations for growth.**

   For example, he had the opportunity with her to be more assertive and less argumentative than he was with his parents. She had the opportunity to practice more direct conflict resolution.

3. **The resistances of the partners/parents prevents growth.**

   For example, when they were in conflict and she began learning how to hold her ground on things, he too easily felt threatened as he had with his parents, and without tools became stubborn and rigid himself, making her withdraw, fearful of the conflict. Over time and behind his back she files for divorce.

4. **The takeaway of the neutralized grief is an invitation to the divorced single person or co-parent to grow through the divorce in ways which were not possible during the relationship.**

   It invites an active process whereby the healthy self 'coaches' the wounded self in ways not possible growing up and not possible in the recently ended relationship.

   For example, his takeaway (invitation) is to learn tools in therapy that demonstrate flexible thinking and speaking, finding his calmer voice when things don't go his way, with:

   a. A new partner in a new relationship.
   b. His ex-partner in the co-parenting.
   c. His children.

Her takeaway is to become more comfortable with conflict:

   a. Voicing her opinions directly with her new partner.
   b. Finding her voice to negotiate a fair separation agreement.
   c. Asserting herself with her children, while maintaining her flexibility.

I developed a specialized grief therapeutic writing program based on developmental theory and the Imago Therapy Approach. This is prepared at home, then completed in sessions toward an effective therapeutic writing and sentence completion exercise. This proved to be a game changer for the divorcing clients I would work with.

It goes something like this: (briefly described)

Try rewriting your love story:

- I grew up with _____ (positives and negatives) and that felt _____ and I reacted by _____ing.
- So, what I need most in my romantic relationship is _____ (what wasn't achieved in childhood).
- My partner grew up with _____ (positives and negatives) and felt _____ and reacted by _____ing.
- So, what they need most in a romantic relationship is _____ (what they didn't achieve in childhood).
- I was attracted to _____ (initial signs that having wounds repaired in the relationship will be possible).

- But, over time those attractions became _____ (frustrations that developed when wounds were not repaired).
- It began breaking down when _____ (clues of failure, or red flags).
- I missed the opportunity to _____ (identified wound that did not get mastered and why).
- They missed the opportunity to _____ (identified wound that did not get mastered and why).
- So, we ended because _____ (the tipping point).
- My takeaway is to _____ (the message in the lost opportunity not achieved in the relationship).

How did you do?

Ultimately, it's about achieving a deeper sense of peace by getting behind the power of learning what you were meant to figure out about yourself in the relationship but didn't before it ended and clarifying how you could live your life now, knowing now what you didn't learn then.

I have many clients who actually download the completed session exercise onto their mobile devices to anchor them when inevitable emotional triggers of the divorce loss occur.

We call these triggers *the waves of grief.* These usually get activated by sensory experiences of seeing, hearing, feeling, or smelling something that painfully reminds you of the loss. Heightened waves (the seventh waves) often occur on expected dates such as agonizing 'firsts' or recurring dating or family rituals now without your partner, important birthdays, anniversaries, or being in places that were special or meaningful to the relationship in some way. These *waves* can also be provoked upon receiving unexpected news about or exposures to your ex and their new life without you. These can overwhelm you, as it did me that day on the driveway when Madeline left for our annual camping trip without me for the first time.

If you like what you wrote in your grief story, try these three steps the next time you get hit with a wave.

1. Like waves on the ocean, loss creates surges of anger, fear, resentment, anxiety, despair, shame, and guilt, etc. They build, they peak, *and* they break. *Remembering that although these triggers feel permanent, especially at the beginning of the loss, when waves are relentless and you are drowning, they will break and a settling of emotions will occur, is powerful.*
2. Breathing through the wave is important. People drown when they panic or give up. People float into shore when they don't. So, breathe.

3. And then the grounding is required. This is when clients pull out their pages to remember what *really* happened. Blame will drown you. So will shame. So will fear. But, compassion. Self-compassion. Acceptance. Power. These will give you the ride of your life capitalizing on the neutral story and the invitations to grow, missed during the relationship. The takeaways become key features of how the healthy self is helping you develop resilience and reach for excellence in your life moving forward. Mostly, but not exclusively, with romantic relationships

Waves eventually get less frequent and less deep. Grief is tricky and the water at the end of the beach feels the same as the water at the beginning. This can fool us into thinking we've made no progress when we have.

The *KG* Method for Couples

I invite you to think about the couples therapy you may have tried and how accountable it was.

Do you have a tool to calm reactions for better communication?

The KG Method creatively combines Couple CBT (Cognitive Behavioral Therapy) with Imago (Images from Childhood) programs to ensure partners gain the necessary insights of past and present and master the needed tools and opportunities to grow the wounded self up within the relationship.

Instead of staying stuck and breaking down at the conflict intersection, they free themselves to love better. Couples:
1. Create visions to unify (from Imago).
2. Heal betrayals to rebuild trust as discussed in chapter 4 (the Structured Healing Conversations).
3. Improve their stress reactions to each other (The Couple Cognitive Behavioral Change Tool).
   And…
4. Deepen love (Imago Dialoguing).
These are achieved when partners learn how to:
- Master the CBT *KG* 'Change' Program together, replacing otherwise hurtful reactions to each other with assertive communications instead.
  And…
- Take a direct pathway from the CBT to the Imago dialogues (intense effective thirty-minute step-by-step conversations that include 'I' messages, active listening, empathy, validation, connecting the problems in the relationship with

pre-existing wounding experiences, and advocate for needs). This pathway is illustrated in Appendix D.

I use the classic Hendrix Dialogue. I developed micro-dialoguing steps for couples who are short on time in real-life circumstances and don't have the full thirty minutes. I also facilitate even deeper sentence-completion dialogue formats in sessions, which work extremely well to amplify and shift the reenacted negative narratives of earlier wounding experiences playing out in the relationship.

This route from the CBT to the Imago serves the dual purpose of:

1. Solving current problems more effectively; with less passive, aggressive or passive-aggressive reactivity.
2. Strengthening the relationship with deeper communication that goes well beyond the surface symptoms to uncover the original wound and offers us a way to talk and listen in ways not possible before.

The CBT prepares the partners *for* the dialogue. The Imago provides the effective conflict and intimacy scripts not previously available to us with others who hurt us in the earlier parts of our life. This carries the relationship from conflict to intimacy. Not back to the romantic more superficial love from the beginning of the relationship, but forward to a deeper, more trusting love. Judgment becomes insight. Personalization becomes empathy. Shame becomes vulnerability.

Consider the woman who finds her voice in her relationship, instead of shutting down (using the CBT to directly dialogue 'I' messages of what she feels and needs) with a partner who criticizes her like her mother used to do while growing up. In turn, the partner is challenged to develop clearer insights and translatable responses repairing his own insecurities that are driving his critical reactions.

The man (A) uses the CBT to bite his tongue in the heat of an argument and drops into a quieter Imago dialogue to raise his concerns calmly without feeling like he 'lost' the fight, as he had felt earlier in his life.

His partner (B), living with her own negative, past-conflict script of being unheard, hears the calmer disagreement more easily, addresses her own disempowerment and speaks up to be heard.

By responding calmly and directly, (A) and (B) mutually offer a better conflict script, different from (A)'s father who yelled over him to win the argument and (B)'s parents who didn't 'hear' her. The partners learn better ways to disagree, heal deeper wounds of control, and the love deepens.

The man who had to prematurely leave his unwavering, rigid family before finishing secondary school finds a way to be vulnerable with and embrace his partner's loving, albeit overbearing family, inviting flexibility that helps her too.

We grow and so does the relationship. We are accountable to ourselves and to our partners for a healthier love. The bottom line is if our partner is present when we grow, and if we grow because of what (and how) we asked from our partner, if we grow because of how our partner responds, the love grows too. The love matures. The love is real. Instead of breaking down, the invitation within the conflict, is opened, recognized, and taken.

A beautiful new dance is created, synchronized to a deeper rhythm that feels magical.

Graduating *KG* couples don't dread the conversations. They look forward to weekly dialogues at home to nurture and strengthen this newfound deeper level of love. Brown was right. We *are* hardwired for connection and, when it happens, the electricity brings us back to life!

A Word About Sex

Sometimes the broken physical relationship heals with the repaired emotional relationship. Other times the sexual relationship requires its own specialized attention. Generally speaking, gender stereotypical roles do play a part where men need sex for intimacy, and women need intimacy for sex (*Fresh Start Therapy & Consulting*, 2017). This is taken into account. As well, we know that anxiety is known to be the biggest *buster* in the bedroom, followed by depression, trauma, and body image. All of this needs specific attention. With accountable therapy, we find a way. Anxiety is managed, depression is reduced, trust and connection are repaired, mindfulness and presence are increased, and the physical intimacy is rebuilt. While trauma-informed strategies bring safety, body work reclaims healthier images, and where indicated, related eating disorders are treated.

Modern Love

Intimacy shifted again at the turn of the century as millennials grew up, not only in the not uncommon hurtful shadows of their parents' divorces, but also in the age of 'digital love'. The search for authentic connections is still happening. But so is the increase of casual encounters, group dating, open relationships, group sex, hookups, and friends with benefits which, if made from the wounded self, sabotages.

Authors are now 'players.' Love on the internet impedes intimacy via technology including raising unrealistic expectations for immediate responses, overreliance on tech versus in-person interactions, use of anonymous or false identities, scrolling habits increasing avoidance, distractions and ADHD symptoms, cyber bullying and sexual exploitation, and easier access to infidelities—all while undermining needed quietness and stillness for the brain, mind, and heart to sit in the intimacy of vulnerability.

Social media also seems to prolong and complicate the grief process by presenting a view of our ex's seemingly perfect, happier, life post-breakup without us.

But what's more interesting from the other side is this generation's healthy questioning of the previous generation's inclinations to marriage and divorce, and their increasing openness for embracing nontraditional relationship structures and sexual fluidity (Mittleman, 2023).

Society is redefining gender roles, and prioritizing emotional intelligence and mental health. I am excitedly seeing a new generation of client couples. Millennial couples are coming in for *premarital and pre-parenting* counselling to strengthen their love and protect their families before taking major steps that they could otherwise not be ideally prepared for. These encouraging trends could very well be the new modern dance of intimacy.

Finding Our Inner Pickle Men. Finding Home

In 2003, the year I turned forty, Craig and I went to New York City to celebrate. I insisted we go to the Lower East Side. There we stood at 87 Orchard Street—Guss' Pickle Store. Craig had no idea why I stood there with tears in my eyes. That didn't matter to me. I stayed a long time. I looked, I mean, I really looked around me to take it all in, all the history and the meaning of that store and that street. Then I closed my eyes. I tried to picture the men and women who had traveled across the ocean, just like my Baba and Gigi, to make a better life for their families living in the tenement buildings here on Orchard St. I replayed the scenes from the film. I pictured Amy Irving running across the street, finding Guss stinking of vinegar and then, distracted by Anton, running on. She just kept running. Then I watched my own lifetime of Authors flash before me in a speed reel, smiling and crying at the same time, as I watched frame after frame. I had been running too, until thankfully, I stopped.

Turns out, Guss' life commitments had healthy ingredients, well beyond his pickles and were a great reminder to all of us—more is not always more and simplifying otherwise overly complex steps means just a little bit more...

The real Guss, the original Pickle Man, had arrived in 1910 as a Polish Immigrant, Isidor Guss. At the time when he opened his shop, there were eighty other pickle shops on the street. In 1979, Harry Baker and his partner took over the operations of the business but kept its name, withstood economic difficulties, and when it closed in 2009, Guss' ended up being the last store standing of those original eighty. Guss' Pickles had no plans to raise prices or expand into wholesale when demand for the local pickles waned. Guss just wanted to sell pickles to the average guy. Guss kept it simple. Guss didn't get swayed by trends or commercialism. Guss had heart. Guss had commitment. He just kept making pickles, and when he stopped, he just went home to his family.

Think about this:

1. What have you noticed in your romantic relationships? Who do you choose? How does the intimacy and conflict play out? What common feedback have you been given by partners? How/why have your relationships ended?

2. How easy/hard is it for you to share your fears, needs, and joys with others? How much do the others in your life share theirs?

3. What were the main wounding experiences in your life that impacted your romantic connections in negative ways? How has that changed your journeys with romance so far?

4. What would you need to 'cure' yourself of, or to improve the quality of intimacy in your life?

CHAPTER 7
THE TRIBE: BEING A GOOD FRIEND TO YOURSELF FIRST

You've got a friend in me

You've got a friend in me

When the road looks rough ahead

And you're miles and miles

From your nice warm bed

You just remember what your old pal said

Boy, you've got a friend in me

Yeah, you've got a friend in me

(Randy Newman - You've Got a Friend in Me, 1995)

Why Friendships Are so Important: The Theory

If we *are* hardwired for connection, then it goes without saying that the intimacy of friendship fills us up while friendship breakdown hurts.

How we pick our friendship tribe can be as important as our choices and patterns with lovers. And, similarly, there's nothing random about it. The quality of our attachment with our caretakers contributes to it. The quality of our relationships with our first peers, our siblings, matters (Lee, 2023). And how successful we've been at earlier stages of trust and control makes a difference (Cherry, 2024).

As with other developmental disruptions, there is a cascading effect. When the interdependence through friendships is held back due to unresolved conflicts or loss of self, subsequent stages of worthiness and identity are compromised. Future intimacy is undermined. And as is the case with most other mental health issues, the negative effects take on a life of their own and double downs develop, creating a secondary layer of pain, reducing energy, motivation, and confidence further. Social isolation worsens, it continues to perpetuate by itself, sending us into the spiral from boredom through anxiety toward anger onward to self-loathing and depression (McLeod, 2024).

The Story

As you read about my friendships, I invite you to think what you have brought to your friendships, positive and negative.

Think about how your healthy friendships are indicators of your growth.

"Meeting to order! Meeting to order." My friend looked at me strangely. Yes, at about nine years old, I was the founder and president of *The Bachelor Girls Club*. We held regular meetings in my parents' five-by-five-foot canned goods storage room, which contained all the homemade peaches, pears, pickles, and relishes my mother made every year, as well as an oversized, old-fashioned fridge. There was only room for my small, red, fold-out children's table with nursery-rhyme images pressed into the surface and our two smaller red fold-out chairs. But that didn't matter because I had found the perfect club house space. Cozy and most of all, private.

Yes, I had signed out a book at the local library on how to operate a successful club. Yes, I had learned how to make a motion and how to properly pass that motion. Yes, our club had only two members: my best friend and me. We passed the motion on the name, which I loved. After all, we were proud to be bachelors! In the mid-seventies, it felt ambitious to acknowledge that not only men but also females were bachelors! After that, I literally have no memory of what else our club achieved. I do remember that I loved learning how to manage and operate a club. I loved organizing the club. But, most of all, I loved being in charge.

My bold personality with friends was also apparent when playing 'wedding' as children, with longtime family friends. I'd been exposed to 'big fat Ukrainian weddings' and fantasized about getting married from a young age. We recreated the church ceremony again and again. And yes, I insisted on being the bride every time. My friend, by default, always had to be the groom, and her sister, the priest. Our house in the Maritimes had a long upstairs hallway outside the bedrooms that provided an ideal aisle for me as the bride to walk down to meet her groom. So, when they visited from Ontario, we could re-create the church scene perfectly!

At my actual wedding, many years later, that same friend (and first groom) told stories of our theatrics in a surprise speech to our guests, all laughing about the fact that I had never 'let' her be the bride. She then presented me with our framed 'wedding' photo. We looked both innocent and ridiculous, and it brought back such fun memories. She stayed in the small town where my family and I were born near the onion farms and was married more than a couple of years before me to her high school sweetheart—a truly amazing guy. My life, on the other hand, had been radically different.

I never questioned what I thought were terrific ideas of bringing people together. Even as young as elementary school, I would hold meetings behind the front bushes during recess to exchange important information about our lives. I remember one meeting in particular that I dedicated specifically to our budding sexuality. Yes, you got that right. I convinced the grade-five-and-six girls to give up their playground games to participate in serious conversations about our prepubescence. At that meeting, I led a topic debating the use of tampons versus sanitary pads. What I wouldn't do, to watch a video recording of that. I honestly don't think the participation rate of the discussion was very active. I don't think any of us had even started menstruating at that time, or that the others really cared about which sanitary products they would choose. Even funnier, years later, when I did get my period, all hell broke loose (my BFF could attest to that)!

I preferred to lead the meetings, rather than use the information, back then. Leading wouldn't change as I grew up. Learning how to *use* the information definitely did, and, as with most humans, that came the hard way.

When I ventured out into the world as a school child, with the task of building a sense of interdependence through social relationships, I was not quite prepared. Not having enough say with my parents and fearing a repeat of not belonging as I had with my siblings, fused with my lively personality type and the aggressive side of the wound. I overshot with my peers through stubborn, albeit enthusiastic leadership, all to regain control and restore my fragile self-worth.

Along the way, I made a lot of friends, I participated in a lot of community and social events, and I had a lot of fun. But there were signs that I was struggling. I clung to my BFF, being sensitive if she tried to take space, and at times, even causing disruption in the class if I felt she was distancing from me. I also remember being extra hurt if she cancelled social plans. At one point, we even went to the extent of organizing meetings with the school principal to insist on room assignment changes to ensure we would be in the same class together the following school year. This kind of clinginess protected me in the short term but stressed her and isolated us from the larger peer group.

I could also be confrontational and demanding, especially if I felt threatened in a group of three. For me, this reenactment meant that I was running the risk of being the *third* one out again, and I couldn't take that chance. I even bordered on being the mean girl, projecting my own fear of not belonging by excluding those *I* deemed not to belong, even once excluding the girl who later became my lifelong BFF. This is a classic example of what is called identification with the aggressor, adopting the traits of someone you felt hurt by to feel better. It is part of an unconscious deal you make from your wounded self to not be hurt in the same way again. If I rejected before being rejected, I wouldn't be rejected. Of course, this backfires, indulges our wounded self, and takes the healthy self out of the equation. This, for me, meant being badmouthed by others for being mean, and not figuring out how to risk rejection by leading *without* aggression, only to discover that I may not be rejected at all.

These kinds of reactions are not about being *bad*. They are about being *wounded*. If we are unaware, we project our pain, easily under- or overshoot as we struggle, easily indulge and set ourselves up for deeper fears to be confirmed. We ultimately sabotage our development, compromising subsequent stages. I was trying to regain the control I had lost. I was searching for a sister. I was searching for a place to belong. I was short-sightedly taking charge to control the dynamics to reduce vulnerability and rejection that had felt unbearable, and at times, projecting my own unworthiness by rejecting others.

As life would have it, I was by all accounts an awkward nerd and that worked against me too, undermining my otherwise desperate efforts to fit in and belong, but at a loss of what to do differently. With a conservative mother and no sisters, I had poor fashion sense. I was ridiculed for wearing running shoes with dresses. I had thick glasses, full orthodontic braces, and I experimented with the then-popular, clown-personified hair perms. Luckily, my healthy drive toward success didn't let me down. I 'hired' a more fashionable friend who had older sisters as role models to teach me how to apply make-up, style my hair and clothing, and update my look. Then, something even more important happened. Despite being highly unathletic, my drive led me toward dedicated practice and determination to make the highly regarded cheerleading squad at our high school. It was worth every sweat and tear. My status as the unnoticeable, under-socialized nerd was instantly upgraded. Being a cheerleader opened doors with boys as well as with friends. This may seem superficial, but at this stage of development, these kinds of events can change the direction of life in interesting ways.

These key turning points gave me some badly needed confidence and I had a lot of fun on the way. But for the most part, I would continue to be underestimated by most of the popular kids until a high school reunion twenty-five years later brought us back together again. I showed up beaming, proud, and sexy, and finally got the recognition I deserved, only made possible because I had finally recognized my true self-worth first (living the high life after **Invitation Seven**).

As the years passed, I did in some ways re-experience the separation I had felt with my siblings in my friendships. That's no coincidence. One of my best friends from high school suffered a major mental breakdown the first month into university, had to move back home, and was later diagnosed with bipolar disorder. I remembered her as a sharp, extraordinarily witty girl. Her crisis happened the same week I had won that DJ contest. In fact, we had often played DJ together (she was actually an integral part of me entering the contest in the first place). Suddenly, life felt really serious. I knew about her background and knew she was facing huge pressures, including starting a university program that she didn't choose for herself. I was very present for her and supported her in ways I knew best at the time. Our worlds divided though, partly because of the stage of life we were in, no longer seeing each other daily at high school, but mostly because of the diverse directions our lives were taking. What was once a vibrant friendship severely diminished.

Shortly after I was married, my other childhood BFF (the other member of *The Bachelor Girls' Club*) who was my maid of honour and stood by me that day not knowing my secret, relocated to the West Coast on her own complicated adventures with life and love. She stayed there for over *twenty-five years* during a time before internet and cellular phone service and during the hardest times of my life, when I got sick and lost my career and marriage. That was hard for me, like losing a sibling all over again. Somehow though, we stayed connected. She was that friend who you can easily pick up where you last left off, regardless of how long it has been since talking together.

But, honestly, one of the biggest gifts I received in my life was from my BFF as she remained committed and dedicated to me throughout the years, despite my earlier childhood reactions to her and despite our prolonged geographical distance. My sister from another mother. In fact, as I write this, we have known each other for over fifty years. She has been *the* constant in my life, listening unconditionally with astonishing mindfulness, compassion, and humor to my crashes, and championing my wins, every time. That has meant everything. Being there for each other in good times and bad. More evidence for my healthy self that I was, in fact, worthy the whole time. She is right up there with Grandma.

My divorce dramatically impacted my friendships. I did go to support groups at the time, but everyone's experience in the crisis seemed to inhibit our capacity to socialize outside the group. My daughter was three years old at the time. Building new friendships with other young mothers at our play groups was exciting to me, particularly because of how alone I felt after my husband had left. To my disappointment, the social gatherings outside the groups centered around intact couples and families for the most part, and although I really tried, I was left out. Married friends from my past also seemed to move on with their lives, raising their families together without me. Even when my daughter competed in swimming, years later, the hopes for expanding my social network died again when my daughter's elite level took her much further and faster than the other swimmers and the unexpected toxic layer of competition between the parents ousted me.

There was one other detrimental component to my social life overlapping with those post-divorce years—my failed health. Bedridden and house bound for many months, I found myself separated, yet again. It was a very, very lonely time for me. By then, I had already lost hope of rebuilding after my separation and taking advantage of the new network of parents. Any further attempts trying at these were now blocked by my physical disability to socialize.

As my health gradually improved, I slowly learned to live within my new physical limits, and I gained more strength, resilience, and stamina for social interaction. Of even more importance was that this was happening at a time when I was beginning to make progress on my emotional health. The gift of the illness invited me to protect my health at any cost, including reducing social interaction that could make me sicker and in doing so taught me to withstand disconnection from a place of empowerment instead of loneliness. This ultimately helped me reach a developmental task that for me had been missing this whole time—*object permanence* (to feel loved even in the physical absence of the other). Even if the few friends I did still have in my life went on without me to gatherings I couldn't and shouldn't attend, I could still be loved. Loving myself had been building, and this increased tolerance for separation would be a product of that journey.

I also knew I was making progress when I continued to find myself in groupings of three, when the other two knew each other better than I knew either of them, reactivating the 'third wheel' role again. By then, I knew about my wounded self and could recognize that part of me when I inaccurately misinterpreted and personalized 'rejection.' I was able to lead with my healthy, secure self and settle my reactions by *de*personalizing and calming internally. I stopped clinging. I stopped stammering. I stopped overworking. I learned to just be me. In fact, I learned to be the best version of me. Even more, I let people come to me.

While I continued to feel better over the years, I renewed my commitment to myself to show up with more balance, sharing the spotlight, being very particular with whom I socialized, and creating healthier friendships overall. I looked for male and female friends who had energy, creativity, integrity, maturity, honesty, and stability—and I found them. I found support, and I found intimacy. I got involved in more community activities including renewing my interest in acting, where I met fabulously creative, like-minded intense people. I resumed some athletic activities when my health allowed, including tennis, and helped create the infamous 'Davisville Divas,' a group of the most inspiring, brave, creative, and entertaining women I know.

From there, I met my second BFF, someone who demonstrates such grace and integrity and positivity, which truly grounds me and lifts me up at the same time. She tells me I help her grow too. I think that's because I model direct conflict resolution and vulnerability, toned down from my more aggressive days.

I joined a private women's club filled with exceptionally successful, ambitious women of all ages. I won't lie, this was initially quite intimidating for me before I found my footing through steady patience. I could truly reach for more and be more in my life without trying to be too much.

The success of my private practice took off, sometimes in unexpected ways, and my confidence grew exponentially. Of course, I brought that pride and strength back into nurturing healthier and authentic friendships, which helped me rediscover a sense of belonging and a sense of worthiness, while finessing better ways to set boundaries. At times throughout the years, this led to difficult and painful decisions to end friendships which were unhealthy. These experiences paralleled how I had ended those unhealthy dating connections, both being supported by increased self-value and mastering the wound that endings could be tolerated, sometimes even necessary. I found ways to handle delicate conflicts more tactfully and strive to be a better person without feeling so sensitive or trying so hard to prove my worth.

This growth with friendships is indeed a great example of the spiralling up of the healthy self (same momentum but completely opposite direction of the spiralling down of the wounded self). Mastery from the healthy self opens up the space where one good decision from a stronger place leads to healthier exposures that motivate you toward being an even better person and inviting more growth. As my healthy self gained more airtime from places of optimal control and confidence, my wounded self needed less attention (like the immature child who settles down from a temper tantrum). Experiencing that shift firsthand would teach me how to teach this to clients.

When writing this chapter, I asked my two BFFs to identify my strengths and flaws. They told me they valued my passion and *com*passion, my generosity, and my steadfast fearless resilience. They also told me about my shortcomings: overdoing and stubborn willfulness. Like everyone, I'm a work in progress.

Understanding Friendship Patterns

I invite you to think about what has hurt your friendships.

Understanding the history of friendships provides very useful information about who has supported us, who has hurt us, and what it all means. It's why any good, comprehensive clinical assessment includes tracing the history, development, and themes of our friendships. Who we pick and how the intimacy and conflicts are managed are good indicators of not only the quality of one's past and current network, but the state of our overall mental health. Examining our friendships reveals our experiences in previous developmental stages. Specifically, how successful we were at achieving trust and control when we entered school age to master interdependence, self-worth, and eventually identity with peers *outside* the family. In a deeper sense, when we connect the friendship themes to earlier attachment styles with our primary caregivers, traumas, conflict narratives, and losses, we expand our knowledge even further. This usually clarifies why our fulfillment with friends happened as it did and how earlier struggles were projected onto peers causing breakage.

I help a lot of individuals presenting with issues in their social worlds and who show up with hypersensitivity and dysregulation. Who are being aggressive or narcissistic—instances where they cut off, punish, bully, abuse, and push away people they care about. More frequently than not though, I treat those with social anxiety, and/or passive isolation who are indulging in what I call 'low-risk living,' created from, and reinforced by, over-controlled vulnerability and conflict avoidance. It continues to concern me how alone and isolated people really are. Not just hidden in their bedrooms, recently named 'bed rotting' and closely correlated with internet and gaming addictions, many people are also lonely in crowded rooms, alone 'in plain sight.'

The higher rates of internet and gaming addictions I observe are especially apparent with teens who create virtual peers in simulated worlds that replace in person interactions and otherwise meaningful social skill building. This was never more concerning than during and after the COVID-19 pandemic that began in 2020 and sent everyone home. If you were a school-aged child or teenager, such home detention had greater negative impacts because the timing intersected with a vital stage of social development. This stage invites you to gain a sense of greater autonomy and clearer identity, and also requires interpersonal socialization, that was no longer available during COVID.

Even more so, for those with pre-existing social anxiety, the pandemic created a convenient way to hide, further reinforcing core beliefs that they would not be accepted by others whom they believed were better than them. Those individuals had a harder time during what I called 'COVID 2.0,' when the world reopened with expectations to 'get back out there'. Remote learning is still more available than before the pandemic, which one could argue offers flexible educational platforms to help everyone succeed, especially those with learning styles not supported in traditional curriculums. But more often, I see it as an unhelpful crutch for those functioning at lower social levels, indulging social fears and insecurities.

There are other significant factors that impede a healthy social life. High levels of depression and global disenchantment are rampant and easily reinforce loneliness, emptiness, obsessions, addictions, emotional dysregulation, fears, and paranoia which increase social separation. ADHD (Attention-Deficit Hyperactivity Disorder) (Gill & Hosker, 2021) and spectrum diagnoses (ASD) can be complex interferences as well (Bellini, 2023).

Being a Good Friend

Positive changes with friendships begin when we:

A. **Improve** our Self-Care: Altering eating, sleeping, exercising, and leisure as much as possible, with sheer willpower, before feeling the benefits of more advanced therapy tools, before we feel better emotionally. For social health it means doing more if we are 'flighters'. Being kinder if we are 'fighters'. I invite clients to make a commitment of at least once weekly interactions that are not at home or work, with at least one other person, in-person, without 'problem-talk'. There is a time to be vulnerable and go to your people for support. But there is also the power of positive distraction by making your life bigger by re-charging your brain outside of problems.

What have you done for fun with others in the last week?

B. **Change** our Thinking: Restructuring negative thoughts that are impeding positive social interaction (introduced in chapter two). Thoughts which exist within the walls of anger, anxiety, and depression (overt *or* covert). Bottom line, if we want to 'do' our friendships differently, we have to think differently.

What kind of thoughts impede your social interactions?

Remember, we don't just wake up thinking differently because we want to. Our brain needs daily practice. This is why it is so important to do those quick, five-minute CBT tracks every day for brain health.

Here's another example of the CHANGE program as it pertains to social anxiety.

1. Noticing the **Cues** our brain body and behavior are telling us we are indulging trigger reactions. Brain: *"No one likes me at school."*. Body. Tired. Behavior: Bed rotting. Device scrolling.

2. **Honeymooning** by taking a much-needed short break, e.g. I force myself out of my room.

3. **Adjusting** our stress by discharging, soothing, or distracting, e.g. I have a hot shower.

4. Correcting with **New Thoughts** that are present, specific, neutral, and factual. *"The fact is I'm at a new school and I don't know many people. They don't know me. When I last went to school, I just sat alone and didn't talk to anyone. I didn't actually give people a chance to like me. I am good at Math. I'm good at skateboarding."* This directly includes outwitting those stinky thoughts where, *"It's never worked out for me to make friends, so why try?"* becomes *"The fact is if I don't try, I won't make friends."* *"I'm too tired to go out,"* becomes *"Going out will actually give me energy."* *"I can't do this,"* becomes *"That's not true, I can do more than I think, others have actually complimented me on my skateboarding."* *"Let's see how long it takes her to...,"* becomes *"I'm expecting her to read my mind, and I am setting this up to fail."*

5. **Getting** honest about what is most important: e.g. *"I really want to have friends. I really want to stop feeling so lonely."* Separating out healthy 'really wants for interaction,' from stinky 'wants for avoidance,' is key here.

6. **Empowering** ourselves by speaking up, deciding, or planning: e.g. I make a plan to find one person tomorrow who looks friendly and ask them two questions about themself. If they ignore me, I will ask someone else or join an activity I enjoy.

Have you started practicing factual thinking? Are you clarifying what you really want toward speaking, deciding, or planning something powerful for you?

C. **Regulate** our **Negative Emotions**: Learn advanced emotional regulation techniques. There is a specific part of the DBT program (the bridging of the head and heart that is mostly connected to improving relationships) named Interpersonal Scripting, and it includes:

1. Depersonalizing others' 'bad' behaviors by identifying alternate explanations (what else could this [someone's negative reactions to me] be about if it's *not* about me?)

2. Establishing common ground called 'clouding' when there are differences, toward improved negotiation in disagreements. I call these the emotional Venn diagrams, the vertically or horizontally overlapping clouds.

3. Doing voice work to utilize the feedback loop between the words, tone, volume, and speed of what we say and what we hear ourselves saying, to train our speech in ways that invites rather than breaks social connection.

I teach clients to take something that is hard to say and record and rehearse it on devices until they sound how they want to sound. They practice sounding like someone they know personally who they admire during conflicts, or someone they look up to in the media, study videos of the voice they use, and come up with three adjectives of the voice they want to emulate (Interpersonal Effectiveness, n.d.).

4. Establishing balance with often opposing needs between yourself and the other person, so there is not too much or too little of 'you' or 'me', letting it go 'the other person's way' sometimes, advocating for it to go 'my way' other times.

5. Using assertive delays (slowing down the overly urgent interactions as anxiety or frustration increases). I use the imagery here of grabbing the ping-pong ball flying over the net to slow the game down, while we breathe and act with intention about what we say or do next.

Pick one of those five to practice in your social interactions.

D. **Mend** our **Broken Hearts** (the heart surgery of the deeper emotionally focused work). This goes after the root causes and early, related interruptions of attachment and developmental disruptions of trust, control, autonomy, self-worth, and identity. Past problems in social relationships and situations I commonly find include bullying, loss, betrayal, abuse, ostracization, multiple moves, and school changes among others. Healing from these is obviously crucial at this stage and the deeper healing program helps by:

- **Mapping out** the wounded vs. healthy self—e.g., the bullying that forced me to believe **I was not likeable**, made me feel unimportant, and that shuts me down vs. the time I competed in skateboarding, reminding me that I can be **disciplined** and talented, feeling proud made possible by being persistent.

- Exploring and discovering the pain of the wounds. **Creating the images of the pain**—e.g., bullying represented by a dead forest, burned, desolate, lifeless (social death, being 'burned' by the bullies, alone and flattened bed rotting).

- Using **the wisdom of the healthy self** to offer gifts to the wounded self, e.g., new growth by **disciplining myself** to talk to one new person tomorrow. Having a picture of a green leaf surrounded by dead wood on my home screen with the caption 'One Leaf at a Time', where I am reminded of my potential multiple times a day. Taking one small step each day to rebuild my forest.

- **Deconstructing and disowning others' projections, depersonalizing**—e.g., recognizing the bullies were dealing with powerlessness that had nothing to do with me, creating the image of powerless represented by a squished worm and passing the worm over to the bullies in an empty chair intervention. Passing over something that was never mine to begin with, thereby tapping into the freedom of reclaiming who I really am, not who the bullies needed me to be to suit their need for power.

- Confronting the bullies in a therapeutic letter, inviting my healthy self to **help the wounded self who had become my personal bully by tricking me into shutting down and bed rotting,** recovering unconditional love to myself, accepting my imperfections, building resilience in the imperfection of others, and **the reality that not everyone needs to like me all the time to be good enough.**

What is a good visual representation of your social pain? What would be the gift to help with that, from your healthy self?

Family Therapy

As part of the KG systemic and comprehensive model of therapy, we invite families into the process, including the treatment of social problems. School phobia, acting out with peers, under-socialization, and failures to individuate and launch are symptoms of greater familial problems. They are unconsciously or indirectly inviting the family system toward needed change, but are getting blocked. Negative familial conflict scripts, inappropriate roles, insecure or anxious attachments, overwhelming unmet needs of other family members, unhealthy boundaries and expectations, misaligned communications, and intergenerational trauma easily cause interference for children and teens building relationships and vying to individuate.

Family therapy works toward softening and removing those blocks. This is the case for school-avoidant children who have insecure or anxious attachments with their parents and, unable to manage the separation anxiety, resist attending school. This is the case for self-centered children and teens who are being overindulged by guilt-ridden, divorcing parents. This is the case for children who are aggressive or passive with peers, witnessing persistent arguments and worse in the family. This is the case for under-socialized children and teens who are extensively taking care of younger siblings to compensate for parental anxiety, depression, addiction, or health issues. This is the case for teenagers who fail to progress to postsecondary education and campus residences, unconsciously worrying about their parents who are stuck in conflictual marriages, or who are single depressed parents, especially if they are the youngest and there aren't younger siblings at home to pick up that responsibility for them if they leave.

Creative three-part child-and-parent sessions for symptom management include:
1. Parent check ins.
2. Active work with the child.
3. Passing over the specific work to the parents for in-home practice.

The active work includes: child-adapted CBT to change unhelpful thinking patterns, using storybook or video characters familiar to the child facing their own problems; narrative techniques to rewrite negative internalised stories; externalization techniques to animate and empower the child against an outside negative 'force'; and psychodrama to improve social behaviors, assertiveness, and empathy.

Associated, deeper family problems feeding the symptoms often include parenting, divorce co-parenting, and blended family co-parenting. Individual therapy for the parents' unresolved issues is common, addressing addiction, depression, intergenerational trauma, parental abandonment, grief etc. Otherwise, parents easily expect their children to be 'fixed' while a large portion of the problem remains unaddressed.

Teenagers, although this is much more delicately planned due to their independence, benefit from parental involvement in the process. Often parents are 'working in the dark,' and at cross purposes, causing more harm unintentionally. This comes from either a lack of understanding of the core issues, distractions and negative experiences of their own struggles, or from the accumulated dysregulated, misunderstood frustrations and powerlessness with their teen's struggles. Unless these issues are resolved, any progress the teen makes is often minimized or short-lived, as it is undermined and sabotaged on the home front. This is preventable.

Parents attend to learn how to support the teen's therapy including the improved daily decision-making of self-care, the restructured thoughts by the CBT, the emotional regulation plans by the DBT, and ultimately in a family CBT program (the pathway from CBT to dialoguing in Appendix D).

Most importantly, attending family sessions addresses earlier childhood ruptures in familial relationships, underlying problems with attachment, trust, control, boundaries, loss, trauma, or transitions through divorce/blended families. Those structured betrayal and healing conversations, discussed previously are very effective here. All of this leads to improved mental health planning not only for the child and teen who is freed to master interdependence with peers and be more prepared to explore who they want to be in life (identity) and experience optimal adult intimacy, but also for the parents' wellbeing and the overall functioning of the family. There are clear takeaways that change the trajectory for everyone.

What family issues are sabotaging your child's social health?

Divorce

The social transition when a marriage ends often brings its own challenges to the partners who now find themselves single, separated from their partner, their partners' family members, and even sometimes mutual friends. Such displacement is a common *secondary* loss at this stage. A working-through of these losses is very present in the work I do with divorcing clients.

Reconstructing a social life takes effort, often over a longer period than we think, and it takes persistence. I knew it could be done. It took me ten years. I knew it took time. Not just the passive passing of time. Time to better use the healthy self. Growing up to be a better friend, first to myself and then to others, was part of my invitation.

It's part of the loss. It's part of the rebuild.

Cultural Shifts

There have been some positive impacts post-COVID, raising the volume on conversations about the dangers of isolation and the deep need for human social connection. As gender roles continue evolving, I have also observed the deepening of male friendships. I am encouraged to hear male clients describe the deep conversations they are having with their peers that echo the therapeutic conversations from sessions and reverberate back to the clinical progress. Finally, I have seen the increase in recent years of positive social activities, including sober curiosity, mindfulness, mental health retreats, yoga, sound baths, plunge pools, and wellness, which aligns with what was already being talked about in private therapy spaces. All these improve awareness and self-care, and level up overall social health. And maybe even more important than we realized.

Friends Do More Than We May Realize...

We started hearing the word tribe more often after the 2023 release of the Netflix Documentary: *Live to 100: Secrets of the Blue Zones*.

In 2004, Dan Buettner teamed with National Geographic, the National Institute on Aging, and the world's best longevity researchers to identify pockets around the world where people lived measurably better and longer. He discovered five areas he dubbed 'blue zones' where they found people reaching the age of one hundred at a rate *ten* times greater than in the United States and with lower rates of chronic disease. One of the principles which Buettner concluded was common amongst the populations in these pockets was having the *right tribe*. "Health behaviors are contagious," Buettner said. Deleterious behaviors (e.g., obesity, smoking, excessive drinking, loneliness, unhappiness) are also contagious. The world's longest-lived people curate social circles around themselves that support healthy behaviors (Blue Zones Project, 2021).

It seems that surrounding ourselves with healthy peers is no longer just about making our worlds bigger, no longer just about fun and support and connectivity, no longer just about social and mental and emotional health. Hanging out with healthy people doing healthy things could actually prolong the length of our life.

Finding *my* tribe meant everything to me. Finding yours will, too.

Think about this:

1. If you interviewed your friends, what do you think they would say about you? What would you say about them?

2. How do your friendships represent your core wound and your adaptions to your wound?

3. How would your healthy self level up your friendships to fit with your best self? To have better conflict resolution and higher intimacy?

CHAPTER 8
MOTHERING MADELINE/
MOTHERING ME:
CONSCIOUS PARENTING OF THE SELF

She's just a girl and she's on fire

Hotter than a fantasy

Lonely like a highway

She's livin' in a world and it's on fire

Filled with catastrophe

But she knows she can fly away

Oh… she got both feet on the ground

And she's burning it down.

Oh… she got her head in the clouds.

And she's not backing down.

….

Oh…. We got our feet on the ground.

And we're burning it down.

Oh… Got our head in the clouds,

And we're not coming down.

(Alicia Keys - Girl on Fire, 2012)

The Happy Parent

Where has the happiness been for you, as a parent?

I have always loved kids. No, I mean really loved kids. I am a kid at heart, and it shows. In our extended family, I always gravitated to the kids, and quite frankly, usually enjoyed their company more than the adults. I was always the one who organized creative events for the kids. At the cottage, I turned normal hikes into scavenger hunts or an otherwise predictable day swimming at the dock into a full-scale family Olympic event, with everyone involved, including the adults, whether they wanted to or not.

Kids are innocent. Kids are free. Kids are curious. Kids express intensely. Kids speak my language. And I speak theirs.

When I began babysitting at thirteen, I developed a full craft program I called 'Karen's Crafts'. By the time I showed up for the job, I had planned a major project for the kids and me to work on together while the parents were out. I loved it, and the kids loved it. I also remember regularly taking my niece and nephew for the weekend when they were young, one time including all their little cousins as well. There we were all squished into my tiny apartment at Yonge and Eligible during Christmas for fun-filled activities for the whole weekend. We did paper mâché, foot painting, sculptures, baking, parades, and more. I thrived on those kinds of experiences and so did they.

Becoming pregnant was over-the-top joyous for me. I meticulously planned the birth, the nursery, and the post-delivery care. When the doctors announced, 'It's a girl!' I shrieked.

Having a daughter has been the single most important thing in my life, so it made complete sense to me that I named her Madeline after my paternal grandmother, one of the most important people in my life. Mothering has been the best gift to me and has given me some of my proudest and most unforgettable moments. Alongside my seventh invitation, parenting truly was the best way to keep me growing. After all, we do generally have three chances to grow—through ourselves and the problems we get into, through our lovers and the attractions that become our frustrations, and through our children and the reflections they give us of our own childhoods that make us uncomfortable.

I interviewed Madeline, now twenty-six and living in the UK, for this book. She said, "You always make me feel loved and supported."

It can be delicate to have a therapist as a parent, but she told me, "Having a mother as a therapist meant open honest conversations with really helpful advice that made me feel incredibly understood."

Making sense to others helps us make sense to ourselves and that necessarily builds needed inner security. So, I was especially thrilled Madeline experienced and benefitted from that validation from me, and I know that will continue to serve her well.

Honestly, it was completely natural to be present and loving to her. An organic maternal instinct perhaps, but I also believe wholeheartedly that Grandma's spirit and essence of bubbles and giggles lived in me. My heart was so full and open for my daughter. I saw the positive impacts as she blossomed and excelled.

The Conscious Parent

Madeline also told me, "You aren't normal—you do more than anyone I know, put more into everything than I know, and you always go above what is expected." (Funny, as I write this, lately, I have been telling her that I thought she was 'above average' in her achievements, resilience, and resourcefulness). She added, "You had high expectations of me, sometimes overly high, sometimes looking like OCD (Obsessive Compulsive Disorder)—and that stressed me out."

Madeline was right about this. I do throw everything into everything. Oftentimes, too much. As much as Grandma filled my heart with love I could shower onto my daughter, I would be guilty of overdoing and being overbearing for sure, and that easily overwhelmed, confused, and disempowered her. I needed to work on those parts. With experiences growing up and the disappointments I faced, it made sense that my journey to regain control and self-worth would not only show up with friends and lovers, but also showed up in how I mothered.

Even more relevant, though, was that the most significant losses of control and experiences of unworthiness I had in my entire life from my worsened health and divorce, began when Madeline was only 1-1/2 years old. These understandably challenged my ability for conscious parenting. Luckily, the yellow paint wake-up happened only 1-1/2 years later, when Madeline was three. That wake-up eventually made me a better person, and a much more conscious parent. I learned so much about myself at that bottom, and the power of that made it possible to restore my career, my relationships and most importantly, re-set my parenting before Madeline got much older. Fully opening the invitation comes with many gifts. Not everyone's wake-up falls in line so neatly. The fact is none of us have it all figured out by the time we become parents.

I invite you to think about what could be getting in the way of your parenting.

Conscious parenting makes it possible for parents to provide unconditional love to their children by being aware of where *they* are currently in their journeys and what they are bringing into their parenting from their incomplete past. What remains from unresolved experiences play out in the parent/child relationship as reenactments of our unresolved pain. We are given yet another and often one of the last major chances 'to get it right.' The more aware we are of what is unfinished for us, and how to make progress with that, the more likely we are to show up as the best version of ourselves (our healthy self) including our parenting, and the more likely our children are free to show up with their best versions as well.

The fact is, if we don't manage our own wounds, our children absorb them, and they unconsciously take on the role of mastering them for us. Doing so not only negatively alters the relationship they have with us, it also dramatically disturbs the boundaries in their relationships with others outside the family because those absorbed wounds of the parents are projected onto others (as I had done growing up). Children don't deserve to inherit this pathology from their parents' wounds. They need to be free to design the kind of life and relationships they want for themselves, from themselves.

So, the invitation for conscious parenting is for all parents. This is the responsibility for all parents. But it is not easy. There are typical patterns with parents living below optimal levels of consciousness.

The most common reenactments I see that provide the best therapeutic opportunities for parents are:

- Children who show up with normal developmental temper tantrums, power struggles, and defiance in their efforts to find boundaries and flexibility as they grow up.

These can trigger the parent who had too much or too little control in their own childhoods. The parent indulges or becomes too rigid because they are overly threatened by their child's resistance, and too sensitive about losing control.

- Children display otherwise normal outbursts and may even be 'mean' to the parent as they struggle with their own emotional regulation. They are trying to make sense of their internal emotional states and how to articulate their feelings under stress.

Parents who were criticized as children feel these outbursts too deeply and either back down too easily or retort with heavier criticism and shame the child in order to restore internal and external equilibrium.

- Pubescent children and teenagers who are developing normal sexual expression.

Parents with untreated sexual trauma can be either overly protective and interrupt the natural sexual expressions/social experimentation of their children and teens, or, usually due to some level of dissociation, be 'blind' to their child's needs and unintentionally place them in high-risk situations. This can contribute to a pattern of intergenerational trauma.

- 'Pushback' teenagers who show up by not listening, talking back, testing etc., in their search for identity and in figuring out who they are and who they want to be.

The unconscious parent experiences pushbacks as *disrespect* and over-personalize the behavior, especially if they experienced a lack of respect growing up. They feel intensely hurt and, as a result, indulge or conversely, over-punish their teenager when they are, in fact, unconsciously trying to seek approval of or retaliate against the person who disrespected *them* from their past.

- Teens and young adults express an innate need for independence and individuate from the family and begin making decisions without the parents' involvement.

If parents experienced abandonment or premature independence as teens, the separation anxiety is profound, and unconscious resentment sets in. They either don't get involved enough with their teens, contribute negatively, forcing an early, abrupt departure of their teen from the family as they experienced, or they become over-involved to soothe their own anxiety and fears of loneliness and hold their teen back.

Parents who were enmeshed with their own parents growing up or who are currently in unfulfilling marriages/facing above average adult stress of one nature or another can smother their teenagers, replicating their childhood enmeshment, preventing individuation for their teen and contributing to a failure to launch—all driven by an unconscious avoidance of being alone, and the incapacity for autonomy. This is projected onto the teenager.

Do you recognize any of those patterns in your family?

The Divorcing Parent

Madeline faced pressures as an only child of an overdoer. But, at three, when I separated from her father, the divorce heightened the fact that she was also the only child of divorce. This was a double challenge that placed her often at the center of the conflicts between me and her father, without siblings to defer to or confer with. I believe she over-neutralized her own feelings to satisfy the competing needs of us parents, which put her at risk of overaccommodating to others as she grew up. Unlike a lot of only children, Madeline seemed to make peer-aged friends easily, but I know that feeling the burden of the divorce as a child without siblings weighed on her and affected her development, compromising autonomy and self-worth. It weighed on me too. The schedule of continually going back and forth between homes was also hard, and I know heightened separation anxiety for her, not just as a child but as she grew into adulthood. I have done my best to ease and repair this with her. The rule of thumb generally is: the younger the child, the more frequent the transitions between the two homes should be, in consideration of the lower attention spans, and the importance of parent/child bonding while children are young. This only works if there is a low level of conflict between the parents, which we, as parents, back then were observing, so it was probably the best of two evils, but it was still a risk.

Divorce adds a challenging parenting element—co-parenting. It's a stretch for most parents and I was no exception, but the children of divorce deserve their parents to figure this out. Divorcing parents are usually battling a significant lost dream. In many instances they are dealing with betrayal, organizing new homes, managing reduced incomes, facing the realities of their new partners becoming stepparents to their children, and/or their children having stepparents with their ex's new partners, and still trying to show up as good parents themselves. Blended families add a further challenge. In fact, these can be among the most fragile types of families to succeed because of the grief of the lost family, and the intense loyalty binds in the new family. These intense pressures are usually experienced by all members to one degree or another, easily projecting/acting out against the stepparent, scapegoating the children, especially if the new couple aren't strong together, and placing the birth parent in the middle.

No doubt, co-parenting was a challenge for me, and among the darkest moments of my life due to my reduced time with Madeline, which I wasn't expecting and definitely not wanting. The biggest takeaway from my divorce was that I had to let go of the rage I felt for my husband leaving me. I also had to figure out how to manage the enormous amount of anxiety I felt from the sheer loss of control, when I had already lost control of significant *other* parts in my life, including my health, career and lost pregnancy, within the past two years.

These are some profiles of the divorcing parent:

- The angry divorcing co-parent: automatic, negative thoughts (see examples of generalized blaming thoughts listed in the previous chapter) keep them locked into conflict, which *keeps* them angry. Grief for this parent, especially if not grounded as described above, becomes weaponized. This reduces the chance that problems are effectively resolved, prolongs the separation and uncoupling process, and most importantly, pits the child between the two parents (referred to as triangulation) or toward a more extreme and damaging dynamic of parent alienation (Lewis, n.d.).

- The depressed, divorcing co-parent: excessive blaming of self, hijacks the grief process by drowning them into deep shame (generalized self-criticism, past regretting thoughts). The parent becomes immobilized and distracted. Their capacity to take care of themselves is lowered, which can be serious, and most significantly, their capacity to take care of their children is undermined, often inviting the role reversal of their kids taking care of them (*Depression after Divorce*, 2023).

- The anxious co-parent, labelled divorce anxiety: overwhelmed with worry and fear by the lost control they can suffer with catastrophic thoughts (generalized future worrying thoughts) and panic attacks. This frightens the children, especially if the anxiety is displaced directly onto them. Interventions are needed and, in the absence, can cause permanent damage (Amicable, 2022).

Although I was depressed to the point that I was suicidal, this was mostly masked by anger and anxiety until I healed. Feeling extremely powerless, I would lash out and argue on meaningless details. I would also go to hospital suffering panic attacks. My yellow paint wake-up ultimately allowed me to use my divorce as an invitation for growth. It saved me and in doing so, saved Madeline.

For the divorcee, conscious parenting is about having a conscious divorce. Complex at best. But not *impossible*.

What part of your divorce as a parent gave you another opportunity to grow?

KG Therapy for Singles, Parents and Families

Accountable Therapy is comprehensive therapy. Helping all family members is necessary Interventions are needed on all levels with all individuals and integrated back together as a family. The following program details help all clients. Single, married, or divorced. Children, teens, or adults. You can read these no matter what stage or age you are at. Examples are provided to invite conscious parenting. Sometimes that means parenting your children better. It always means parenting yourself better.

I worked extra hard on my journey as a parent because it was so important to me. Because Madeline was so important to me. I was able to work better on myself because I was riding the energy of that seventh invitation. I relied heavily on the programs I was refining with clients, included these below:

CBT- Changing Our Thoughts

Recall the Cognitive Behavioral Therapy:

C - Identify the brain, body and behavioral **C**ues of the trigger.

H - **H**oneymoon and step back.

A - **A**djust by discharging, soothing, or distracting.

N - Replace negative thoughts with **N**ew **N**eutral, specific, and factual thoughts (I call this 'my bottom line').

G - **G**et honest about your goal given the facts (I call this 'what is most important to me?') that help discard any lingering negative thoughts that are still hanging around.

And…

E- **E**mpower by speaking with 'I' messages, deciding or planning that puts you back in the driver's seat in a constructive way, available for active listening.

CBT Therapy is extremely helpful at weeding out the useless negative thoughts that take us further away from what we really want, including thoughts that sabotage the family's needs and the relationships we have with our children. This radically improves our ability for active listening which is so key. It also changes "You" messages, "No" messages, or no messages at all to "I" messages ("I feel _____" and "I need _____") and drives decisions and plans as a parent from a place of response rather than reactivity.

Different pieces of the CBT program resonate differently for different people. For me, especially in my relationship with Madeline, what resonated was the "I." I tried my best to hold myself to the standard, when triggered by her, of biting my lip from the inside (my 'A' adjustment), and quickly correcting negative thoughts, until the first word out of my mouth I knew, was going to be "I". I know this helped tame the aggressive side of the wound for me. I know this protected open communication between us, which was paramount.

CBT also helped me land on the indisputable facts of a trigger, discover what I did have control of, identify what was most important to me, and commit to acting in ways that got me closer to that. I did this instead of indulging what felt good for me in the instant but would have harmed me, Madeline, and my co-parenting relationship further.

This brings me to my second favourite step in the CBT program. In addition to finding the "I" message at the empowerment stage in 'Change' by speaking assertively with less aggression, I fell in love with the 'G' when I got to ask myself "what is most important to me?" (This is the G stage "Get Honest about your Goal).

Here's why:

When I mastered my CBT while I was divorcing, I landed on something that radically changed my internal narrative and, consequently, the entire parenting direction I would take. I identified that what I actually wanted more than anything was to nurture and protect my daughter's self-esteem above my need for control, my need to be right, my desire to punish her father, or my desire to win an argument. From that, much more constructive responses to my ex-husband when we disagreed were more possible.

I pictured Madeline growing into a young woman who believed in herself, thriving and having healthy friendships, having a good career, taking educated risks, needing a good relationship with her father (despite how I had once felt about him), and having healthy relationships with future partners (mastering the stage of intimacy) without losing herself. She needed me to be an anchor amidst the stormy waves. I couldn't anchor her if I didn't anchor myself first. So, I put in the work. I held myself accountable, ensuring that what I did, said, or planned, fit with growing her self-esteem, one step at a time. As long as I had that 'G' on my radar, I could hold myself accountable for how I spoke to her.

Remember, we grow more when things are going badly. There is no better chance to grow than in the heat of a trigger, when you redirect a tempting negative reaction to a positive response. Everyone wins. The messenger and the receiver. So, I dropped the self-indulgent want of immediate gratification in an outburst to be right over my ex-husband, and instead I aimed to listen, speak, decide, and make plans more calmly and directly for Madeline's sake. This is the chess playing of the healthy self, looking two-to-three moves down the board. To protect her self-worth, she had to feel heard, she had to have what she needed to resign from the role of pleasing me, get out from under the pressure of taking care of her father, and stop playing the middle neutral Switzerland in our disagreements.

I supported regular family meetings to build cohesion where I could. I hosted full family, child-centered celebrations regularly. These weren't perfect by any stretch, but I felt empowered, leading the way from a place of love and peace. I even repaired my relationship with my ex's parents, which had been an immediate, albeit short-term, secondary loss after the divorce. We maintain a good bond to this day. All of this helped me chart a different pathway for my anger, anxiety, despair, and grief. And of course, and most importantly, it helped Madeline.

It may seem obvious to you as you read this that any good parent would put their child's needs ahead of their 'baggage'. But this is not easy, and under the stress of the divorce, it was anything but. In fact, the 'G' is not that simple. Clients regularly tell me that they don't know what they want, especially when they are overwhelmed. I show them how the power of clear thinking makes the 'really want' evident. Once what is most important becomes labelled, because you're in neutral factual thinking, the act of empowerment from speaking, deciding, planning, and listening also becomes clear.

What negative thoughts do you need to change to be a more conscious parent?

What part of the CBT resonates the most for you, whether you're a parent or not?

The Family CBT programs teach the child/teen and the parents to have their own individual cognitive restructuring programs, done at the same time individually, but brought back together for a better conversation together. See the joint pathway used for couples and families in Appendix D. The program ensures that all family members speak the same language throughout the CBT C-H-A-N-G-E pathway. Members are able to call breaks when needed, (the Honeymoon), usually using a pre-agreed alert word such as 'pineapple' (for some reason people love picking some kind of fruit as their 'honeymoon' word). This signal is short enough to avoid releasing longer, harder fighting words, but must be at least one word to force flighters to announce their needed break. This ultimately redirects otherwise escalating situations toward the active listening and 'I' messages at the 'E' stage, introduced by saying: "I am ready to talk, are you?" Sometimes waiting is needed until you hear a "Yes" from the other person. Members stay on 'standby' if they hear nothing, or the honeymoon word is repeated indicating the other member is still working through their 'C-H-A-N-G-E', knowing it will be worth the wait to have a more constructive conversation. The 'wait', with practice should not be long. Most CBT experts will tell you, when 'perfected', this process could be completed in twenty minutes. Definitely worth the wait! This pathway leads to much more effective family conversations, inviting the growth of all.

DBT – Regulating our Emotions

Radical Acceptance

Living with radical acceptance, explained in more detail in chapter 9, rests on the belief that resilience comes from working with what is, not with what isn't. It's about believing that authentic worthiness comes from accepting that all humans are imperfect, instead of striving for perfection that is unattainable. I developed a powerful way for clients to live with radical acceptance, with daily practice, by creating and being accountable to act from a *personal slogan* developed in therapy.

Mine was 'Give up control, to find more.' AKA—Let Madeline make mistakes as long as she is safe, and then be there to help her when she asks. This will be more beneficial to her and our relationship in the long run.

I really had to work hard at that if I wanted to be more effective and parent with more consciousness. A lot of radical acceptance slogans point out the irony of finding more with less. e.g., *"Trying too hard to find myself with others, makes me lost"*, *"I am richer from simplicity"*, or *"Overworking creates more work."*

These slogans are usually attached to meaningful photographs and placed on devices for multiple viewings per day, to change our neuropathways and to outwit temptations for perfectionism or any other habit that creates dysregulation.

How could accepting something help you? What would be your slogan?

The Two-Check Rule

Embracing the broken record technique, a 'two-check rule'. Remember when we listened to our vinyls? If we heard a skip, we let the record play around once more and listened very closely, and if it skipped again, we could take it off, try to carefully buff out the scratch with our sleeves, and play it again. If it skipped again, we would take it off the player altogether. This helps with obsessive dysregulation. The invitation here? Drop into a worry with full mindfulness. If there is still a worry, go over it again, with even more attention. And then *let it go*. There is a saturation point when more is *not* more, it is less. Useless worrying. Useless obsessing. We indulge anxiety and fear rather than soothe it. The shake-off comes from knowing we were mindful *both* times. This helps with the classic OCD of checking and rechecking, tapping, and counting habits, and it helps with perfectionism. I learned over time, to express my concerns, to myself and to Madeline, often twice and then left it with her, especially as she got older. That destressed me and her.

Do you need a two-check rule on something you may be obsessing about?

Grief Work

As discussed, neutralizing the losses of divorce to let go of shame and blame for the newly single person helps them move on more effectively. For the divorcing parent, it helps them move on as well and work with the bigger stakes of freeing up energy needed for parenting and co-parenting. Ungrounded grief indulges the anxiety, anger and depression of the uncoupling process. Ungrounded grief for the divorcing parent too easily contributes to over control of, aggression toward, and distancing from the children. This easily leads to inappropriate reactivity to regain lost control, to discharge rage or to isolate. Part of the answer for me was to pin down my grief. Once I neutralized what happened in my marriage, I could begin finding 'real' control without trying to control Madeline or others for that matter. I co-parented better. I lived better. Conscious parents aren't distracted. Neither are they boxers or those dissolving into shame. Enter the grief tool, introduced in Chapter 6 for reference. Bottom line: Grounding the grief for the parent grounds the children.

Healing Deeper Wounds

Depersonalizing flaws in self and others and living from a healthy self invites the parent to be conscious because they are free to live in the present, instead of being entangled by the pain in our histories. As long as we are wrestling with the past, we will easily be reinforcing rather than mastering the wound, affecting all parts of our life, including parenting.

For me, it was about depersonalizing and healing from those family of origin beliefs of strict control in my home growing up. For me, it was about owning my healthy self-power with assertiveness not aggression. Madeline and I could be empowered with direct loving communication because of this.

What could you be wrestling with from your past that is affecting your parenting?

Emotionally focused counseling helps to repair the adult's own inner child, resurfaced in the daily lives with others, including with their children in ways not achieved before. This reduces the projection reaction onto them and breaks negative intergenerational patterns. This is where the adult, conscious parent makes significant gains. Such therapy creates deep awareness, repairs, reframes, and empowers toward strength from what is being reactivated with others in their life, including their children. It invites a level of consciousness which protects the whole family for years to come.

I rely heavily on imagery in the deeper work. A picture is indeed worth a thousand words. When words aren't enough or can't be articulated, especially because we are in overwhelmed states, an image can be a deeply meaningful way to illustrate and move the stories of our lives. In fact, the healthy and wounded selves become specific pictorial representations in the mapping out process of the EFT therapy for clients of any age. This is particularly powerful to the clients as we sketch out these 'portraits.'

Guided meditations specifically done in session, while the brain is quieter:

- *explore the stories of our life,*
- *reframe the narrative, and*
- *direct a specific, improved way of living from the exploration and reframing.*

The portrayals become effective daily tools to help clients do things differently by regularly and frequently exposing their brain to the therapeutic 'canvas' used in the work (through actual or digital recreations of the images). This invites the 'growing up' of their inner child.

Flowers planted in sidewalks grow with water. Persistent fires are put out with extinguishers. Life preservers save people who are drowning. Umbrellas offer needed protection to those otherwise soaked by pelting rain. Hurricanes are survived by shelters. Black holes burn out. Dangerous river rapids are crossed with bridges...

EFT can be used with clients of any age, not just adults. Teens find their way in the world without carrying their parents' wounds. Children's language is through their play, including their art, so it is a naturally comfortable modality to use with them.

The emotional focused KG method consists of:

1. Tracing out the history, of the good and of the bad (the healthy and wounded self) e.g., represented overall, by a gorgeous rainbow when someone took control of their life, moved out, and graduated university vs. the cold harsh pelting rain from experiences with a narcissistic mother.

2. Making specific emotional, cognitive, and behavioral discoveries of the healthy and wounded self, the wounded self specifying our negative associations with control, e.g., the feelings (powerlessness, unworthiness), the thoughts/core beliefs (I have no say, My thoughts and feelings don't matter, Others always have the last say, Life is useless, Love steals) and the reactions (shut down with fear to protect myself from getting hurt if I voice my thoughts and am punished for it).

3. Broadening the real story through imagery, guided meditations, letter writing, and empty-chair techniques, by depersonalizing the experiences without blame or shame and by understanding the actual reason of why others hurt us and had little to do with us e.g., my mother was controlling me because she had an abusive mother which was unresolved for her.

4. Using the 'gifts' offered by the healthy self to help with the specific pains of the wounded self through the imagery work, e.g., providing warm candlelight to an invisible wounded self hiding in the shadows with the caption: "*I deserve to be seen, as imperfect as I am*".

5. Rejecting the other person's projections by 'passing over' the ownership of the damaging situations/relationships to those who caused us harm in this area, e.g., passing back the self in the shadows to a mother who felt powerless with her mother. This invites the mother to do her work, which she may or may not do. But the client no longer carries her mother's invisibility either way, and reclaims a more visible self in her life, no longer living in the shadows. This frees the client up to use the self-care, CBT, and DBT tools to guide her journey.

6. Confronting others to restore healthy control with letter writing from the healthy self to the wounding person or from the healthy self to the wounded part of self with key messages identifying the true source of the wound, what the client's true value was/is that was overlooked or punished by the wounded part of the other person, how this triggers in current life, and what the healthy will commit to doing to master the wound, e.g. written excerpts such as:

    "Dear Wounded Self,

    Growing up you felt invisible with a mother who could be cold and harsh. You felt powerless and unworthy as a child and as you grew up, you learned to shut down in the face of conflict to protect yourself from getting further hurt. The consequence of that is that you only lost yourself more, sometimes with people who actually cared about you. Moving forward, I will help you be on the lookout for shadows. I will help you look for warm candles to bring you into the light, especially in the face of conflicts, when you feel most misunderstood but where you do matter. Where your thoughts and feelings count for something. I will help you take better care of yourself than your mother could. Not because she didn't care. Because she was in a shadow herself that she didn't figure out. I will teach you how to think more factually toward clearer speaking, especially when you are afraid of conflict. I will teach you to breathe and accept your imperfections without unworthiness. I will help you look for others holding out their candles to you." Love, your healthy self.

7. The 'passing over' and 'confrontation parts can be done alone metaphorically with the single client (as described in the above example) or, if the actual mother is emotionally available for the work, she is brought into sessions where the metaphors are explained with compassion and/or the structured healing betrayal conversions described in chapter 4 are facilitated.

8. Giving ourselves very specific daily actions to practice healthy control in our present lives, e.g., carrying a picture of the candle/caption to look at/read every day. Becoming a 'shadow expert' on the lookout for others who may also be trying to put us in the shadows and set boundaries not possible with my mother. Reminding ourselves of the healthy self-advice that we deserve to have our say. Using the CBT toward 'I' messages to express feelings and needs directly. Using the DBT by saying these twice. Using radical acceptance if necessary to accept that this person (who may be controlling me like my mother) is not emotionally

available to hear me, and using a grief tool to grieve the lost relationship if all the previous tools were ineffective in rebalancing the relationship.

How can you acquaint yourself with your wounded and healthy self?

What would be good images to represent each part?

What would be a good 'gift' from your healthy self?

How could you imagine using an image of that to motivate you every day?

What would the meaningful caption of that picture be?

Millennials who are coming in for premarital/pre-parenting therapy, as mentioned in Chapter 6, are ahead of the game on this when they work out their childhoods as they prepare to parent. Demystifying negative legacies of what they witnessed in their own parents' painful experiences (evidence of their parents' unresolved wounds), while preparing for parenthood themselves, is truly liberating and important work.

Coloroso Backbone Parenting

I invite you to think about what type of parenting you received and what type you provide: brick wall, jelly fish, or backbone.

On a more pragmatic basis, clients often come to me to learn better parenting than they received. The parenting tools I teach reflect the work of Barbara Coloroso from her original book, *Kids Are Worth It* (Coloroso, 2010) . The theory underpinning her work overlapped with what I was already teaching parents about conscious parenting so the strategies would complement the KG Methods described above.

In her book Coloroso delineated three types of parents—brick wall, jelly fish, and backbone.

Brick-wall parents rely on fear-based rules and authority. You can spot them by phrases like, "Because I said so," "You're grounded for the next month," or "Go to your room and think about what you've done."

Kids from brick wall parents are punished and obey from a place of fear rather than an internalized sense of discipline, *or* they rebel and act out against the strict rigidity. It's the kind of parenting I experienced, along with a lot of kids growing up in the sixties and seventies. At that time, authoritarian-style parenting was popular. There was the commonly accepted paradigm that kids should be seen and not heard, and discipline was emphasized over nurturing as the key ingredient for creating successful adults.

Jellyfish parents parent without structure and boundaries and try to be friends with their children. (Another way of describing the enmeshed bond between parent and child). This can result in overindulgence and cause children to ultimately lack their own self-driven discipline and motivation. Frequently, children of jellyfish parents are pleasers, accommodators, or underperformers, and easily end up being caretakers with the people in their life, who are emotionally dependent on them. Typically, they avoid leaving the nest or prematurely escape, as listed above, repeat the pattern of enmeshment by being suffocated by or suffocating others, or distance themselves from others because they fear engulfment.

Backbone parents, however, as the spinal cord supports the body while giving it the neurons to bend, somehow find that balance between consistency and flexibility. They parent by teaching good decision-making skills to their children while instilling positive self-confidence.

Parents raised by brick walls naturally become brick walls or overcompensate by jelly fishing. Parents who had jellyfish as parents easily replicate that approach or counterbalance by brick walling.

It can be enlightening to identify the style you grew up with and connect that insight to where you are now as a parent on the continuum between brick wall and jellyfish, and whether you are replicating the same or overshooting to the opposite of how you were parented. This can help you find the middle backbone. With motivation, curiosity, and insight it *is* possible to change your inherited parenting style.

I received brick wall and worked especially hard to find a way to be a backbone. It worked for me. It's why I know I can bring the same tools I used, as well as hope to the parents I work with.

I created an acronym with the clients in my practice from my review of the Coloroso Backbone method. Parents can retrieve and practice the steps in the heat of the moment when they are triggered and their child needs support. G-O-O-D parenting teaches parents the language to use to help their children identify, take responsibility for, and solve a problem together with encouragement instead of fear, humiliation, or giving in.

Here's how it works:

"We…"

G-ot a problem: help the child see how the consequences of not fixing the problem will work against *them* (without blame).

Need to **O**-wn the problem: help the child see how *they* are contributing to the problem (again, with curiosity not humiliation or shame).

Have **O**ptions for solving the problem: engage in brainstorming solutions together, prompting, using play, art and/or multiple-choice 'answers' as necessary. Parents can sometimes limit or vet the choices but do it in a way that makes the child/teen feel like they are contributing their ideas.

Can preserve **D**-ignity: give heavy doses of encouragement to help the child believe *they* have the capacity to solve the problem.

This results in: the setting up of a **specific plan**, and then sticking to it, providing support as you go, then reviewing the progress or lack thereof at the end of the week, and, if need be, revising the plan until there is success.

G-O-O-D parenting is *not* a lecture. It is not a handoff approach. It is a **short**, animated, light but clear dialogue-not-monologue, and can be used with children from two to twenty-two!

I used 'GOOD' in my own parenting with Madeline. This helped our relationship and gave me first-hand experience to use with the parents I work with. Somehow, despite the pressures of being the only child and the chaos of her parents' divorce, she was so easy to parent—she only got 'in trouble' twice. I'm serious! And I really don't think that was about pleasing me.

One time, at about seven, she was caught playing on the roof at a friend's house, and secondly, when she was in grade seven, she intended to go with a friend to meet a boy unknown to either of them at a park blocks away from their school. Funny, she called me first to tell me not to pick her up from school that day so she could venture out to do this.

- **G**ot a problem— 'Meeting strangers without an adult can be dangerous.'
- **O**wnership— 'If it is dangerous, you could be hurt and get stuck.'
- **O**ption—'Invite the new friend to meet up at home, with an adult nearby, or in a busy public place with lots of people close by.' (or any other good ideas the child offers that could be considered)
- **D**ignity—'I want you to have new friends, and I understand you are getting curious about boys. Let's figure out how you can do this and be safe.' She opted to let her friend meet the boy separately, making a plan with her own parents, and she took herself out of the equation.

The Coloroso method had actually started succeeding for us when Madeline was only about five, when we worked together to help her with sleeping. Like me, she had been a 'poor' sleeper. Before the separation, with a lot of support, she was sleeping in her own bedroom, but, as is often the case during high periods of stress, there is a regression in previously mastered stages. For Madeline, this meant reverting back to the family bed. I see this a lot: families struggling with over-extended family-bed situations or musical-beds throughout the night with no one waking up rested, especially when there are big changes occurring in the family, intergenerational patterns of poor sleep management, or compromised attachment issues.

Madeline and I applied the G-O-O-D Backbone method with this 'problem'. We worked out a ten-night sleep transition plan that we drew out on paper together for fun, to incrementally move her from my bed back to hers, reducing anxiety, fear and rejection. Instead, she felt empowered by contributing to the plan, which heightened her investment in the steps and ultimately increased the likelihood it would succeed. She also felt supported and loved during the process. She slept better in the end, and so did I.

One final note about brick-wall/jelly-fish parents can be helped with the G-O-O-D method. 'Brick Wallers' will easily exert too much force to control their teen's behavior, but what easily results is that their teen's behavior becomes *more* out of control in an effort to offset the power struggle that ensues. There is a useful metaphor that I regularly use to teach parents that goes something like this: Your teenager is driving on a motorcycle toward a brick wall (pardon the pun). Most brick wall parents will stand in front to stop them, to prevent a crash. The teen, with their natural instinct to be their own person will likely speed up, swerve or run their parents over, and hit the brick wall harder than originally planned.

The answer, instead, is to stand *beside* the motorcycle, providing calm opinions, ideas, even predictions to help the teen problem-solve for themselves and find their own confidence in making a better choice, and then be there to pick up the pieces if the teen still crashes. It is more about empowering the teen and less about indulging the fears or frustrations of the parent. Easier said than done. I know. But it works. In addition, parents often have to make improvements to their approach and *stick* to it longer than they may think they need to, made even harder if they continue to get pushbacks and negative reactions from their teenager. This is because by the time they have to dig themselves out of a pattern of poor parenting that has usually been in place for months, if not years, they need to prove themselves repeatedly with better parenting before their teen catches up, trusts them more, starts improving *their* behavior and shows up better in the relationship with the parent.

A lot of parents don't understand that this delayed reaction is normal and give up prematurely, especially brickwall parents who believe the *teen* has to prove to *them* and not vice versa. When they *do* stick it out, the repair is evident and the direction of the relationship changes, usually long term.

The same metaphor also invites jellyfish parents to take a stand (as a parent offering advice versus being a friend who jumps on the motorcycle with them) or engage in a meaningful way that is not suffocating (stand beside stating the opinion without incessant repeating).

A final note about safety. Clearly in circumstances when health and safety are at clear imminent risk, the parent does make the choice and does stand in front to stop the motorcycle. But my experience is that this can easily be over- or misused and is often a demonstration of the parent's fear and anxiety versus actual risk.

Understanding the motorcycle crash was particularly important to me with my control wound—I wanted to accept that trying to control Madeline would backfire, and I was deeply committed to raising her to be successful, empowered, gutsy, and confident.

I loved how this helped me move from brick to backbone. Again, a picture says a thousand words, whether it be the more pleasing picture of a flexible life-giving backbone over the cold hard brick wall, or the spineless jellyfish, or using the picture of the motorcycle crash scene toward finding the powerful image of 'standing beside'.

Parenting Sexual Health

How do your attitudes about sex influence your parenting?

Of particular importance to me was parenting Madeline in a way that took shame out of the equation, especially as she developed sexually. My parents did their best from the parenting they had received during an ultra-conservative time, especially for girls. But those attitudes made me feel uncomfortable, confused, and upset. This made me hide and do things in secret, leaving me ill-prepared for the situations I would find myself in.

I knew the number one goal with parenting was to keep the communication lines open. That, indeed, is the best way for parents to have the strongest positive influence they are trying to provide. A shut-down child. An unprepared preadolescent overwhelmed in new situations. An acting out dishonest teen. These need to be minimized, and the best way to accomplish this is by leading in a way that sends the message that no matter what is happening, the door is always open. Our family physician gave that message to us, and it was great advice. I promised myself 1000 percent that I would commit to that and promote positive sexual health in Madeline. Without going into details that would embarrass her, trust me, I showed complete openness well beyond slipping pamphlets through doorways to ensure she grew from a curious child through heightened puberty into a healthy woman sexually, safe, and feeling positive about her body and its natural urges.

With this in mind, I was excited to find the work of Laura Berman, an American relationship therapist whose work in the nineties was highly refreshing, some of which focused on raising girls to honor and embrace their needs without depending solely on partners, particularly male partners, to satisfy them. This opened up a lot of important dialogue including the normalizing and promotion, of self-pleasuring for females, including young females. The liberal approach was controversial at the time. I do remember shocking clients with Berman's progressive attitudes as I guided them through the delicate waters of providing sex education to their children. But I knew it was the right direction. In the end, clients learned a lot and their teens made better decisions and still do. And I definitely used The Berman Method with Madeline which, if nothing else sent the message about how open and accessible conversations about normal sexual urges would be. Berman also demystified the belief that people with STI's are marked with dirt.

She turned that idea on its back and suggested carriers use it to screen out 'less than' partners and when advocating for compassionate relationships.

Madeline made good choices in her relationships growing up, including who she picked as partners and how she managed her developing sexual needs. Much better than I had. I am proud of her, and I am proud of me. Breaking intergenerational patterns of parenting is one of the hardest things we do, and when we do, it frees us, and if it frees us, it frees our children.

Slowing Down: The Conscious Parent Reframes and Finds Mindfulness

I invite you to think about what you would need to shift, that could be blocking your parenting as you read this.

Mothering Madeline had taught me about unstinking perfection, accepting imperfection and limiting obsessive thinking, grounding over flighting and depersonalizing my control wound. I had two more things to learn: pacing over rushing and reassurance over worrying.

You know those images of mothers cuddling their cooing babies? I had longed to embrace that experience. Instead, Madeline would dig her heels into my lap and push with her legs to squat up and down with fervor. She was colicky for months on end. While other mothers breastfed for at least thirty minutes, she'd empty one breast and then the other in no more than five minutes flat, causing me to seek out assistance from Dr. Jack Newman, the 'Breastfeeding Guru' at the time who said to me, "This won't help you much now, but babies like this go on to big things as teens." He was right on both counts. The advice didn't help because I only wanted to sleep and never got it. And, as she grew, she did go onto big things.

Madeline ran before she walked. While other children sat joyfully in their parents' laps in music classes tinging their triangles, Madeline would be seen running around the room, wiping sweat from her head, and running some more. She raced through her schoolwork and raced through the water while learning to swim. In fact, as she grew up, she would compete at her elementary school, and no one could beat her in the pool. That's when we really knew we had a superstar on our hands and entered her into the world of competitive swimming, which at the time began to unify an otherwise divided family. As a teen, she became an elite swimmer, holding a national first place in her age group for over a year, and achieving an Olympic qualifying time in the fifty-meter freestyle event, making it look almost effortless.

Madeline is a great combination of both of us. Out of the pool, she was cool and calm like her dad and most definitely inherited his athletic agility. In the pool, she was like me, driven and focused. And she was *fast*. Unfortunately, a significant concussion prevented her advancement to international competition. She never made it to the Olympics, but the discipline, dedication, and confidence in her training and achievements have continued to benefit her, and I believe made up for some of the psychological injuries from the divorce. Although she had to resign from competitive swimming, she could use the acquired skills and tenacity she used to compete, win, *and* take the setback to fuel her passions when faced with challenges in other areas of her life, just like I had done.

Although her speed worked for her in the water, outside of the pool, Madeline had to learn to slow down, especially in her schoolwork. This ended up being a double win for both of us. As I taught her to slow down, I had to slow down, which I had probably needed my whole life.

It's funny that way. When we decide to parent consciously, we teach our kids what they need for them not for us, but to pull this off, we need to be it to teach it. Finding the language to slow her forced me to put into words my needs for the same. I was motivated to help her and do a good job as a mother, and if it helped her, it helped me, and vice versa. Slow down, not stop. Be more mindful and intentional, but always stay driven.

This gift of slowing down for me was never more evident than when I became sick. Madeline was one and a half years at the time when my body forced me to not only slow down but to stop. The colic, the vicarious trauma in my career, my crumbling marriage, and the overdoing of my wounded self set into motion a chronic dysregulation of my immune system. I remember sitting at the window watching my father play with her in the snow when the cold temperatures and energy needed were beyond my reach. I remember sleeping while her father picked her up to take her to activities that I could not participate in. Months went by when all I could do was watch Disney movies with her. So, we watched movie after movie after movie. Madeline still remembers the films. So, do I.

At the time I remember telling a mother's group I had joined before becoming ill about the devastation I faced in not doing as much as the mother I had always dreamt about being. They told me about their own frantic lives doing and overdoing. As 'healthier' mothers, they worried that they were not mothering the way they had wanted because they did too much.

Those mothers have no idea how meaningful those conversations were to me at the time. It helped me to completely rethink my mothering of Madeline while I was sick and tune into what was most important. This allowed me to value the quietness and stillness over activity, which my body and mind desperately needed. Turns out Madeline, although young and active, needed that too. It gave Madeline and I a chance to be quiet together. I reframed my illness, and I reframed my role. I redefined that doing everything all the time actually wasn't everything. I will always overachieve (trying to be excellent, not perfect), but being present instead of overattaching to the outcome would make me happier than checking off predetermined boxes. So, we look back at the Disney movies and smile, recognizing now more than ever before how beautiful that time really was.

Taming the Worrying Mind: The Conscious Parent finds Reassurance

Can you benefit from reassuring yourself of something, to reduce your worrying?

I had more to learn. I had been a constant worrier, and this showed up as a mother mostly with how much I worried about Madeline's education. And I worried about this a lot. While I thrived in organizing, constructing, writing, and memorizing, Madeline struggled. I loved school. My parents were very involved in my learning and that was a good thing. I still love technical learning and embracing theories and applications, especially about uncovering the human experience. Madeline, however, has more of her father's wiring. She is an athlete more than a student. She is more intuitive than logical. She is more kinetic than cerebral.

Indulging worrying leads to all kinds of problems. The overly worried parent is suffering. The overly worried parent is not present. The overly worried parent is unconscious. The child of the overly worried parent worries too much or not enough.

I worked on this, and instead of indulging, I took action—which was my forte—but I would have to act in a way that didn't overlook the emotional growth needed to help Madeline not only become the good decision-maker in her education, but also be confident in her learning—the Coloroso Way.

The psychoeducational assessments I usually recommend for the students I work with when academic performance is an issue, are useful for students and their parents by identifying specific learning issues (which for Madeline were identified as executive functioning gaps), and providing specific tools and strategies to improve learning capacity. As hard as it was to hear about the deficits, the evaluation gave Madeline and me a structure so we could work together on her education. This structure was determined by her learning style (different from mine) and focused on her needs rather than my unrealistic expectations, while at the same time meeting the goal of improving her schoolwork. I won't lie, this was challenging. I struggled with impatience and taking over, worrying too much about results and not enough about process. But the framework from the assessment gave us a specific plan which is key for all parents trying to figure out the best way to support their child's learning strengths and challenges. It certainly helped us and gave me less to worry about.

Providing quality tutoring to ensure Madeline received educational support from someone other than me was also important. It established a very clear process to get me out of the way, without worrying about her academics. Interestingly, tutors always told me that despite some of her learning gaps she would excel due to her infectious energy and likeability (qualities she shared with her father), and they were right.

In addition, I also applied therapeutic tools discussed earlier (CBT, Coloroso Backbone Parenting, Grounding Grief, and Emotionally Focused Therapy—*see more on these in the Glossary.)* to calm my worries about her future. It allowed her to feel my deep support and commitment toward the 'excellent' success she is today, allowing her to be herself, and separate from who my inner child needed her to be. A great example of this was when Madeline was in grade ten and we were backing out of the driveway on our way to the college and university fair. I was 'on top' of my worrying triggers. As I backed out, I stopped the car, took a breath, and said to her, with true compassion, something like: "I really don't mind if you decide to be a doctor, a garbage collector, a coach, or a fashion stylist. What matters most is that *you* come up with something that is going to make *you* happy, not just now but in the long run. And, even if you start with something and then change your mind, that's really okay. Just get in the running with something, and you can tweak it as you go if you need to." I found a place *beside* her in her education and career planning. Needless to say, Madeline found her groove, and then some.

Academically, she was not a likely candidate for postsecondary education. Despite this, today, she has a four-year undergraduate degree, a postgraduate certificate, and is working in a field she loves. When I initially wrote this chapter, we had just learned that Madeline had been offered a position at a thriving global company based in over sixty countries, after successfully competing against *three hundred* other applicants. More recently, she received positive recognition from *two* levels of upper management for a presentation she gave. Go figure. It was a great lesson that, in the end, the excessive worries of our wounded self are unhelpful indulgences. We frequently worry about a lot of things that never happen. Things often end up being okay, usually better than okay.

In 2020, I hosted Madeline's University Graduation in our backyard, when the world had shut down in the pandemic. Of course, I set the stage with videos from teachers and coaches, school pictures, and artwork from JK to university. The gardens completely covered in purple tuille, symbolized her university colours. I choreographed it 'excellently' for her to come down the patio steps, adorned in a prefab graduation cap, as I played Tina Turner's *Simply the Best.* She was beaming that day, and so was I. I spoke profoundly in my own speech to the family gathered; who included my parents, my friends, Madeline's father, his new partner, his parents, and our family therapist as the keynote speaker. She spoke eloquently of Madeline's resilience that day and we all knew what she was talking about. Madeline had really made it. We had really made it. In more ways than one.

The Conscious Parent Lets Go (Parenting with Boundaries)

How are you preparing your children for individuation and intimacy?

Often the measurement of parenting is demonstrated by how successful children move through those important developmental stages of trust, control, interdependence, and worthiness. The end result of this lies in the degree of clarity the young adult develops in knowing themselves and knowing who they want to become toward making a successful independent transition into the world. The end result of this also lies in the quality of intimacy the young adult develops in their relationships. Boundaries with the parents are relevant. Too much disengagement with parents disrupts this and either thrusts the child out prematurely or with anger and resentment. Too much enmeshment disrupts this, and the child avoids leaving or leaves smothering others or living an isolating life.

Because of Madeline being an only child and the only child of divorce. Because of my perfectionistic tendencies and control wound, I ran the risk of enmeshing Madeline. I ran the risk of helicoptering parenting. That ran the risk of Madeline struggling to find her independence.

Despite how hard I was working on mothering; it was tough for me and Madeline to be a one-child family. As initially described in chapter five, each birth-order effect has its own indicative patterns, including how only children are often extra *special*. Such preciousness easily results in over-indulgent parenting when the over attention to and from the child becomes excessive. Enmeshment begins to occur when it is unclear where one person's needs end (in this case, the parent's) and another's needs begin (the child's). It can be unclear who is caring for who, sometimes taking the shape of role reversal, where the child is in some way 'parenting' the parent.

There seems to be a higher rate of enmeshment, not only with families who endured pregnancy or infant loss, maternal ill health, or in other situations where the parents have a high level of need, but also with single mothers and single daughters in divorce families, especially where there is high co-parental conflict or absent fathers.

I had to be careful of this given how we fit that demographic and given my higher needs due to poor health, my desire to be more lenient with her than I had experienced, which combined, could transform our relationship into more of a friendship. No doubt Madeline and I teetered on being 'best friends', but I was aware of the boundary. I made sure I had resources to support me and that she knew, without detail, how I was taking care of myself. That no doubt helped Madeline find trust, control, interdependence, worthiness, and identity. It helped me clarify a sense of self as I forged ahead.

Inevitably, I would have to let go of Madeline completely. Well, not 'completely', but I think you know what I mean. We are still very close, and always will be, but I needed to let her go on to lead an independent life.

When she was in her fourth year at university, I encouraged her to take advantage of the global learning opportunities offered at her school. She came home that Christmas announcing, to my complete surprise, that she was in love. She'd met an Englishman while studying in Australia. They were set to build a life 'down under' when COVID-19 struck. Australia and New Zealand had the strictest borders in most of the world. Madeline and her boyfriend would be separated from each other for nineteen months. Then, she moved away from home to join him in England, where he had returned to be with family.

Madeline had indeed grown into that woman who I had pictured so many years ago. I guess in the end, we must have done more right than wrong despite how hard it was at times. She takes risks with boldness, she ambitiously reaches for excellence at work, she builds extraordinary networks of friends wherever she goes, she works hard at setting boundaries amidst conflicts to advocate for herself instead of losing herself, and she recognizes her growth as she continues to learn about herself. We are close and she has a good relationship with her father. So, if part of parenting is about making each generation stronger and ensuring your children end up being better than you were, I can tell you she is much more mature, confident, and self-aware, and making much better decisions for herself than I was at her age.

I can't lie. Madeline's final move from home across the ocean was extraordinarily difficult for me. It was not the same as when she'd left home for postsecondary school five years prior. I had actually *handled* that quite well. This time, it was likely permanent. This time, she was across the world. This time could mean grandchildren growing up far away. Her move to the UK became one of my most recent reasons to mother myself.

I had created an independent, successful woman who was reaching for her full potential; what did I expect? Wasn't that what I wanted? Wasn't that what she wanted? Then, why was I in so much pain?

The invitation was clear. I had to master being left by the most important person in my life without feeling abandoned. That was what I called **Invitation Number Seven, Part Two**, delivered right to my door from my healthy self. But, as with all invitations for growth, it was rather messy. I re-grieved my divorce (as is often the case that we face previous losses during a current loss). I began to believe that the pressure of being the only child and having to be a neutral between two conflicting co-parents growing up thrust her across the world to escape (me). I blamed him. I shamed myself even more. I did my work again. I reframed it, and then I let go—because here's the thing—growing never stops.

A mentor of mine once told me that life is like flowing down a river. It's great when we are moving. We have places to go! So, it's incredibly hard when we inevitably get stuck at one of those bends in the river, when opportunistic crises or developmental transitions cause our wounded selves to be activated and pull us over. Our job is to learn how to move our sticks around so that we can flow again.

So, I found my flow. If I found my flow, so would Madeline. After the all the work we had done, it definitely wasn't the time to undo all of that.

My mentor also told me that the job of therapists was to help people 'move *their* sticks' around when they come to your door because *they* are stuck on that same curvy river. That also made a lot of sense to me.

(Re)making sense of the divorce and our family's stages, finding gratitude in the deep relationship we shared as mother/daughter, and embracing my life as a sixty-year-old divorcee provided the peace and clarity I needed and had always needed. All of this gave me a new rhythm to be me at my best. I could be separated without being unworthy. I could live, even thrive amidst major decisions made solely by others, without being powerless. In fact, I could be strong, confident, creative, and engaged without losing control, vying for control, or personalizing something that had nothing to do with me.

Instead of feeling unimportant, I felt relevant. Instead of feeling abandoned, I felt free. By letting go, I could finally take hold of the person I was always meant to be, and so could she. Instead of seeing Madeline leaving me, I saw her finding herself and going to live the life I had taught her to live. She was growing and so was I.

The Conscious Parent Gives Gifts

I don't know exactly what Madeline would say was my most positive influence on her, but she knows the divorce was hard, and she knows my illness was depressing. I also know that she watched me rebuild my entire life, recover my medical health, rebuild my social network, restore my mental health, and build a thriving business despite it all. I know that, as a mother, I ended up modelling drive, focus, and determination to make the most out of life and always reach higher and further.

And I know that most definitely I became a better person from mothering Madeline.

I do sometimes think about the day when she was only three, as she bounced down the driveway without a care in the world. Sometimes, I think about what would have happened if I *had* given up. Sometimes I think about what would have happened to Madeline if I did.

Then, I think about how my biggest gift as a mother has been about showing how to achieve your full potential from *not* giving up when that's all you wanted to do. It turns out the darkest moment for me would not only be the turning point I needed and deserved; it would enable the brightest future for her. As a human, I had discovered how to dig deep and then throw myself into something higher. Maybe, as a mother, that showed Madeline everything she needed to know.

One day, about five years ago, I sat downstairs with Madeline right where the yellow apartment used to be. I told her the whole story of the blackness and my yellow paint. She was at a stage where I thought she could hear it. I remember she listened intently, shocked to hear about how weakened I had felt, surprised to hear about how the yellow paint had saved me, and awestruck about how I had dug myself out, starting with the walls. She paused and then said, "Mom, you have to write a book."

So, I did. I knew then I had a story that meant something to me, something to her, and perhaps could also mean something to someone else in need of a little yellow.

Think about this:

1. If you are a parent, are you consciously parenting? What do you need to resolve in your journey to ensure your children master their stages of development from trust to intimacy?

2. If you aren't a parent, how did the CBT, DBT and EFT in this chapter inform you to be a better parent to yourself?

3. How is the dynamic with your children giving you an opportunity to heal, in ways that wasn't possible with your parents or with your partners? How are you stepping up to take full advantage of that opportunity?

4. What kind of parenting did you receive: Backbone? Jellyfish? Or brick wall? And how do you think this has impacted you? And if you are a parent, how has this impacted your parenting?

5. Are you flowing down your river? Or are you stuck at the sides? What do you need to recognize to get flowing again?

CHAPTER 9
THE AUTOIMMUNE GIFT:
HOW HEALTH PROBLEMS BECOME AN INVITATION

I'm a rolling thunder, pouring rain

I'm coming on like a hurricane

White lightning's flashing across the sky

You're only young, but you're gonna die

I won't take no prisoners, won't spare no lives

Nobody's putting up a fight

I got my bell, I'm gonna take you to hell

(AC/DC - Hells Bells, 1980)

I sat down with this chapter like all the others. Framing out the information and then writing.

I've referred to my health challenges from the beginning, starting with that dark day in 1994 when I was first diagnosed with my STI.

Now it was time to tell the 'rest of the story'...

I spread the papers out and started combing over the reports, lab results, and assessments.

I hadn't looked at these for close to fifteen years. At that time, I had intentionally packed all of these papers away. My entire identity had become saturated by being 'sick' and I had to rediscover who I was outside of the illness which had consumed me for close to ten years.

I felt shocked, confused, and overwhelmed about what I started to read.

In my practice today, I regularly use my health experiences to motivate and teach clients how to manage their own chronic pain and illness.

So, why was opening the reports so complicating for me to read?

The Beginning

The world was preparing for the turn of the century, and we were gearing up to party like it was 1999, because it was! Not only did I miss that monumental New Year's Eve. I didn't fully show up for my life again for another decade.

In October 1999, it had started like all the other sinus infections I'd had in my life. I honestly thought nothing of it. I knew the drill: rest, fluids, compresses, nasal rinses, vitamin C, massage therapy, chiropractic adjustments, and, as a last resort, a course of antibiotic medicines. Taking the medication didn't feel like a bad decision. At that time, we were just beginning to hear about the risk of overusing antibiotics. Taking probiotics during and after antibiotic use wasn't even a thing. I would only learn later that *my* frequent use was reducing the efficiency of my immune system.

By December, I remember I wasn't feeling much better despite efforts, so I pushed on, treating myself like I had many times before with these sinus issues. I kept working, and slowly resumed exercising. I felt like I just had to tolerate the symptoms and believed I would eventually get better. That was until I realized that I really wasn't getting anywhere. In fact, I was starting to feel worse, much worse. By the end of December that year, I had:

- No energy, hardly any to think, walk, or talk.
- Little concentration to absorb, store, or process information.
- Sensitivity to light, smell, and sounds.
- Joint and muscle pain.
- Skin that was overstimulated, making touch painful.
- Little to no ability to multitask as I had so easily done before.
And…
- Little to no ability to *sleep* so I could rest and get better.

If I did anything from my regular toolkit for getting better, I stayed sick. If I did nothing, I stayed sick. I felt like I was stuck, having no control over what was happening. I honestly believed I was dying (no one could feel this badly and *not* be dying). When my own and my physician's initial efforts to get better had failed and my symptoms worsened, I actually thought I was dying from AIDS, which had been getting huge media attention at that time.

Although I couldn't sleep, I went to bed. I stayed in bed. I lost my health. I lost the ability to parent in ways that I had dreamt about (I didn't have the physical energy or mental concentration for the responsibility and relationship I was hoping for, nowhere close to what I had babysitting so many years ago, and that was devastating to me). I lost my social life. I lost my ability to work. My marriage was crumbling, which was part of the problem but also made my capacity to recover much harder. My husband wasn't happy about being the caretaker either, and it showed. Like it had been with the STI diagnosis, he just couldn't carry that amount of responsibility and step up. My deep despairs made me angry, and my husband got most of that anger. I was hell to live with, but I was so lost by that time, I didn't care. I raged at him and of course that only pushed him further away.

There was no improvement in the new year. My family doctor, although lacking a personal bedside manner, was extremely knowledgeable. She queried whether I could have chronic fatigue syndrome (CFS), also known at that time as 'yuppie flu.' (Like Cher and had been aptly named because those who were ill with CFS were the young, overtaxed professionals of the generation, like me.) I looked up the criteria:

- Post-exertion fatigue ✓ ✓
- Non-restorative sleep ✓ ✓
- Impaired memory or concentration ✓✓
- Muscle pain ✓
- Polyarthralgia ✓
- Sore throat ✓
- Tender lymph nodes ✓
- Persistent Headaches ✓

In the early 2000s, the existence of symptoms for a minimum period of three months was required to meet those standards, which was exactly the time frame my doctor was using to diagnose me. I didn't realize until much later how 'lucky' I was that she made conclusions about my symptoms within that ninety-day mark. (All I knew immediately was that if I had the diagnosis of CFS, I had to stop working and I had to stop exercising.) But at least I had something to work with.

I was surprised to learn from fellow sufferers that most of them had been unwell for five years or longer before being properly diagnosed and during those years, had not only not been diagnosed, but had been misdiagnosed, or even worse, wrongly labeled as depressed, faking symptoms to get off work, or lazy (which was ironic, given that most patients were guilty of overdoing, not under doing). Misunderstood and neglected by the health professionals of the time—therefore lacking direction to manage their health—they were suffering in significantly greater ways than I was.

Twenty years later, that ninety-day requirement has doubled to six months. I worry what the impact of this lengthened criteria period is having on patients, delaying diagnoses and necessary care even further. Hopefully, the medical field has advanced and new doctors have more awareness of the disease, recognising it sooner despite this change.

To be fair, the diagnosis of CFS is complex because it is a 'diagnosis of elimination.' There wasn't and still isn't a blood test, urine test, MRI, scan, or x-ray to detect the illness (Myalgic Encephalomyelitis/Chronic Fatigue Syndrome (ME/CFS) - Diagnosis and Treatment - Mayo Clinic, 2024).

I was a strong health advocate and pushed my way through the system, relentlessly researching who should examine me to get clearer directions and more importantly how to get an effective treatment plan. I began the endless search for answers, creating opportunities to be seen by specialists in the fields of immunology and neurology. As a way to confirm a diagnosis, I had to exclude a wide range of other illnesses that could explain my symptoms: cancers of multiple types, HIV, early onset Alzheimer's, Lyme Disease, Lupus, Meningitis, Multiple Sclerosis, Tuberculosis. A lot of these tests at that time had to be purchased privately and sent to the United States for results.

Test Results

Natural Killer Cells
- These are white blood cells functioning to destroy infected and diseased cells, but at high levels, dysregulate immunity and **attack the body's healthy cells,** creating negative reactions from the immune system that make you feel like the worst flu you've ever had and worse.
- **Normal**—CD, 53-80 millimole/litre: **Results—90 mmol/L**
- **A Different Calibration: Normal**—CD, 8-32 millimole/litre: **Results— 37 mmol /L**

Cortisol
- A steroid hormone that increases with stress to assist body, but chronically high levels overtax the adrenal system and cause **adrenal fatigue, poor sleep.**
- **Normal**—167 nanomoles/litre: **Results—375 nmol/L**

DHEA
- This is a hormone produced by the body's adrenal glands; hyper levels at birth, slowly decreases with aging, and contributes to osteoporosis, heart disease, **memory loss,** and cancer.
- **Normal**—for a thirty-six-year-old woman—7.3-14 Umol/L Micromoles/litre: **Results—3.4 Umol/L, equivalent to a 90-year-old woman.**

Mercury

- Even in small amounts, causes serious health issues and has toxic effects on the nervous digestive immune systems, and on lungs, kidneys, **skin,** and eyes; **causes lack of coordination, muscle weakness, impairment to speech.**
- **Normal**—0-3 micrograms/litre: **Results—21 micrograms/L**

Lead

- There are no safe levels; causes headaches, stomach cramps, constipation, muscle and joint pain, trouble sleeping, fatigue, irritability.
- **Normal**—under 1 part per million: **Results—3.07 ppm,**
- **A Different Calibration: Normal**—0-15 micrograms/litre: **Results—33 micrograms/L**

Sleep Study

- Restorative sleep allows the body to repair and replete cellular components necessary for biological functions.
- **Normal**—four to six sleep cycles/24 hours, three non-rapid eye movement and one rapid eye movement period, presence of slow wave sleep when the electrical brain activity changes while the body relaxes into a deep restorative rest to promote energy and cell restoration, increasing blood supply to the muscular system, supporting growth and repair of tissues and bone, and strengthening the immune system.
- **Results—markedly delayed REM** sleep by 289 minutes**, increased proportion of lighter** sleep**, reduced REM** sleep**, total absence of slow wave sleep, sleep fragmentation** due to intervening arousals and awakenings.

The Etiology

When did your health hold you back? What has made you sick?

The origins of CFS are multi-faceted and systemic. These elements described below contribute to the development of the illness singularly *and* increase the risk for and negative impact on the others. Even worse, as is common with most auto-immune disorders, the breakdowns in the body are progressive, usually over a prolonged period, silently going unnoticed until they aren't.

Immunity

The foundation for understanding the development of the CFS in my body was in my immune system, and the results were alarming.

I was initially told that the outbreaks of CFS were usually related to a respiratory infection—for me, sinus—or a catastrophic event to the body such as a car accident or physical injury. Most patients I would meet fit these explanations.

I questioned further and learned that prolonged exposures to stress weakens the immune system, which elevates cortisol long term, and in that process, depletes the adrenal system (now more commonly known as adrenal fatigue). The adrenal system regulates metabolism, the sleep/wake cycle, and energy—all leading to further deterioration (Adrenal Fatigue, n.d.). A dysregulated immune system disrupts the number of killer cells. This impairs the system's normal function of protecting the body and attacks it instead (Cleveland Clinic, 2023).

The combination of these factors leaves the body defenseless and susceptible to environmental chemicals in the air and water, toxins which healthy people can usually tolerate and flush out. It appeared the mercury amalgams in my mouth from cavity fillings, chemical dark hair-colour products I had been using for years, and lead paint that had been removed from my home were overloading my body. Although out of the house at the time of the paint removal, I later discovered through environmental testing that high levels of lead particles were still lingering in the air when I returned home. Lastly, I also knew I had ingested a high level of nitrates from fertilizers (a test I could not find to include in this book), which I had traced back to a significant food poisoning incident in 1995. These incidents explained the absorption of chemicals and combined, and were likely further culprits my weakened system could not deal with.

Immune issues also lead to secondary symptoms from the body 'overfighting.' One doctor told me only one-third of the symptoms we get from the flu are from the actual virus. The other two-thirds are from the symptoms created by the body's fight *against* the virus, which results in fatigue and achiness. For CFS patients, these secondary set of symptoms are significant and persistent. Instead of protecting us, the cells over-protect, and their fight paradoxically intensifies symptoms.

At a cellular level, I also questioned my shameful STI secret and its continued impact on my body, specifically on my immune system. Once diagnosed with CFS, I relived the resentment of contracting herpes from my husband when it was explained to me that the immune system becomes less effective the more demand it is carrying. There is no clear cause and effect between herpes and CFS, but it adding to the load definitely pressured my system long term and compromised its efficiency. Learning this added to my emotional stress and unraveled my marriage further.

Friendly Bacteria

Connected to understanding the immune inefficiencies in the body, I began learning about why the good bacteria in my body wasn't doing its job. Antibiotics kill bacteria and prevent it from regrowing. That's a good thing, and their discovery has been lifesaving. Our bodies, however, also need the good bacteria which helps fight off the bad, aids in the digestion of food for energy, and produces vitamins. Here's the problem: antibiotics cannot distinguish between the good and bad. *Over-use* of antibiotics not only disables the good bacteria, lowering the ability to fight the bad bacteria but, over time, leads to bacterial resistance. Bacterial resistance renders antibiotics ineffective and can lead to the worsening of symptoms or the development of others, compromising the immune system.

In my case, chronic sinusitis, common in my family, had led to me using antibiotics regularly and frequently for many years, probably since I was thirteen, without ever using probiotics. Unknown to me, this over-use severely disrupted the balance of the bacteria in my body, added to general dysfunction, and lowered my body's overall resilience. Advancements about the proper use of antibiotics including prioritizing its usage for resistant infections, eliminating its usage for viruses, and using probiotics to regenerate the good bacteria should help prevent some serious chronic illnesses, including CFS, and improve general health.

Lack of Sleep

I had been a chronic bad sleeper since childhood. Bad sleeping habits were most definitely linked to my DNA from my father's side of the family. I remember listening to the clicking over of the minutes on my 1970s alarm clock keeping me awake night after night. I also seemed to be more negatively affected by poor sleep than others. I remember suffering from terrible sore throats as far back as childhood when I didn't get a good night's sleep. Even so, I thought the problems sleeping were nuisances, not the origin of what would become a serious illness years later.

Somehow, I pushed through until I had a daughter, who, as I've described was active. Active in the day and even more active at night. She had prolonged colic for close to eighteen months. During the first six months, she relentlessly cried from 10:00 pm to 6:00 am; despite many efforts by friends, family members, and specialists to intervene. The sleep deprivation seemed to affect me much more than her father. What became obvious to me initially, was that my blood pressure lowered significantly, making it hard to function. What I didn't know about was how the chronic, non-restorative, fragmented sleep I had been having for years had been slowly disabling my body's cellular functions. That had left me with little to no resilience for postnatal sleep deprivation, which for most new mothers is challenging, but for me would be harmful. Sleep studies were just beginning to be used more often in the late 1990s. Until then, I didn't have any specific data on how poor my sleep really was and what it was doing to me, let alone what to do about it.

Stress

That the depletion and dysregulation to the immune system described above, from chronic exposure to high levels of stress raises the risk of illness, is real. That perpetual processes where negative reactions to stressors increase the likelihood that additional stressors are created, causing further depletion and dysregulation, is also real. The fact is that living emotionally unconscious enables disproportionate reactions, and over time, upsets the natural balance in our bodies beyond emotion and thought, and makes us sick. Sometimes the symptoms are overt and obvious. Other times, as was the case with me, the breakdowns in the body are more covert, and were debilitating me, silently.

It wasn't that I was never getting sick, but the symptoms seemed minor and unrelated to each other. Internalizers get sick more often because the load the body ends up carrying is heavier. Externalizers like me, although better at discharging the stress and freeing up the body, still get sick if those sources of stress are multiple, persistent, and worsening. *How* we get sick is based on the vulnerabilities of our DNA. I was battling anxiety, marital breakdown, and vicarious trauma stress (detailed below), all worsened by the sleep problems.

By the time I was an adult, I had been living with chronic anxiety for many years, and I had just carried on, not knowing that beyond the discomfort of the emotional stress was the more severe biological stress.

As my marriage deteriorated, I became devastated by our poor communication patterns and the accumulative disconnection between us. We had numerous problems, but by the time I got sick, the unresolved guilt and shame of the STI had held my husband and me emotional hostage from each other for eight years. I was regularly having STI outbreaks that were painful, both physically and emotionally, and reliving the contamination broke me down each time. Learning that the STI contributed to the load of my immune system added fuel to the fire and frankly, nailed the coffin for me, but I felt trapped to stay. I even met with a gestational immunologist to understand if my compromised health and related medication use had caused my pregnancy loss. It was inconclusive that they had, but the possibility of this was overwhelming and added more layers on what had become by then a heaping pile too big for us as a couple to deal with.

Plus, I was battling with a different kind of tension that was much more insidious and mysterious than the anxiety and marital problems.

Vicarious Trauma

As therapists, we study countertransference, an important element of the clinical relationship in which the client redirects feelings for others onto the therapist. Understanding and using these projections maximizes the effectiveness of therapy.

Much later, by the 1990s, burnout was a well-known long term stress condition linked to workplace conflicts, overloaded responsibilities, perceived inequality, inadequate rewards, and consistent exposure to traumatic content, all leading to depersonalization and apathy for therapists. From this, compassion fatigue was considered as a secondary traumatic stress reaction connected to the demand on helping professionals, including therapists and emphasized the need for self-care.

Looking back as far back as 1986, when I began working with an extremely high-risk, highly damaged, sexually traumatized population of teenagers, I began suffering with a different type of stress. I remember temporarily losing an otherwise healthy sex drive and becoming hyper-alert to individuals I saw in the community who were similar in ways to the offenders of the clients with whom I was working. None of this was being discussed or addressed. It would not be for another thirteen years (and continuing to work in the field of trauma) until falling ill at the end of 1999, while I was desperately trying to understand why I was so sick that I was diagnosed with VT (Vicarious Trauma).

'Vicarious' comes from the Latin word 'to substitute'. The idea is that *you* experience what *someone else* is experiencing second hand—an occurrence that is particularly damaging when those experiences are traumatic in nature. Vicarious trauma is its own separate beast. Beyond countertransference. Beyond burnout. Beyond compassion fatigue. As of 2013, VT is classified in the DSM-5 of psychiatric conditions to include a stressor-related cluster of symptoms, recognizing important workplace factors of overwork, conflicts, lack of appreciation, and low flexibility, as well as individual manifestations of sleep disturbances, *weakened immune systems*, troubles concentrating, fears/numbness, preoccupations of clients' material, hyperarousals and hyperalertness to situations of safety, disenchantments with the world, and social isolation (Fact Sheet: Vicarious Trauma, 2021).

Therapists who were regularly exposed to their clients' graphic images of pain and intrusion, helplessness, powerlessness, manipulation, and humiliation were at higher risk for VT. Trauma for the clients had been a core part of clinical education and training for years, and evidence-based research about how to treat trauma and the trauma brain was widely recognized and expanding. Trauma for the *therapist*, however in the '90s, was still hidden for the most part; sometimes even viewed as a weakness, or an absence of skill or boundary with the client. Consequently, the incidence of illness, depression, anxiety, personal relationship breakdown, and poor physical health among therapists soared, and had sadly stayed too far under the radar for too long.

By the time I was diagnosed, I had been working in trauma for thirteen years, specializing in the assessment and treatment of sexual trauma for ten of those years counselling clients, providing province-wide training, and supervising therapists in the work with sex offenders, victims, and their families. At one time, I also co-led a specific group of overcontrolled adolescents who were either molesters or murderers. I remember when I first took that job, I wondered about the long-term effects. The team, however, seemed dynamic and supportive, and I went for it.

I was eager to learn everything I could, and I was privileged to be given many outstanding opportunities that would be relevant to my career success for many years to come. I was good at what I did, but I stayed in the work too long and overlooked the signs from my body of increasing fatigue, headaches, illness, nightmares, fears of being unsafe in the community, imbalances in my life, and constant attention to work. I became too self-critical and started losing my perspective. Then, there seemed to be a cascade of negative experiences that pushed me over the edge; a particularly high-risk case of a university campus rapist I was working with challenged me, when in the past, it wouldn't have. I began receiving prank calls at home, and then one night while out for my usual walk in my neighborhood, I literally walked into a murder scene/investigation taking place over the back fence of my yard.

Then, I gave birth to a daughter, and the expectation of protecting my little girl in what had become, for me, an unsafe world was overwhelming. I started dissociating when further prank calls came in. After years of quietly breaking me down, it all came to an abrupt halt. I stopped work. I went to bed for many months. I wouldn't work again for more than several years.

Despite all of this, some positive things began to happen.

A couple of years prior to me becoming more seriously sick, in 1996, the VT disorder was covered in a publication, *Transforming the Pain,* (Saakvitne & Pearlman, 1996). The work of these two psychologists and trauma specialists finally began a more serious discussion on therapists' experiences of VT. That was encouraging.

Other therapists where I had been working saw me as the 'canary in the gold mine'. Many of them left before they got sick too. For those who stayed, support groups, specific to VT, began running for the team and that truly inspired me.

About a year after I quit (when I was stronger) I returned to the clinic and gave a full presentation on the incidence, cause, treatment, and support for VT. That was an extremely critical day for me in my recovery.

Despite how bad everything was, I also had good luck again, as I had with my family physician. This time, luck came to me through a very experienced therapist who specialized in VT and diagnosed me, then took me on as a long-term client. That changed my life. She helped me. She helped my daughter. She helped my ex-husband. She helped my family.

If you are in the helping profession or in a career regularly exposed to lack or safety or graphic images, how would you rate the supports you have to protect your health?

The Treatment

With my own personal health experiences, I became deeply passionate to help those with chronic pain and illness. It was part of my gift to teach what I had learned, so that others could open their gifts too.

I invite you to read this section and see what could help **your** health?

Advocacy

While researching who would be best to care for my medical needs, I heard about a doctor in Niagara who was suffering from CFS and specializing in the treatment of the disease. She was speaking at a lecture at the University of Toronto. I somehow dug up the details of this clandestine meeting and just showed up to hear the presentation. It turned out to be a very small gathering of eight physicians in a tiny boardroom (and me). Little did I know how much that day would change my life forever.

Unfortunately, the doctor presenting was not able to continue her practice as she became too ill to work, but at that meeting I sat right next to Dr. Alison Bested. She was a haematological specialist who had struggled with her own health and decided to focus on CFS. Since meeting her in 2000, Dr. Bested has gone on to become a leading international expert in the field (Dr. Alison Bested - Environmental Health Institute Canada, 2023).

I desperately told her my story, and she listened closely. She had a two-year waiting list at that time serving clients at her dinky little office next to a pharmacy in a plaza out in Scarborough, near the Toronto Zoo. She asked me about my symptoms, and specifically, if I had received any indications of absorbed metals in my body. I had. And luckily (because of the testing) I *knew* I had. Dr. Bested immediately suggested I bypass her waitlist to sign up for the chelation treatment (slow intravenous administration of a chemical solution known as EDTA that binds with absorbed metals and is urinated out of the body) which she offered at her clinic (Wikipedia Contributors, 2019). Directly from that treatment protocol, I could become a regular patient. That's exactly what I did.

I remember the day I first stepped into the clinic. The waiting room was filled with what looked like near-death patients—women who I later learned were type A over-achievers like me. As mentioned earlier, these patients had been unwell a lot longer than I had and consequently had similar but worse symptoms. I had just entered a world where I lived for the next decade. Amidst this nightmare, I had found home. I know, most definitely, I would not be where I am today without this angel of a doctor and the healing community she created with her expertise and complete dedication to her patients. I would go on to teach clients how to be good health advocates for themselves, knowing firsthand how crucial that had been for me.

Clearing the Metals

With Dr. Bested at my side now, I began a long multiple series of chelation. My numbers for mercury went from 21 to 2.4 ug/L. My numbers for lead went from 33 ug/L to 1.7 ug/L. The fillings in my mouth remained, as replacements often release even more mercury to the body during the procedure, which I could not tolerate medically.

Specialized procedures were done to clean the air and water in my home where I continued to live, deciding not to move as it would likely add too much to my stress, and my doctor agreed. I stopped using chemical hair dyes and switched to herbal products, which I still use to this day. I had other extensive testing done to determine my food intolerances which were considerable and then improved my diet, particularly removing foods that contained mould, gluten, or chemicals that contributed to major brain fog as well as sugars, preservatives, and caffeine that overstimulated me.

I stay dedicated toward living with as decontaminated an environment as best I can and sharing the wealth of information I collected about chemical absorption, environmental testing, and food sensitivities with the clients I work with. Our understanding of these topics continues to expand, giving everyone better choices.

Sleep Management

I had developed a secondary diagnosis of Fibromyalgia related to the trigger-point musculoskeletal pain I was experiencing. These feel like darts shooting in my body at very specific targets. Fibromyalgia has nineteen possible trigger points from the neck, shoulder, back, forearm, buttocks, upper legs, and knees. Some of the patients at the clinic had this pain worse than I did and described their pain to me as if all of their bodily bones were breaking. What many do not know is that Fibromyalgia is strongly associated with major sleep problems, and without restorative sleep (which as noted, was a significant part of my medical picture), the trigger points developed are manifested by the lack of cell restoration while at rest (Fibromyalgia and Sleep: Sleep Disturbances & Coping, 2020).

My CFS was far more debilitating than the Fibromyalgia, but if I had a 'worse' day, the trigger pain started. However, while being assessed for this secondary condition, a pain doctor recommended a tricyclic antidepressant that helped control that pain *and* had a sedative effect to help with sleep, which I desperately needed. For me, this was the beginning of where pharmacological trials as dreams turned into nightmares, then back into dreams. What looked like an initial solution became less effective as my body built up resistance and the benefit wore off, or what sedated others, stimulated me, and I had to go back to square one. For me, all of this meant no sleep, again. Medication trials are commonly complicated, and even more so for auto-immune or chemically sensitive patients.

Luckily, that lifesaving day that landed me at Dr. Bested's office led to her recommending a special cocktail using medications that worked better *for me*. Trazadone has sedative effects for sleep, and doxepin, also an antidepressant, is known to treat insomnia. The sleep study I'd been part of was helpful in identifying the key disruptions in my sleep cycle, and with Bested's expertise led to the clear recommendations for medications that targeted my specific, sleep-stage problems.

For me, my chronic sleep problems were not just part of more serious sleep and anxiety disorders. It was, and still is, directly and mostly connected to the previously mentioned food intolerances causing overstimulation. Certain foods place my body into a significant hyperalert physical state inconsistent with rest. What causes a bad night for most people, means no sleep for me at all. Not just tired, sick.

My sleep became my number one priority and continues to be a primary focus of mine. I had to make peace with it. I had learned the hard way how the lack of it is a quiet killer to the body, so protecting it would be necessary to recover and stay well. I need ten hours a night to feel good. I rarely attend early morning activities, and I carefully plan overnight stays. I bookend extra rest days around demanding activities. Madeline and my friends respect and support my sleeping needs and have shown incredible flexibility and planning with me, which makes it possible for me to partake in activities that would otherwise still be out of reach to me. It's not perfect, but I'm in a hell of a better place than I was twenty-five years ago. Sleep really is *everything* for good health.

I knew that in the daily self-care programs offered to clients, sleep had to be a serious consideration and not just for CFS and Fibromyalgia clients. The cause and effect are clear. Poor sleep depleting physical health reduces mental health which worsens physical health. Depression makes it hard to go to bed (postponing bedtime to avoid feeling the pain that surfaces when there is stillness, is a key symptom of depression that surprises most people). It also wakes you up earlier than you need to and then makes it harder to get out of bed. Anxiety makes it hard to fall asleep, interrupts the sleep once you are, prolongs the time to get back to sleep, and then starts your day with early morning anxiety before even getting out of bed.

There are three levels of interventions offered to KG clients to improve sleep that I called the '3 S's': **S**leep Hygiene, **S**upplements and **S**edatives. Clients are specifically supported in how best to manage their sleep to protect their mental and physical health, which unless there is a major risk, starts with the least intrusive good sleep hygiene habits. Sleep studies are regularly recommended, for obvious reasons, for those clients with significant struggles in this area.

In Dr. Bested's words, "a lot of patients cure their sleep disorder but struggle during the day, others suffer with sleep disorders but find ways to live better during the day." Pros and cons to each, I suppose. I fell into that latter category. Over the years, with specific attention to my wellbeing, my 'daytime health' became more normalized, but my 'nighttime health' never did. I've tried many alternative treatments for sleep, including making more than several attempts to wean off the meds, but never succeeded. There's insufficient research to conclude the adverse effects of the long-term sedative medications I am taking—potential cardiac issues and increased risk of falls, and I've accepted those risks because the meds provide me with a reasonable quality of life during the day, and that is worth more to me. Having said that, I am not heavily attached to treating clients with medications. In fact, psychotherapy, not medication, is viewed as the treatment of choice, integrated with other disciplines including nutrition, massage, naturopathy, mindfulness-based stress reduction, personal training, and somatic work, except in the presence of high risks, major illnesses, major psychiatric illnesses or ADHD, and even so medications in conjunction with therapy is usually advised.

Supplements

I spent a better part of ten years assessing the need for supplements to go beyond the pharmacological interventions to repair my body at a deeper level.

The natural hormone, DHEA, was the first priority in order to rebuild my cells and energy (For, 2023).

Categorized as a 'controlled drug' in Canada since 1992, the supplement had to be purchased out of a 'secret back cabinet' of a highly reputable downtown pharmacy known only to an underground population of patients and care providers. By 2005, my DHEA number had gone from 3.4 μmol/L to 7.3, which brought me within a normal range for my age. Over that time, I began to watch my energy resume. Through Dr. Bested, I also obtained slow-release IV drips for vitamin C and Myers drips (much less known at that time than they are now) to correct my immune regulation. The effects of these were less noticeable, but I did feel like I was feeding my body at the cellular level.

The probiotics I started taking began to restore levels of friendly bacteria. I also took milk thistle to support my liver, especially given the medications I continued to take, and multiple adrenal system supports to help regulate the cortisol. By 2004, my cortisol levels dropped from 375 nmol/l to 162 by 2004. I regularly detoxed with 'Ultra Clear' products, and in the early days, could actually feel my brain and bowels physically releasing 'junk.' I also took valerian root and magnesium, and later, CBD for pain, anxiety, and sleep.

Supplements are a key part of the holistic treatment of autoimmunity but require careful planning and self-awareness to determine what is helping and what isn't for the unique state of your immune system. When taking supplements, it is critical for the autoimmune patient to find the point where supplements could help without overdoing things. CFS patients do not suffer with what is more commonly known as a *depleted* immune system which benefits from boosting supplements. The *dysregulated* immunity of CFS is often not only not helped by the boost, it actually often makes the patient sicker.

The best example of this happening was when I was recommended vitamin B injections. For most people, vitamin B boosts energy properly. On the surface it looked like exactly what I needed, but vitamin B pushes those with CFS and similar conditions into having way *too much* energy. With excessive energy, the CFS person is unable to sleep, and their symptoms worsen. It is a bit of a mind game because the first day, you feel you've won the lottery, only to crash forty-eight hours later and be worse off than before you began. This is also true of iron, licorice, and most of the more common over-the-counter energy and immune boosters, anti-inflammatories, tinctures, and teas.

As part of the *KG* self-care management program, I share my knowledge of how tricky managing supplements can be with autoimmunity and regularly advocate for specialized naturopathic consultations with doctors trained in dysregulated, not depleted, immunity.

Cognitive Behavioral Therapy (CBT)

At the time, cognitive-behavioral therapy (CBT) for treating chronic illness was a relatively novel idea, which may surprise many readers. Dr Bested was right on the mark with this research and provided CBT group therapy to her patients to improve stress responses. She said, "Healthy people struggle enough having negative thoughts, but sick people simply cannot afford to carry the extra load of those thoughts when their systems are already overloaded." She was right.

As a therapist, I knew CBT. As a patient, there would never be a better time for me to start improving the management of my anxiety, anger, and grief that was now keeping me sick. Re-routing negative thoughts to stress toward empowering responses would calm my internal state, reduce the likelihood of exposures to further stressors, and most importantly, give my immune system a chance to repair. Dr. Bested's CBT groups were incredibly helpful, and doing my own CBT made me a better CBT therapist.

How could the CBT we've discussed in previous chapters improve your physical health?

Mindfulness-Based Stress Reduction (MBSR)

Do you have a mindfulness practice that is protecting your health?

In 2002, two years after I was diagnosed, Harvard began publishing research on the mind/body connection in treating chronic pain and illness, intended to build on the CBT tools (Grassini, 2022). Accordingly, Dr Bested referred me to the workbook, *Managing Pain Before It Manages You (Caudill & Benson, 2016)* to teach effective mindfulness, relaxation, and somatic practices for pain management. I expanded this methodology to include Jon Kabit Zim's work on MBSR from his book, *Full Catastrophe Living: Illness (Kabat-Zinn, 2013)*. I was lucky to get into Dr. Lucinda Sykes' group in Toronto. She was one of the first Canadian Doctors to go to California to study with Dr. Zim, learn his techniques, and bring them home.

While I attended her group things started to register. I came face-to-face with my monkey mind. I finally recognized the chatter that had been running in the background without realizing it and without knowing—to my serious detriment—that I had been feeding that monkey with bananas for years, consuming *a lot* of energy that I had needed elsewhere in my body. I learned to be present with meditation and body-scan exercises, which began for me by regularly *feeling* the warm water and suds while washing my face in the mornings (as if I had never used/felt them before), instead of distracting my attention with useless worries of the coming day. I still notice this every day. It's a blessing.

But the best example by far of my developing mindfulness practice happened in a most unexpected moment. I had purchased a new car after my marriage dissolved, and with less than 100 kilometres on the odometer and my three-year-old daughter in the back seat, a guy T-boned me when he ran a stop sign and totaled my car. I had just finished the MBSR course. I sat in the driver's seat and imagined my old self jumping out of the car to scream and swear, letting the monkey mind trick me into believing that my rant would fix my car (the stinky thinking of fighting). But instead, I checked Madeline, then gripped the steering wheel and breathed. Yes, breathed. I radically accepted my arguing would not bring the car back. I faced the facts of the situation. I embraced what I really wanted was to figure out a plan and do it in a way that minimized stress to my daughter. The guy came over apologetically, explaining he was on his way to his wedding rehearsal dinner and was nervous and distracted. The car was towed. A new car was rented. I was calm. Madeline was calm, and within an hour, we proceeded with our plan to drive up to the family cottage for the weekend, to everyone's pleasure.

I was onto something. My mind would thank me. My body would thank me. Years later, clients thank me. Incorporating mindfulness tools as part of the DBT Bridged Program became particularly important for treating chronically ill clients. Mindfulness training and meditation is not only a regular part of my personal life, but a key part of clients' lives, including the four-part meditation I teach, introduced in chapter 3, which tames the monkey mind for brain health through the breath. Every day I do it, I reset to the breath, to self-compassion, self-affirmation and wise gut channelling.

My mindfulness practice also fulfills a proactive measure for me. Regular body scans and having a keen body awareness, I can usually detect actual vibrations activated in my body from my overtaxed immune system (uncomfortable sensitivities in my head or on my skin) telling me I am approaching the stage of doing too much. I scale back early enough to override most immune crashes before they fully develop. If I miss it, the body begins to block mobility for me. That is my last chance to stop. This truly is where the mind heals the body, and the body teaches the brain.

Pacing Daily Activities

How are you doing at pacing your life for improved health?

More is not always more. In fact, there is a saturation point when more is less and less is more. The law of diminishing returns is real and if you're in poor health, you can't afford to be in a deficit.

I had been speeding through life, living (or at least trying to live) on 'more' and as long as I continued to do that, I would get sicker.

It may seem obvious to just do less if you're tired and sick from doing too much. Trust me, I am not alone. It turns out most autoimmune patients are suffering with the same fight of overdoing, despite how sick they are. Suffering and denying their limits. Suffering with trying to outwit limits they never will. Suffering with believing that surrendering would be a loss, an unbearable loss worth avoiding. It turned out a lot of people were losing the same fight I was.

By far the most frustrating but most helpful intervention of my recovery was re-pacing my daily life. Dr. Bested had me document my activities of daily living *and* measure my concurrent stress, pain, and energy levels, every hour of every day to look for patterns of crashes. The purpose was to use the data to determine bedtimes, rest times, length of, frequency of and location for social interactions, type and number of chores and tasks, food intake, and physical movement on any given day. There was one single goal. Reduce the frequency and severity of the crashes. I hated doing this, but she was strict about it: no records, no care. If I wanted to keep her as a doctor, I had to produce the hourly logs at every appointment. She was all I had.

Although I initially resisted this, over time I realized her approach was liquid gold to me. I learned to redirect my methodical type-A approach to life from hurting me to serving me. I ran the pacing charts like a machine, matching daily routines of tasks, meals, social interactions, stress, rest periods, food, and body movement with the stress, pain and energy numbers I recorded on the logs, to determine my optimal activity levels. For example, I started with a pedometer measuring my daily steps around my home for one week, then without crashes, I increased the movement to one minute out to the end of my driveway and back the next, then two minutes out, two minutes back, continuing to increase the daily levels each week as long as there were no setbacks. Then I began sit-ups, one sit-up daily for a week, and then two, etc. gradually building up tolerance for higher levels of exercise. Inevitably I would overdo, crash, and need to start from the beginning. I did this hundreds of times.

This rehabilitation is difficult because recovery involves not only determining what the set points are to avoid crashes, it also involves realizing that the set points of not overdoing is a moving target and can change on any given day, sometimes even within a given hour because of uncontrollable stressors in our often-unpredictable lives or fluctuations within the state of the autoimmunity itself. The overall capacity for mental, physical, and emotional exertion is lower than normal, but it is always shifting and requires flexible and tight management at the same time. What you did yesterday may not automatically be what is possible today. The goal is about being steady and patient while being acutely aware of stress, pain, and energy, making necessary adjustments as you go, minimizing the interfering variables where you can, and ultimately reducing the severity and frequency of the crashes. As much as I hated doing it, and as imperfect as I was at it, it worked for me, and still does.

Since this worked so well, I knew it was worth teaching the chronically ill clients in my practice. In fact, there are now apps that help clients document daily activities and corresponding symptoms in much easier ways than the pen and paper of those early 2000s. Clients still complain like I did, until they see the clarity, get behind the power of what they can control, and use the determination and awareness themselves like I did, to achieve better health. It makes the inconvenience and annoyance completely worth it.

Footnote about Exercise: Because of what I had to do to recover, starting from such minimal levels of physical movement, you will *never* hear me complain about exercising. Just the opposite. As is often the case for us humans, only when something is taken away from us, do we realize how much we were taking it for granted. We miss it. We want it back, and we will do what we can to not lose it again. The fact is, over time I was able to move my body more, but I can never exercise with the great cardiovascular fervor as most others, and this will always disappoint me. So, when I can work out or play active sports, I embrace it fully.

KG clients benefit from the power of this and find ways to include body movement starting at *their* physical and emotional capacities as part of their medical recovery and/or mental health management. Exercise, when planned correctly, is a key part of discharging stress, increasing energy, improving sleep and appetite, connecting with our breath and mind, and feeling inner power. In particular, outdoor mindful walking is incorporated into the depression management programs (Grassini, 2022).

Surrender Without Defeat

I invite you to reflect on what your body might be trying to teach you.

Learning what my limits were on a practical level, from the daily logs, was necessary for my recovery, but one of the best gifts of the illness was figuring out how to work these limits *mentally* from a place of strength and power, not failure. I could decide to be stubborn and fight with my illness, as I had done with other stress in my life, and, similar to those other situations, I would lose. This time, the stakes were higher. I wouldn't just lose a relationship; I would lose my health, and I was already on the course to achieving that. The reality was that I had finally met my match. My body was *more* stubborn than me.

This was why my diagnosis was my ***Invitation Number Six.*** Inviting me, in a very dramatic way, to rewrite my control scripts and find power in a different way. The game of tricking myself into overdoing in order to have control was over. I could see this as a total failure and loss. Or I could see it an invitation. I could keep overdoing what I was doing and lose even more. Or I could become curious about the deeper meaning of the illness. Doing my deeper work led me to the unexpected invitation of changing my *relationship* to the CFS. If I wasn't going anywhere and it wasn't going anywhere, no matter how hard I denied it, minimized it, or argued with it, then we would have to somehow learn to get along. If we were going to co-exist, I would have to make friends with the CFS. I took the upper hand in the relationship in a different way than in the past. I paid attention to what CFS was telling me. Not one down, and not one up, but as an equal. I reframed my experience where less was more and where my power came from letting go rather than pushing. I decided to surrender without losing. I took all the stubbornness and transferred it over to my recovery by setting up competitions with myself to see what I could scale back on the least *and* still prevent a crash. I called my win: 'Surrender without Defeat.'

Of course, I had to grieve what I couldn't do, but the focus became more about getting behind the power of what I could achieve for my health by doing less. I eventually mastered that system only because I had redefined 'the win.' I hadn't lost after all by giving in. What has become even more meaningful to me over time was that the inherent gifts of the CFS, of listening and pacing went well beyond my medical recovery. Those gifts improved my overall stress management, my communication with others and my relationships with myself. Those gifts keep on giving in all parts of my life and will as long as I live.

Is there something that you would benefit from surrendering to?

The EFT of the deeper healing programs with chronically ill *KG* clients had to tap into the relatable deeper messages unique to *their* life journeys. Only then could they really make 'friends' with *their* body and mind as I had and find gratitude in the helpful invitations that came with their difficult illnesses, not only to reduce symptoms but to ultimately live a better life. That would be a big exhale. I needed to help clients find out what *their* deeper messages from their illnesses were and what to do about those.

In the bridged DBT program, clients learn about Radical Acceptance (see glossary), first introduced in chapter nine. It is a key part of regulating emotions. Recall how Radical Acceptance specifically targets how as humans we so easily 'forget' that we are imperfect, so we too easily equate our self-worth with our ability to achieve perfection. Accepting our imperfection helps us let go of what is not possible and get behind what is. That makes us more powerful. That makes us happier. That makes us healthier ("PCL-R Demonstrates Inadequate Field Reliability and Validity," 2017).

We tell this story:

A man who goes to the gym to strengthen his legs by working the leg-press machine. He loads up the weights but cannot do a full press because his legs are too weak. He goes through the motions, day in, day out, trying to prove to himself that his legs are as strong as the others he sees at the gym, but he knows he is faking. Even worse, not only are his legs not getting stronger, they are still weak. Only by accepting that his legs are weak, does he choose to lessen the weight on the machine. Only by lessening the weight can he do a full leg press. Only by doing a full leg press does he begin to strengthen his legs (2000 Books, 2018).

As discussed in the previous chapter, user-friendly tools are always necessary to link theory to practice. Those links come out of the therapeutic conversations in sessions so are specifically relevant to the person's journey. Personal daily slogans drive the radical acceptance. Mine to improve my health, definitely became 'Less is More' 'Short term Pain (missing out on what others could do physically or socially without penalty) for Long Term Gain'.

I would do better mentally, emotionally, socially, and physically if I accepted the limits of the illness. That I would always be different; having more sleep, doing less high intensity exercise and keeping stress minimized would be needed if I was to be as healthy as I could. I failed at this many times before I accepted my truth. Sometimes, I still do, but once I bought into the restrictions, my health was more consistent. Like the man on the leg press, I got stronger if I admitted the imperfection that I was weak and stopped tricking myself into thinking I could do more.

Leave your House, Leave Your Spouse, Leave your Job

Do you need to 'leave' anything to feel better?

There is an informal saying among autoimmune patients that says: "To get healthy you have to *leave your house, leave your spouse, leave your job.*" Although I never left my house, as explained above, there were significant 'leavings' in my life.

There truly is a point when poor health becomes the biggest and sometimes last signal we get, telling us that something is very wrong with our life. For me, it wouldn't be my last, but it was close (second last, **Invitation Number Six**). Although I learned so much in the rehabilitation of the CFS, I wouldn't fully surrender to what I really needed to learn about my life until my husband left, about two years after I was diagnosed.

As catastrophic as it was when my husband left, ending the marriage was needed if it wasn't going to get better. In fact, DBT theory equates living in a toxic relationship with negative self-care including poor diet, sleep deprivation, and no exercise. Staying and indulging in the chronic negativity of my marriage no doubt contributed to me getting sick as much as the poor sleep and the vicarious trauma. Period. I needed to radically accept that my need for control tricked me into believing that I could still fix it, and that prevented me from accepting it was over. For me, the ultimate lesson was about finding control not by hanging on but by letting go.

Leaving work that was exclusive to trauma was almost as difficult as the marriage ending. My role in helping sexual abuse victims and offenders continues to be among some of the proudest parts of my career. I know the model that we were working with at the time rehabilitated offenders, reunited families safely and most importantly, prevented future victims. But there was no way at the time, as things were, I could have continued that work without becoming sicker. Sadly, the program has since closed.

Helping clients bravely leave what was once so important turned harmful is delicate and necessary.

How the *KG Method* Grew—Saving Marriages When There Is Disability, Treating Vicarious Trauma

Do any relationships in your life need a different type of attention, because of prolonged poor health?

The statistics tell us that marital breakdown when one partner is disabled is double the average (Vikström et al., 2020). There are clear reasons why. As it was in my life, the sick partner feels the other partner isn't empathic enough, and the well partner feels that the sick partner isn't trying enough. I knew what we did wrong, and I knew how to help others love better in similar circumstances. I have become passionate about saving these marriages, so that no one goes through what we did. We carefully work our way through the same couple CBT and Imago Approaches but with a specialized lens on the presence and impact of the chronic health problems for both partners. Extended family programs also help to protect and strengthen the relationships depleted by illness.

I also commit part of my practice to other therapists suffering from vicarious trauma and burnout. I provide therapy, career coaching, and business coaching to keep good therapists in the field, keep good therapists healthy, and prevent the development of serious illness while doing the work they love.

If you are a therapist, what is your mental health plan?

Not Going It Alone

A lot of people who have autoimmune illnesses are on their own. It is a silent invisible sickness. I never had any scars to show. I never had any wounds that bled. I never had broken bones. As sick as I was, I never stayed in hospital. Many in my life had no idea how sick I was. Some of them still don't. The isolation, misunderstanding, and underestimation of severity of the health problems make the journey, both physically and emotionally, much harder than it could be. Much harder than it should be.

Dr. Bested once remarked on my determination to keep pushing for my own health and the value of my parent's support through those difficult times. She said their 'showing up' for me was something that truly set me apart from her other patients whose prognoses were significantly poorer because of the lack of similar support they had in their lives.

Without a doubt, my parents were part of my healing journey. Their support was demonstrated by keeping my home going, caring for Madeline when I was too sick to get out of bed, driving me to my appointments and her to school and social events, showing up day after day, week after week, and month after month, for over a year.

It takes a village to recover health. It was my luck that I had a village. I help clients build theirs, because no one should go through this alone. Make sure you have yours.

For a summary of this Chapter, you may wish to use this checklist to identify your potential risks and to develop a better health plan. This is not an exhaustive list by any means but could be a helpful review for you.

The ABCs of Health Risks

Present/Not Present	Health Risks, A-D
A	
	Abnormal Blood Work including hormone levels, immune system scores, killer cell counts, DHEA, cortisol, chemicals, etc.
	Abnormal Sleep Study Results
	Antibiotics, Overuse and/or No use of Probiotics
	Abusive, Toxic, Codependent Relationships, Workplaces, History of Trauma
	Advocating (Not) for Self, Resourcing, Networking, Second Opinions
	Avoiding Problems, Internalizing Stress and Conflicts
B	
	Body Pain - Ongoing/ Recurring Muscle/ Trigger Points/Joints
	Behavioral Habits of Overdoing/Perfectionism
	Bad Intake of Food including Processed Foods, Gluten, Caffeine, Allergens, Intolerances, Sugars, Unsafe Consumption of Drugs and/or Alcohol
	Brain Fog, Reduced Tasking
C	
	Consistent Persistent Exposures to Stress
	Career that is High Risk with Regular Exposures to Trauma, Danger, Suffering, Graphic Violence, Lack of Safety, Lack of Support
	Chronic Persistent Worsening Fatigue, Post-Exertion Fatigue, Non-Restorative Sleep.

		Chronic Recurring Sore Throats, Swollen Lymph Nodes, Headaches
		Cognitive Impairments of Reduced Concentration, Focus and Memory
D		
		Deficient Exercise, Stretching, or Regular Body Movement
		Dysfunctional Work/Life Balance
		Dysregulated Anger, Anxiety and/or Depression
		Dangerous Exposure to Toxic Metals, Chemicals, Unsafe Environments
		Dealing with Divorce, Grief, Loss
		Deferring Diagnoses/Testing/ Assessments

How did you do?

You may wish to use this 15-Point Plan to Begin Taking Back Your Health:

The 15-Point Health Plan

Number	Present/Not Present	Health Plan
1.		Sleep Management-the 3 S's of sleep hygiene, supplements or sedative, Sleep Study Follow Up
2.		Blood Work Follow up to Assess Needs for Supplements, Medications, Further Assessment, Chelation
3.		Change of House, Spouse or Job
4.		Alternative Safer Treatments for Viruses
5.		Probiotics
6.		Naturopathic Assessment for Immune Dysregulation
7.		Fibromyalgia-Specialized Assessment for Trigger-Point Pain
8.		CBT Therapy to Change Behavioral Habits and Improve Pacing
9.		DBT Therapy to Improve Emotional Regulation
10.		EFT Therapy to Repair Underlying Trauma, Abandonment, Loss
11.		Self-Care Management for Improved Eating, Exercising, Leisure
12.		Somatic Therapy to Release Body Somatised Pain and Stress
13.		Neurological Follow Up
14.		Therapy to Improve Level of Supports
15.		Mindfulness Based Stress Reduction Course, daily meditation Practice

Did you see a gap in anything you would benefit from?

Final Thoughts

I would never be fully recovered. Not from the CFS. Not from the Fibromyalgia. Not from the Sexually Transmitted Illness. But we are no longer enemies. We are friends. As with all other invitations, the health problems gave me an opportunity that I badly needed to wake me up and do life differently. One could even argue that my commitment to the difference was made accessible to me because of the pain.

Years later, when my health allowed, after the ending of my marriage and after I had found the freedom from all that had been aching at me physically and mentally, I returned to that same campground my daughter and her father were traveling to on the day of the Yellow Paint, where we would visit as a family. I found myself on a bike. I was weaving through the beautiful trails; super smooth pathways underneath the wheels, feathery strong trees lining the edges, and the bright blue sky overhead. But what I remembered the most, and still do, was how the breeze felt on my face as I gently picked up speed; so fresh, like I was flying I felt so grateful to be moving again. I felt alive. I felt grateful to *be* alive.

It's remarkable that the body can usually heal if we let it.

It's remarkable how resilient our mind and spirit are when we free them.

It's remarkable how we learn to live again.

Think about this:

1. How would you describe your current state of health?
2. How do you think your home environment, food, work, mental, and emotional stress are impacting your body?
3. What do you believe your bodily symptoms may be telling you from a deeper level?
4. What is one thing you could start doing differently that would make a difference to your health? In your daily living? From underneath the pain?

CHAPTER 10
THE PRINCIPLES BEHIND
THE KG METHOD

(Jimmy Cliff - I Can See Clearly Now, 1993)

I was at a friend's cottage several summers ago and after a thunderous storm the night before, we awoke to beautiful bright sunshine the next morning and my friends belted out this tune. We all started to sing. It seemed like an obvious song of choice for this chapter- as my personal and professional journeys gained speed and power and yes clarity for myself, my client and now for my readers.

Developing the KG Programs for Individuals, Couples and Families has been one of the proudest achievements of my life.

Throughout this book you have read through common life experiences, the good and the bad, the impacts of those, and the overviews of the techniques I offer clients for accountable healing and growth.

What follows are some of the key principles that underly those tools and programs.

At the end of this chapter is a short essay I wrote discussing human development and attachment theories and how those underpin the *KG Method of Therapy*.

For Individuals

Self-Care

The relationship between body and mind is key.

We start with the basics. Eating. Sleeping. Exercising. Leisure. We are what we eat. We eat who we are. Over-sleeping is depression's best friend, as is sleep deprivation is with anxiety. Depression loves under-exercising. Over-exercising is often connected to obsessive thinking and/or an eating disorder/control wound. Isolation feeds depression and anxiety. Covering these off, if in only in a minimal way, prepares us for using more advanced mental health strategies.

How we feel physically affects how we feel mentally. How we feel mentally affects how we treat ourselves physically. Mechanically Functioning (I call the Daily Self-Care) adopts the belief that we can 'push' ourselves (even if only small steps) toward:

- Diet improvements to reduce hangry/over-stuffing (with appetite awareness), stabilizing the glycemic roller coaster, (focusing on protein with vegetables and replenishing sugars after work outs), and reducing caffeine, processed foods, and gluten to improve anxiety management and reduce brain fog.
- Restorative sleep (with the three Ss of sleep hygiene, supplements, and sedatives).
- Exercise (to discharge stress, improve sleep), at least a daily outside 20-minute walk.

    And…

- Productive leisure (weekly in-person interactions outside of work and home with non-problem talk). The bigger our worlds, the smaller our problems. The smaller our worlds, the bigger our problems.

…even before we 'feel' better.

Growing is not just internal, it is also helped by *outside* changes from a myriad of circumstances we push ourselves into including fitness, appearance, environmental space, and organization, housing, career changes, etc.

Addressing any medical conditions, injuries and illnesses including naturopathic/pharmacological/holistic treatments is helpful, sometimes necessary before we move forward.

Cognitive Behavioral Therapy

Believe that you choose your happiness. Happiness is 99 percent internal. How we think determines how we feel, determines what we do.

Knowledge is power. Make connections with that information. Build bridges. Create your aha moments. Be informed. Neutralize the facts of a problem. Let how the past shows up in the present, inform you, then inform others with 'I' messages about what you know, feel, and need. It is through this relevant, neutral information that full potential is gained, and relationships are healed.

CBT requires having the awareness that you're being triggered and using discipline to take a break to correct what you're thinking when you're triggered. You can only do this if you're not drinking, drugging, or delusional. If needed, develop a relapse prevention plan for addiction, or arrange a psychiatric assessment to review the need for medication to help you in your therapeutic process. You don't get a pass for not doing the CBT, and with practice you can change your thinking.

You are with yourself twenty-four hours a day. That means every time you are triggered, you are there. That means only you can be accountable for managing your triggers.

When 'perfected,' CBT takes twenty minutes to complete. It takes the disciplined vigorous relationship with your brain based on, *"I own you. You don't own me. You don't tell me what to think, I tell you what to think."*

There is a way to be sad without shame. There is a way to be afraid without panic. There is a way to be angry without judgment.

Yes, depression is real, weighing you down like a wet, heavy blanket, but if you don't cut a hole out from the inside, you won't see the light, breathe the air, and see what's possible on the other side. Yes, it is one step at a time—often mechanically at first—but single, small steps are necessary when all you think you want to do is suffocate yourself. Be prepared to outwit the stinky thoughts of depression that tell you the effort won't be worth it.

Yes, anxiety is about control. Control is also not a four-letter word. Reframe the control, whether you have had too much or too little or never had the chance to reset your internal thermostat to the centre. It is in this middle place where you can live a life with less panic and more acceptance of imperfections. Be prepared to outwit the stinky thoughts of anxiety that doing more or delaying/distracting to something more appealing in the moment, gives you more control.

Procrastinators are not lazy people. The opposite: they are perfectionists acting out a control wound no different than over-doers, but who avoid tasks and situations which put them face-to-face with the possibility that they aren't perfect, which feels unbearable to them. Consequently, they delay getting started or avoid finishing a task and trick themselves into stinky thinking that control is achieved by doing what they *want* in the heat of the moment (but distracts them away from the important task) rather than coming face to face with the possibility of doing something imperfectly. They ultimately *lose*, not gain, control.

Yes, aggressive anger is the overt expression of hurt. Blame is only trying to reduce your vulnerability. You can get tricked by making a secret deal with yourself that judgment will recover your pain. But judgment only serves to hurt you more as you push people you care about away and you push yourself away from your own pain that needs your attention. Be prepared to uncover how your internal self-critic turned inside out.

Learned helplessness is a thing. The mouse stops moving if repeatedly shocked while moving toward the bowls of food. It eventually stopped moving. It starves to death with food in its bowl even *after* the shocks are removed. Get ready to unstink the stinky thoughts of helplessness, which convince you that 'there's no point' or that 'you can't' and get the tools to build up to learned optimism instead.

The CBT 'Change' Program

The Cues:

Practice awareness in knowing specifically how your *brain*, *body* and *behavior* changed when something thematically similar to your unresolved past is showing up in the present and triggered you.

Categorize your thoughts to know if you are:
- Future worrying or past regretting.
- Generalizing,
- Self-criticizing or judging.
- Mind reading, and/or
- Stinky thinking.

Honeymoon:

If you're in fight mode, you will easily resist the 'honeymoon' to stay in the fight to convince the other person how you're right, and they're wrong. If you stay in flight mode, you will honeymoon and not come back. Force the honeymoon to physically and/or mentally move away from the specific stressor. Mentally honeymoon if you are in a meeting, that you cannot leave or in a moving car. Honeymooning may look like flighting. It is not, for three good reasons:

1. It is a conscious decision to step away, not a reactive one.
2. It is time limited, not random floating.
3. It has a specific clear purpose of leading you to the remaining four steps (the A-N-G-E), without indulging avoidance.

Adjust:

If your stress is above a 6/10, discharge, soothe, or distract your stress to bring it under a 6/10.

For example, vigorous walking, deep breathing, screaming, bathing, music, pressing fingernails into palm, cleaning.

New Thought:

With your stress under 6/10, get rid of negative thoughts that are not serving you, indulging anger, depression, anxiety, obsessions, addictions, tricking you into immediate gratification. Force a one-sentence factual report of the problem. I call this 'my bottom line'.

CBT is *not* about positive thinking. First of all, it's not always possible to go from negative to positive. Secondly, if we move to the positive too soon, we sugarcoat the problem, and it comes right back up. CBT is the rigorous discipline of forcing neutrality in an otherwise stinky, highly emotional, generalized, catastrophic, deeply regretting place of judgment that will work against you somehow.

Get Honest about What you Really Want (The Goal):

There's a massive difference between what you want as a self-destructive immediate gratifier and what you really want. CBT takes you closer to what you really want. It's the bigger more sustainable win, but it often requires short term discomfort and pain as you delay immediate gratification. The real desire can be specific to the situation, such as "I really want clarity," or broader in scope, relating to your life or the relationship as a whole, like "I really want a relationship built on trust."

Empowerment:

Humans are empowered in four ways including: speaking, actively listening, deciding, or planning based on the facts of the problem and the 'really wants' including:

- 'I' messages of feelings and needs, doing this twice and if negative reactions occur from the other move on to decision-making and planning.
- Active listening to the other's 'I' messages with curiosity.
- Decision-making: Determine one specific thing you will do toward your 'really want.' Understand how one decision impacts the next. It is possible to spiral down to depression, but it is also possible to spiral up to joy.

    Conscious decision-making *not* to say or do, is not passive because it's a response not a reaction. It will look the same as flighting, but *choosing* not to say or do is very different than losing your voice in an unconscious reaction. It is very different than being a victim.
- Planning/ Future Planning: Have a specific plan of what you will do in the event your worst fear comes true.

Addiction and Relapse Prevention Planning

Untreated addicts rely on stinky thinking to maintain their abuse of a substance and/or activity. Others use stinky thinking, to procrastinate, perfectionate, avoid, disengage, lie, obsess, isolate, etc.

Interventions with addicts can be very useful. It can be a perfect *invitation to grow* to change direction when they've reached the bottom.

Addicts need relapse prevention plans to learn their specific cycles and detours. The later they try to detour, the harder it becomes to meet their harm reduction or abstinence goals.

Make full use of crises and breaks and changes to 'punctuate' and recontract what you need differently. Often these can be verbal punctuations made to announce the new rules and expectations to others in your life, to support your relapse prevention.

Beyond this, addicts need to get to the root cause of what made the medicating substances/habits so tempting to them in the first place.

Beyond this, medical detoxes and support can be helpful. Especially if the addiction has a genetic predisposition. Antabuse drugs. Anti-anxiety medications. Naturopathic remedies. Help calm the body's panic reaction coming from the crave center of the brain during withdrawal.

Significant others of addicts need to know the details of the relapse prevention plans and how best to support that plan Not because they are responsible for the addiction, but because they don't want to be working in the dark or at cross purposes, which could undermine the addict's recovery unintentionally.

Untreated addicts can take thirteen people down with them. Letting go with love is an important invitation for both the addict and their loved one if denial and minimization are not reduced, and relapses continue.

Emotional Regulation: The Dialectical Behavioral Therapy Program 'The Bridge Between the Head and Heart'

The power of the breath is real. Finding your breath detaches you from the noise in your brain and puts you back in your body where you have a greater chance of acting with intention. Once you breathe, you can decide with intention what you want to say or do next, and that gets you closer to what you really want, identified in your CBT program.

When breathing, you can feel the full force of gravity without being weighed down by it. In fact, the more grounded you are, the lighter you are, and the freer you are, the more anchored you are.

Your healthy self breathes like a whale with an incredible combination of gentle power. When you achieve that same balance, you discover gentleness in your power and power in your gentleness that moves you through the ocean waters of life with greater ease and control.

Daily grounding and mindfulness invite you to go from unconscious reacting to conscious responding and from living to meta-living (not just living but noticing how you are living), pulling you off the treadmill of robotic tasking to human feeling, and paving the way for more sustainable and deeper fulfillment. This builds resilience and improves emotional regulation.

Mindfulness has you drop into the present as an observer. The four-step daily meditation tool described in chapter three is extremely helpful to practice finding the breath, building self-compassion, increasing self-affirmation, and identifying key intentions and specific actions toward what you really want from the healthy self.

Use self-compassion *and* self-affirmation every day to balance your brain allowing you to feel whatever you feel when things are hard, while at the same time recognizing your goodness. This daily practice toward the ambiguity of seeing the good amidst the bad, in yourself, in others, in situations and in the waves of life, is the highest emotional intelligence skill to have.

Don't just be grateful. That's not enough. It's not enough to notice the good things. When those good things happened, *you were there*. Connect the good things to your goodness. This is self-affirmation. Practice this acknowledgment every day so when the next bad, unexpected, undesirable, unwanted thing happens you're not starting from a one down position from judgment or shame; you're at least neutral, if not one up.

Distress tolerance in DBT for emotional regulation is not passive. It is learning the ability to stand or even sit at the rim of the big dark hole of stress with your legs dangling over, seeing the 'problems' without being sucked in or high-tailing it out of town to get as far away from the problem as possible. Sitting or standing at the hole creates curiosity and insight that is productive without being overwhelmed or escaping.

Use senses for soothing. Identify what combination of the five senses is most soothing for you. Create this as your soft place to land, every day. This relaxes the mind. Most importantly, it builds resilience if you've been to your soothing place within the last twenty-four hours, when the next 'bad' thing happens. I use candles for light and scent (Heart: Virginian Cedar, Base: Haitian Vetiver & Musk, Top: Rose). Of course, I also use music that lights me up every time.

Use the five senses for grounding, especially in managing PTSD to differentiate present from past and to reassure self of safety.

Say the same thing to the same person, twice. If you continue to get negative reactions back, accept that your power will likely be more effective with decision making or planning rather than speaking.

Accept your flaws. Unlock yourself from believing that your self-worth is based on your ability to be perfect. Only by acknowledging your weakness, can you get stronger.

Emotionally Focused Therapy

The longest foot in the world is between your head and your heart. Find ways to clear your thinking but do it in a way that heals your heart. Heal the past and practice what you learned from that healing, in the present. A broken heart will undermine your thoughts, and unrealistic thoughts which will break your heart again, but when the heart and head are synchronized with parallel and mutually reinforcing core beliefs and intentions, it creates the magic of going further than you ever once believed possible.

Live with the curiosity that humans are born into this world as pure, innocent babies, shaped by DNA, birth order, gender, and environment.

Use this to embrace your inner Buddha. Curiosity may have killed the cat, but it rescues the human. Untangle yourself from adversity during times of conflict and pain. Instead, be curious about what the universe is showing and teaching you in otherwise unrecognizable packages. Don't worry if you miss it; the universe will redeliver another invitation to you, usually harder, until you learn (or not). Once fully unwrapped, and only once it is unwrapped, can you receive the gift.

Healing is erratic. It swings like a pendulum from one extreme to the other until you find the middle. The middle is not a boring bland place. It is where you find the magic of assertive empowered joy.

Healing zigs and zags. It goes forwards and backward due to the complexity of your brain. Be patient. Don't give up on the backward otherwise you will miss the chance that was waiting for you that would have taken you forward.

Healing is not about drowning into the past. Deeper healing involves:

1. Visiting the past, setting up specific dialogues between the clarified healthy and wounded self.
2. Making it possible to be informed so that reframing the past is also possible.

And then…

3. Identifying specific actions you will take communicating, deciding, and planning, differently, and better.

Reframing includes:

1. Gifts from the healthy self to soothe the pain of the wounded self.
2. Passing over projections making a deep commitment to yourself, to recover who you were really meant to be instead of being who the wounded part of someone else needed you to be.
3. Depersonalizing something that really had nothing to do with you.

These deeper healing stages can be done in different forms of guided meditation, art, play, music, empty chair, imagery, letter writing, cemetery visits, and dialoguing.

Healing betrayal requires:

1. Receiving answers to the questions you never asked or for which you didn't get full honest answers.
2. Receiving validation for the painful experiences.
3. Receiving apologies and responsibility-taking.
4. Receiving actions that you needed to begin rebuilding trust.

The Wounded Self

Your wounded self is your default setting, directing you naturally toward negative reactions until you heal the original wound. These negative reactions were developed by neuropathways during those times when you were hurt and are trying to protect you, but it overprotects you. Brain-health exercises, some of which described above, over time give your brain a different route to take. Learn and practice them daily. Then, do the deeper work to heal.

The wounded self originates from: abandonment, trauma and abuse, unreliable care taking, too much or too little control, isolation or over busyness, shaming, over or under restrictions for exploration of self in the world, betrayal, failure, or illness.

Your wounded self holds negative core beliefs about self, others, life, and love.

The wounded self is your immature part of self, regressed or fixated at a stage of immediate gratification, shaming, blaming, over- or under-trusting, over- or under-controlling, over- or under-depending, isolating, overdoing, feeling unworthy, lacking identify and/or an inability to be truly intimate.

Your wounded self makes secrets with you, dirty deals that trick you into immediate gratification that may feel great in the moment but hurt you more in the long term, one way or another.

Secrets reinforce shame. Shame, caused by judging ourselves for something we did 'wrong' is one of the most common weapons of the wounded self. It convinces us of our badness, projects that belief onto others, so we mind read others will also blame us. It separates us. It increases a likelihood that we will create more problems.

Chances are you witnessed or received negative conflict narratives that cause you to resist or overwork hard conversations. There is a way to embrace conflict and rewrite the avoidance/aggression scripts from your life. Only by communicating and listening more openly can you find true intimacy and connections that fill your heart. Prove to yourself that when spoken from a place of love, you can truly say anything to anyone. If the other person doesn't do their work on their side of the line, chances are they are struggling in their journey, not making enough progress and not really emotionally available to you as you deserve.

There's identification of the aggressor (chapter seven). There's also (over) identification with the victim. We project our past victimization into a situation and leads to over-empathy toward someone who appears weak. This creates inaccurate mind reading (being overly concerned about the other person, overly concerned about what others think of us). From there, we reorganize our actions according to those assumptions, so we easily enable or become enmeshed with someone who could be stronger or we get revictimized by not advocating enough for ourselves.

Your own insecurity and unworthiness make you believe you are the only one on the stage with a single spotlight, while the rest of the world waits at the edge of their seats, gripping as you take your next breath. But, actually, all the world's a stage, and there are multiple lights. Everyone is playing and consumed by their own character. Mind reading and Spotlighting only indulge negative narratives which increase social anxiety and is sure to play out in a way that creates a self-fulfilling prophecy.

Intergenerational trauma and patterns can be supported by the blind spots of your pain. Only by uncovering these blinders of your own resentment, intrusions, shame, rage, and powerlessness can you protect yourself, and the people you love.

The Healthy Self

Healing doesn't just involve repairing your wounded self. It involves embellishing your healthy self, so get to know that part of you just as well. Your healthy self can pick up where the people who hurt you left off if you let it, and then you get a second chance to love yourself in ways others couldn't.

The healthy self comes from experiencing unconditional love, achieving something that was important to you, or from overcoming something that was hard.

The healthy self has positive core beliefs of self, others, life, and love.

The healthy self is more mature, insightful, delays immediate gratification, moderately trusts and controls, is mostly interdependent, worthy, has clearer identity, and is more available for intimacy.

Good therapy has you utilize that part of you that already exists but is getting underutilized.

The healthy self knows:

- Growth also comes with growing pains; the mourning of that moment when we recognize the lost time and lost opportunities of the past as we begin to feel and do better. This is part of the evidence that you are making progress. Grief is part of the growth process as you come face-to-face with what could have been if *only*, you'd known sooner, what you're learning now. Keep going.

- The chemical compound of tears is the same as sweat. Cleansing crying is productive. It is in the why, the what, and the how of grief that ultimately heals you toward finding power in the legacy of the loss.

- Not everybody will get you all of the time. We operate on different frequencies. Our lives are unique, so what we like and what bothers us is different. Don't be so surprised by that difference. Don't personalize the difference.

- There is an art to the shake-off. Letting go in the moment when things go 'wrong', comes from a deeper level, by believing the past could not have been any different given what and how life unfolded. Thinking this way is not an excuse for or a pass to others who hurt you. It's an explanation that frees you through acceptance into living a fuller, happier life, not holding the wounded self of the other person.

- If your poor reactions with others are the projections of your pain, the same goes for others who you trigger just by being you. Know that you are doing your best wherever you are on your pathway and others are doing their best as well. The double record of saying the same thing twice to make your point, still applies, giving people chances to do their work, if they can. If they are important to you, you may communicate differently and make decisions or plans, that move them to an outer circle of trust in your life (seeing or sharing less with them) without cutting them off completely.

- Intergenerational trauma and patterns can be supported by the blind spots of your pain. Only by uncovering these blinders of your own resentment, intrusions, shame, rage, and powerlessness can you protect the people you love.

One sign of growing is that you are excited and nervous at the same time. Learn to tolerate the anxiety so you are able to capitalize on the opportunity right in front of you.

Entitlement is not a four-letter word meaning greediness or selfishness. The healthy self lives with a measured sense of entitlement (with the small letter 'e') as evidence of worthiness, knowing you deserve good things.

The 'Forrest Gump Factor' is real. Run off whatever you need to, and then go home. Throw yourself fully into the pain you feel, believing that you *will* find a way to tolerate the emotions and thoughts. Only by doing this, can you reframe and change associations that direct you to a place that's safe, a place that's calm, and a place that's beautiful. Forrest kept running until he felt that place inside him, and then he was free to go home.

For Couples

The Couple CBT

You're only as strong as your weakest member. It is essential that each partner knows how to manage their triggers. Have a couple CBT program, (see appendix for this pathway), using the 'Change' program to reduce trigger reactions by promoting conscious 'I' message responses and active listening. These are necessary for healthy dialoguing toward a stronger relationship. If we are still reacting, we will be unable to listen, unable to be assertive, unable to have empathy, unable to validate, and unable to work with our partner's needs.

From Conflict to Intimacy

Intimacy develops from working through the conflicts; not just solving problems but doing it in way that deepens love. The pathway from conflict to intimacy is the couple's version of how painful experiences for the individual invites growth.

Intimacy is only truly achieved by revealing and talking about the hard stuff, which carries you from conflict to true intimacy. These conversations are not about restoring 'how it used to be.' This earlier phase of the relationship is typically the romantic one when we are at our best but don't expose ourselves fully. Deeper intimacy is reached in the full reveal and the unconditional attention and acceptance we show ourselves and our partner shows us despite our revealed flaws. It is through the reveal and acceptance we grow; our partner grows, and we grow as a couple.

Often, what we need differently doesn't just work better for us; it invites our partner to heal a part of themselves they may not have even realized was there. Usually what's better for us is also better for our partner. Everybody wins.

Chronic dialed down intimacy is usually a sign that someone is not only not expressing their feelings, they're likely also not feeling or recognizing their feelings. Feeling journals really work.

Growing Together

When you heal, and your partner is present, you kill two birds with one stone. You both grow and because your partner was there to experience the growth, you fall in love with each other all over again.

The Imago Approach to dialoguing deepens love because your wounded self heals, your partner is present when you do and contributes to that healing.

Couples who make it are those who use the incredible depth of empathy to take off the boxing gloves, stop seeing their partner as the enemy, and learn to love themselves and their partner in deeper ways not otherwise thought possible.

Special Issues

In the nineties, a psychology study on marriage and divorce, *The Good Marriage: How and Why Love Lasts*, lists the nine tasks of a healthy marriage (Wallerstein & Blakeslee, 2006). Task one was about separating from your family of origin. This didn't mean sever ties. It meant that there is a sacred boundary around you as a couple that serves an emotional priority in conflicts, communication, and loyalty. Couples who achieve this task have healthy connections to their families while strengthening their romantic partnership.

Co-dependency means you are letting someone else's needs determine yours. Feeling this way is a sign that you have not yet recovered your own worthiness and are living from a place of deep insecurity.

Trying to heal your relationship without healing betrayal is like trying to build a house on a fractured foundation. You can furnish, paint, and decorate, but eventually there will be leaks, floods, and cracks.

There is a specific way to heal betrayal. See above. Otherwise, it will eat you alive and keep you circling in the "whys", "why nots", "why didn't yous", and "how could yous."

Maya Angelou said: "People show you who they are and when they do, believe them" (Maya Angelou Quotes, n.d.).

Give opportunities to grow, be curious about what does or does not happen and then be honest with yourself.

If someone isn't making you feel bigger, they're too small for you.

Knowing you tried everything, and turned over all of the stones will give you good sense of self integrity and respect if/when you walk away.

Grounding the grief is powerful. If you didn't grow in the relationship, you can grow from its ending. Acting out grief that is not pinned down will cause you to repeat the relationship you just left, with someone new.

Narcissism is not arrogance. It is a sign of deeper inferiority, a state that you alone, as the partner, cannot heal. Some narcissists are untreatable. Some narcissists, especially covert narcissists benefit from longer-term, individual therapy to heal trauma and abandonment to let go of the ego.

The best way to relate with someone suffering from borderline personality disorder is to be firm, friendly, and fair. (The three F's)

The best way to break up with someone suffering with borderline personality disorder is Cold Turkey.

Ninety-nine percent of cheaters do not have the Tiger Woods' Syndrome (Bruns & Richards, 2010), that is, incapable of monogamy. Most are treatable broken individuals who are reenacting abandonment, rejection, and unworthiness. In their effort to feel better, they use blind spots, enmeshment, or externalized passive aggressive disengagement, which can lead to many things including infidelity. Most are broken couples, and the infidelity is an untreated symptom of the relationship.

For Families

We have three chances to grow: through ourselves and the problems we get into, through our lovers and the attractions that become our frustrations, and through our children and the reflections they give us of our own childhoods that make us uncomfortable.

Formulate your family story to understand the legacies you received. Identify what you were predisposed to.

All parents are imperfect and can heal through their children if they allow it.

Children absorb the unresolved wounds of their parents.

Children express the unexpressed pain.

Children often act out to get attention for unmet needs, unify divided inconsistent parents, and sound an alert when there is trouble.

Don't try to fix your kids before you fix yourself.

When healing children, the process is often more important than the content. *How* you talk is more important than *what* you talk. When children *feel* acknowledged, heard, and connected in the delivery of their parents' messages, their fear, anxiety, and sadness are usually eased.

Play is the language of the child. It is found in the choice of toys, colours, and images. Interactions made by the child during play demonstrate the child's inner world of beliefs, feelings, and expectations.

Ignorance is not bliss. It is anxiety. Children need answers and spaces to express themselves. It's the parents' anxiety that stops them from talking, and this increases, not decreases the child's own anxiety.

If you ask closed questions, for example, "Are you ok?", you'll only get responses like *"yes," "no,"* or *"fine."* For example, instead of asking, *"Do you have any questions about our separation?"* try open-ended questions that encourage a more thoughtful response, such as *"What questions do you have about our separation?"* Use multiple-choice questions as a last resort.

Make it a habit to ask meaningful questions every day to show genuine interest. Instead of *"Was school good today?"* or even *"How was school today?"* ask, *"What was the best part of school today?"* or *"What was the hardest part of your day?"*

In my family, we have a daily tradition of asking, *"Tell me something I don't know about you."*

You can also draw inspiration from practices that build intimacy in couples by asking about fears, needs, and joys. For example: *"What scared you today?"* or *"What surprised you today in a good way?"* or *"What would make a real difference to you in your life?"*

The number one goal is always about keeping the line of communication open no matter what you hear. If you're freaking out about what you hear, find a separate place to manage that struggle and redirect yourself toward showing unconditional acceptance to your child and teen from beside the motorcycle giving opinions while empowering (see chapter eight).

Adult siblings deserve the opportunity to repair the natural competition, which the family was unable to help with when they were young.

Family members suffering with personality disorders also benefit from firm, fair, and friendly communication (the three 'F's). You benefit, too. Pervasive, persistent dysregulation can entangle us with expectations that are not attainable and enmesh us. The boundary of the three 'F's' keeps us sane.

Blended families need to simmer like a good-tasting soup not thrown together like a badly tossed salad. This includes numerous stages including having the stepparent move in slowly as a friend, uncle/aunt, etc. while facilitating the grief and working through the loyalty binds.

Don't let your parents die without seeing them fully as vulnerable, imperfect carriers of the legacies they inherited and knowing they did their best. If you miss the chance, visit their gravestones, or hold their ashes close, and take a moment to finally 'see' them.

Set boundaries. Reduce communication or cut off completely with continued abuse, let go with love with addicts, or those showing chronic treatment resistance. Refuse to collude with abuse narratives, secrets, victim blaming, or being passive in the face of mistreatment.

When You Are in Therapy

I couldn't do this for thirty-six years unless I knew it helped, but there is a way to do it.

Nothing changes when nothing changes. Make sure your therapy gives you clear ideas of what to do differently when you wake up tomorrow morning.

Look for tools and processes that make your present and future better; tools that are unique to you, so they help you move forward with the information and reframing you've made about your past.

Learn how to start every sentence with the word 'I.' It's not indulgent, it's informative.

A picture speaks a thousand words. Use imagery to express the pain of your wounded self and the gifts from your healthy self. Find ways to create in words, pictures, and music what it feels like to disown pain which you wrongly personalized—problems that were never yours to begin with.

Use the worst or best consequence of your current pathway to motivate you, in pictures with captions. Every day, look at these pictures and what you wrote, to help the brain live in the strength of better choices.

Spending time, money, and energy on therapy is expensive. Be sure you get the change you are looking for, not just a nice person who listens.

Repairing and rebuilding neuropathways is the hardest thing you'll ever do. We easily default to what is familiar even when it is not working for us. There is value in daily brain health exercises. This help us with the 'less and often' idea that tells us more is achieved when we offer the brain other options regularly and frequently.

Make sure you know or get to know your healthy self, that part of you that knows you the best, always has your interests at heart, and holds all of the answers you are looking for. You don't need to be told what to do. You just need to learn how to listen to the resources you already have within you.

Don't stop until you reach your full potential, and then keep going.

If you are interested in knowing more about how the theories of emotional development and attachment influenced the KG Method, consider reading this short essay.

Human Development and the *KG Method*

Babies are born pure, yearning to be loved and cared for. This natural instinct is the beginning of human emotional development toward fulfillment as an adult. Influencing traits such as the DNA of personality, addiction and mental health, family legacy, gender, and birth order, all predetermined for us, are important in understanding how we become who we become. The rest of our emotional, mental, and social selves are shaped by environmental factors, including the quality of our relationships and experiences (both positive and negative), especially from infancy, during childhood, and into teen years while the neuropathways in our brain are developing. Combined, these elements impact our ability as we grow, (in this order): to achieve trust (or distrust), find moderate control (or powerlessness), live with autonomy (or dependence), feel self-worthy (or ashamed), develop identity (or confusion), all toward the ability, to create and maintain intimacy (or isolation) as adults.

Mastery of these emotional and mental stages is never complete, and humans never stop 'growing.' The stages are progressive in nature; success or failure at earlier stages influences the successes or failures at subsequent stages and the degree of this is greatly determined by the responses we receive from parents, primary caretakers, siblings, and peers. In addition, challenges at specific points in this developmental process directly correlate to adult struggles of the same meaning or theme, and can, as described in chapter one, manifest from either side of the wound; aggressive, passive or passive aggressive. For example, disruptions during the trust phase as an infant from unreliable caretakers easily results in under or over trusting as an adult often leading to either a high degree of conflict, sabotaging, lying or a loss of self in relationships with blurred boundaries, and internalized resentments, all manifested from a trust wound. Likewise, ruptures during the control stage may contribute to over or under controlling by dominating situations, avoiding and procrastinating, or giving the 'silent treatment' or overdoing, underachieving or developing eating disorders all from a dysregulated relationship with control and internalized sense of powerlessness.

An equally important theory of development in explaining current qualities of life and symptoms is the concept of attachment presented by Edward Bowlby in 1969 (McLeod, 2024) was later expanded by Ainsworth (Flaherty & Sadler, 2010) identifying different attachment styles. Secure attachment, by receiving reliable care and attention from others, establishes inner security. The idea is that the attentive caregiver consistently and verbally reflects back to the child, their negative or positive emotions and needs. This lets the child know they are making sense to the parent, which in turn contributes to their capacity of making sense to themself. Consequently, as an adult they will have a better chance of understanding and validating their own emotions and attending to their own needs. In *KG* Language, this increases their abilities for healthy power to speak, decide or plan toward what they *really* want in life, ultimately creating greater experiences for success and joy.

A deeper sense of security also allows for object permanence. We learn to feel an experience of love from and for others, even in the physical absence of those we are closest to. In other words, we learn to feel love, loved *and* love ourselves even when we are alone. Therefore, we are better able to retain a more positive view of ourselves in the face of conflict or rejection because there is a stable layer of strength from within that we can rely on, with less volatility from outside influences. This ultimately prepares adults for healthier intimate relationships and in particular raises capabilities for vulnerability (free to reveal self fully, discuss fears, needs and joys, and tackle conflicts without crushing or being crushed) based on worthiness, trust, and empathy.

Anxious, avoidant, and disorganized attachments develop from inconsistent, distant, or abusive caretaking and leads to future frustrations, insecurities, and fears. Further, the *lack* of object permanence makes the individual's experiences of conflicts or rejections almost unbearable, which combined, easily causes reactions of being emotionally unavailable for commitment, distancing, betraying, abusing, avoiding, dominating, over arguing or clinging. These only serves to reenact and reinforce negative attachments, further lowering capacity for future connection.

We believe that having one secure base/relationship providing nurturance is sufficient in helping the individual move through the stages of emotional growth toward developing a capacity for secure love as an adult. This comes from the internalized states of stability, reliability, responsibility, unconditional love that our feelings and thoughts matter, and that we are good enough simply as we are.

How KG Integrates the Theory

As noted in chapter two, KG clients receive formulations at the assessment phase. These formulations have three key parts. Firstly, clinical interpretations specifically draw on these theories of human behavior by collecting information on the client's history of intergenerational patterns, gender issues, birth-order effects, and style of formative attachments. Secondly, these details are directly connected to the specific impacts on the developmental stages from trust to intimacy as discussed above. Thirdly and usually most importantly, these first two parts are integrated to explain the current, negative, usually persistent and worsening symptoms or consequences clients are being challenged by that brought them to therapy to begin with.

Succinct descriptions of the full breadth of the problems including the relevant causes and the specific consequential effects are extremely therapeutic to clients, and even more so, act as launching pads to the recommended comprehensive treatment plans. I divided the *KG Method* therapy approaches between the more present-centered, mechanical, self-care, relapse prevention, and cognitive restructuring techniques with the deeper emotionally focused treatment interventions; and created bridges between the two, including mindfulness and other emotional regulation tools. These programs came to be the best way I knew how to target the relevant predisposing, precipitating and perpetuating factors in treating depression, anxiety, anger, addiction, grief, trauma, interpersonal conflicts, and chronic pain and illness. The Head and Heart programs are described below. Applications of these as well as details of the mindfulness and emotional regulation DBT 'bridge' are provided throughout the book in chapters four through nine.

The Head ('The Brain Surgery')

The daily self-care management program is provided, linking the cause and effect/perpetuating relationship between physical and mental health. Negative habits usually have long histories and deep purposes to them, identified in the histories from adverse role modeling/childhood scripts, and/or long-term maladapted ways of coping. These serve to maintain a poor state of mental health that need attention for the client to begin making progress *and* to take advantage of more advanced treatment approaches.

This program supports restorative sleeping (explained in fuller detail in chapter nine), healthy eating including improved appetite awareness where eating portions are conscious and serves the purpose of nourishment instead of medicating emotions. It supports, physical and emotional discharge through 'intentional 'exercise targeting specific stress, which in turns motivates better eating and provides better sleeping, and regular(once weekly/ one overnight/quarter, one week/year) interactive non-problem focused leisure and dating in new environments for work/life balance to make worlds bigger and problems smaller; and to reduce isolation, depression, anxiety, and obsessive thinking.

Cognitive Behavioral Theory has been around for years, and I believe is still the gold standard for treating depression, anger, and anxiety, resting on the axiom that what we think determines how we feel, determines why we do what we do. CBT ensures you know what to do about a trigger in the moment when your reactions are problematic. Going after the root causes and the underlying narratives of these negative reactions is for the deeper healing program.

The *KG* CBT I created and named 'Change' demonstrates the important cognitive restructuring steps, and helps clients notice, stop, take momentary space, correct negative or distorted thoughts, clarify longer term goals over immediate gratification, and empower themselves. Fear-driven brains in the triggered state overestimate the problem in the situation to protect us, but in doing so, drain the energy we need to be assertive. Therefore, correcting the thoughts to reproportion the problem is needed to redirect the unhelpful reaction chain and reclaim the otherwise lost energy that is needed.

What triggers us and why, and how we react in ways that sabotage us is directly connected to our unresolved history. Since we all have unique life histories, different people react differently in the same situation. This difference can be hard to remember and is why we easily judge or feel separate from others in the midst of a problem. I mastered my own CBT program and practice it every day in quick five-minute brain health drills, as do graduating KG clients when the imperfections of the day intersect with our negative histories.

Linked to the classic CBT, I added:

A relapse prevention program for compulsive behaviors, helping clients build specific four-stage detours customized to their unique addiction cycles.

and

Family and couple CBT programs to ensure partners and family members could use the same CBT language to support empowered responses over reactions together, and reduce unintentional hurt toward each other, by working in the dark or being triggered themselves.

The Heart ('The Heart Surgery')

The emotionally focused 'heart surgery 'program takes what we know about the emotional stages of development and attachment, includes additional elements from resilience and trauma theories, and blends into those self-care and CBT treatment plans explained briefly above. The EFT approach serves to mend, in a much deeper way, hearts broken from past hurtful life experiences by clarifying, reframing, and repairing root causes, then connecting those important pieces back to inform the brain to help with present triggers. This 'cardiac' repair gives fresh blood to the brain to think even clearer, and these improved neuropathways in turn strengthen the heart to ensure otherwise overwhelming situations play out in powerfully peaceful ways.

To really understand how the emotionally focused therapy became so effective, one additional piece of theory is worth consideration.

As is widely known, Freud called the parts of self: the id, the ego, and the superego, to delineate between unconscious instincts, the ability to manage those impulses, and internalized ideals respectively.

Carl Rogers, who took a more humanistic approach, broke personality down into the ideal self of who you want to be, the self-image of how you see yourself, and self-esteem of how much you value yourself.

Somewhere in my experience, I started thinking about these different parts of self as the healthy self and the wounded self, with the former coming from the major positive life experiences of unconditional love, achievement, acceptance, and resilience, and the latter from negative exposures of rejection, abandonment, abuse, loss, chaos, blame, and shame.

As a result, the *KG* EFT work begins with clients mapping out the different parts of self for clarity. This process is charted with the client to integrate:

1. the *main historical life experiences* connected with each part of self with
2. the main *emotions* associated with these experiences,
3. the *core beliefs/main perceptions* developed of self, others, life and love from these experiences and emotions and
4. the corresponding patterned *reactions*, characteristic of each part of self. We explore together how these elements are clustered to form *two* different cohesive parts of self—the healthy and wounded selves that informs what we like and dislike, what we love and what bothers us, what we feel when satisfied or in pain, how we think with open curious optimism, or with generalized shame, blame, catastrophe, regret, stinky thinking, or mind reading and what we do to empower vs sabotage ourselves.

Knowledge really is power, so connecting the dots between these experiences, emotions, beliefs, and reactions between the past and present creates aha moments. These important insights link the past wounded self to the present, including the common themes between the main painful events in our histories to those which cause the most disruptive reactions in our current life; the main emotions that troubled us before, to the feelings that overwhelm us the most now; and the core reactions of the past to those we continue to regress to under stress. What is also so important about this is that it invites *deep* self-acceptance, as we exhale into the why we react the way we do. This improved self-compassion underpins the success for clients working at this level and is incredibly powerful to be a part of for the client.

The knowledge and compassion combined makes it possible to complete the remaining parts of the program, reframing and shifting meanings of the hurtful past through numerous EFT methods and ultimately defining and disciplining the specific current improvements to make in one's life.

The chart I provide in the appendices provides details of the developmental stages, examples of significant life experiences, and commonly associated beliefs and actions of both the healthy and wounded self at each of those stages.

Other EFT programs developed in the *KG Method* include the deeper couple and family betrayal healing conversations; Imago approaches to deepen love for couples; and family therapy to help families and blended families through conflicts, separation, and divorce. In addition, the grief program incorporates a developmental perspective which draws heavily on clarifying the past histories of pain and helps us discover empowerment in the loss. Most recently, I developed an additional Imago couple dialoguing tool that uses powerful three-part therapeutic narratives overlapping the past childhood, with current relationship triggers, and future partner dedications toward creating powerful growth otherwise not available in childhood.

Negative core beliefs are particularly important to deconstruct because it is common in states of shock, fear, rage, hurt, and overwhelm to comprehend what is happening. We desperately need to find ways to make things 'fit.' However, due to the sheer neuro-overloading of the event, the brain finds faulty/distorted congruence creating inaccurate conclusions about ourselves, others, life, and love, which we generalize and project onto future similar situations sabotaging ourselves.

One of the most dramatic examples of this is when trauma victims groomed by perpetrators as part of The Accommodation Syndrome often 'make sense' of their abuse by believing that *I* am at fault—something is wrong with *me*. (https://en.wikipedia.org/wiki/Child_sexual_abuse_accommodation_syndrome) Victims are at higher risk of adopting inaccurate shame narratives if they were manipulated and overpowered to not say 'No', they were too afraid to report the abuse, contact with the abuser continued, their bodies were physically aroused by the non-consensual intrusions, or if the people they trusted and disclosed their abuse to did not believe or support them. or, even worse blamed them, and prioritized their own relationship with the offender over supporting the victim. The internalized shame core belief easily leads to poor self-care, and underachieving and pleasing, leaving them at higher risk to be re-abused in the future.

The mapping out can also help us understand why intergenerational patterns exist. For example, men abandoned by their fathers as children who suppress or repress feelings of unworthiness can unfairly feel *re-abandoned* by their adult partners when the partner's attention is temporarily diverted onto otherwise normal, expected places i.e. their work, the home, the children, etc. This unworthiness wound could place them at risk of passive-aggressively acting out these reenactments by cheating on their partners with someone outside the daily family life pressures. This person shows them the *unmet attention* of their father projected onto their partners, and they abandon their partners (and often their children) similar to their father.

Realistically, by the time I see someone in therapy, the pain has usually been years in the making and endured long term, and those secondary and tertiary problems have taken on a life of their own. The wounded self is mostly 'running the show,' causing doubling down spirals (driving the momentum for **Invitations** too easily), even when deep down they know their reactions and decisions are not working for them. The wounded self is tricky in providing usually short-lived emotional pay offs offering tempting rewards of minimizing, denying, suppressing, repressing, avoiding, pleasing, blaming, externalizing, and/or medicating. Better efforts to repair the reenacted hurt, which could not be mended growing up are further sabotaged, and reactions serve to reinforce rather than heal the wound.

For example, the emotionally unconscious employee who finds a false sense of security and momentarily feels better by blaming the manager or team at work for poorly evaluated projects or job loss (denial, minimization, avoiding), when in actual fact they are showing up with underperformance related to unresolved control or worthiness wounds. Without resilient insight, such employees are at higher risk of being terminated from their next place of employment as well, making them feel more out of control and unworthy, depleting their performance further until more serious financial and/or emotional, social consequences have the potential impact of forcing the wake up more dramatically through *invitations for growth*.

The deeper healing program had to be strong enough to outwit these tricks of the wounded self.

There are answers. There are solutions. Recovery and repair are possible. I couldn't keep doing what I do if it didn't make a difference, and the answer is waiting in our healthy self.

In fact, the emotionally focused program at KG uses the dialogue *between* the healthy and wounded self, relying on the client's *own* internal wisdom and resources of their healthy self, to discover, understand, validate, reframe, let go, heal, and repair, which ultimately means *much* more to the client than suggestions from me.

My commitment to my clients is to:

- Help them find something pure that, even if very small, signifies the unconditional goodness within their healthy self to build up from.
- Help them use the discovery of this healthy self to calm their minds and open their hearts, to face and reframe the inaccurate core beliefs of their wounded selves in ways not possible before.
- To deconstruct this in ways without being crushed or overwhelmed as they experienced in the original wounding, by using slow meditative energy to make shifts and liberate.
- Be fierce in helping others who find themselves in ugly shaming/blaming places, by not only leaning into powerful pauses, but moreover talks about the untouchable and touches the untalkable. Do not give up, unless they do, when for good reasons, they are not 'ready'.

- Teach how to bring that healthy self out of the ashes, and to learn how to live more from that part. Therapy should evolve so that the wounded self is healed by the gifts, depersonalizations, wisdom, and the discipline of the healthy self, thereby needing *less* 'airtime' in the client's life while at the same time, augmenting the voice and strength of the healthy self, and giving it the *more* 'airtime' it always deserved but had become lost.
- Guide those who are swinging from the passive to the aggressive side of the wound or vice versa toward finding the powerful assertive healthy place in the middle.
- Help them be specific about what they will be thinking, feeling, and doing differently tomorrow morning as evidence that their healthy self is showing up for them more consistently.
- Not only ensure the healthy self informs the wounded self but that also, the healthy self can be on its own, and stand on its own frequently and regularly, stretching clients into their full potential.

Every day clients learn how to notice, affirm, and expand their best versions of themselves, and that leads to brave choices and educated risks while living at a higher frequency where joy is discovered.

Brené Brown talks about this when she says, "Joy is the highest vulnerable emotion" (Brene Brown, 2017). We embrace and announce our wins knowing they may not turn out or last or get us to what we thought they would, and we still rejoice! I believe the capacity to do this relies heavily on our healthy self, based on internalizing unconditional love for ourselves, believing that we are good enough as we are, having resilience for imperfections, taking educated risks to be at our potential, doing something spectacular and not being crushed if it doesn't work out.

It is the healthy self, after all, that leads the wounded self toward learning how to depersonalize and separate from others' imperfections and set better boundaries in relationships from a place of worthiness instead of shame. This creates create greater possibilities for dynamic careers, deep meaningful friendships, and unconditional loving intimate romance, bringing with them, boundless bundles of joy, which is ultimately what matters the most.

CHAPTER 11
LEARNING TO LIVE AGAIN

…A little party never killed nobody

So we gon' dance until we drop

A little party never killed nobody

Right here, right now's all we got

(Fergie - A Little Party Never Killed Nobody, 2013)

Work Hard, Play Harder

By the time I turned fifty, I began hitting my stride and evolving with fulfillment, success, power, and wealth. I decided to live by the mantra 'Work Hard, Play Harder.' I even designed a tattoo and a licence plate to put this out to the world. With growing pride of my achievements, I knew I was beginning to really make it—and the knowledge of this was exuberating. I would never stop working hard. In fact, I had been working hard for a long time, and the results I was getting with clients, in my business, and in my life spurred me on to take more risks, and ultimately be more.

I had methodically 'worked' (imperfectly) on my health toward stress management, mindfulness, and adaptability, prioritizing my sleep, energy, and living as normally as I could. I recognized this would be a life-long project. It requires continued attention to my needs while embracing the deeper messages of surrendering without defeat, doing more by doing less, having balance and boundaries in the work I do, and having people in my life who supported my self-care. What once felt as a curse was now a gift.

I had become a conscious mother. My daughter was living abroad and was finding balance between her father and me, finding ways to communicate her needs to her partner with courage, finding recognition in her work with ambition, finding maturity to face life's choices with guts, and I was finding a way to remain as a close mother from a distance, reframing separation successfully.

I had built up a new network of friends, post-divorce: bright, successful, moral, mindful, talented women who reflected my confidence and levelled up my standards further. They were my new 'tribe,' and they were terrific.

During the pandemic, I turned lemons into lemonade by renovating my home and organizing fun zoom parties to keep us friends connected.

Over thirty-six years, I had become a bold, tenacious therapist, fiercely fighting for my client's lives every day to ensure they had what they needed to find pathways, freedom, opportunities, choices, and decisions that lit them up in ways previously out of reach or only imagined.

I was so proud of the work I was doing, and I knew from the results I was seeing I was making a real difference that changed peoples' lives. Not only did I witness this in the therapy room when there were breakthroughs, connections, brave decisions reached, risks taken, and joy and love experienced. I regularly received messages outside of sessions from clients about engagements, weddings, promotions, businesses opened, sold-out performances, and babies born. I also heard about divorces, moves, and most of all, suicides prevented because of the work that we did together. All from clients who at one point had come to me depressed, anxious, fearful, isolated, angry, traumatized, or chronically ill. We had turned tragedies into important invitations accepted.

With the help of a business coach, I better understood the true value of the work I was doing and upped my game even more. I wasn't quite sure when or how I would retire, but I wanted *KG & Associates* to grow. I wanted the *KG Method* to leave a legacy of what therapy should look like and lead to in peoples' lives. I wanted to train other therapists to be as effective as I was. I wanted the methods to live on beyond me. To this end, I began hiring associates and that was a beautiful thing. As I now begin to cultivate my retirement vision, I get excited. Serena Williams recently said when she left tournament play, it was more of an evolution than retirement (Nast, 2022). That's right. That fits. The practice will keep evolving and so will I!

The bitch *was* back, but much better than before, a whole lot more refined, mature, and aware, *and* evolved from the highest/deepest level of discovery that she had *always* been enough. I was finally free to be myself, and when that fell into place, there was no stopping me. I was a foolish kid at heart, playing and singing and dancing around the world—literally (as if no one and everyone was listening and watching). Now that I could be myself, everything clicked. Now, it was time to play.

It was like bursting out of a bubble at full speed, acceleration that I had only glimpses of in those childhood days of writing those awesome cards and letters, leading premenstrual seminars at recess, and opening the 'Bachelor Girls' club, but now, on the other side of *invitation number seven*, my healthy self was in full bloom.

I had already traveled to Europe alone.

I had already climbed Ayers' Rock.

I dove the Great Barrier Reef.

I swam with sharks.

I had already bungy jumped over a valley in New Zealand.

I had seen (and heard) lions mating on the plains.

I had watched giant tortoises' mate in the jungles.

Where else could I play?

I spent two days with the Silverback Gorillas in the volcanic mountains of Rwanda.

I joined private safaris in Kenya.

I gave back to a village of female agriculturists in Viet Nam where I exchanged powerful ideas about communism, domestic violence, and addiction with the Chief and women of the village, while the children taught me to fish and my daughter taught them to swim. Madeline's eighteenth birthday. One of *the* best days of my life.

I had been skydiving in Dubai.

I stayed at the only seven-star hotel in the world for a *whole* week and listened to sweet harpists serenade me every morning at breakfast.

I had:

- Laid in the sun rises and sun sets of the Nile, the Dubai glow, the Moroccan desert, and the constant light of the South Pole.
- Ziplined the longest fastest zipline in the world.
- Hiked the Great Wall of China.
- Co-piloted an eighteen-passenger cargo plane to the South Pole (for real).
- Camped at what is deemed as the most isolated place in the planet (the fuel depot coming back from the South Pole).
- Swam for twenty minutes in the Antarctic Ocean before being hauled back to my pod by the physician who accompanied our group of eight travelers who had flown to the continent on a private jet from South Africa to Antarctica. Our two weeks in the monochromatic quietness of Antarctica culminated in that swim in the icy waters which for me was strangely exhilarating and comforting at the same time. Like I was being baptized or something. As onlookers stared on in awe, including plungers who had survived the typical two minutes, I fell into the deepest meditation of my life, releasing left-over, guttural pain from a place deep within that I didn't know was still there. A forensic psychologist and photographer from Manhattan in our group who witnessed my breakthrough gently touched my shoulder as he puffed on his thick cigar and remarked, *"This is why I come back here, every year."*
- Steered a yacht on the Atlantic Ocean off the coast of South Carolina.
- Sat where Forrest Gump's bench used to be in Chippewa Square, Savannah, and cried as I channeled my Inner Gump. He had found home and now I had too!

Working hard and playing harder had been a beautiful thing for a decade and now, as I was turning sixty...

I Wanted More

As I wrote this chapter, I was flying with my BFF to Cairo. She had been there with me for the last fifty-two years, and we were off to the pyramids of Giza, dressed in the matching Egyptian shirts and snake necklaces I had presented to her at our pre-trip cocktail launch. We would laugh and dance our way through what can only be described as unbelievable temples constructed by the Egyptians with unparalleled diligence, determination, and dedications.

As my BFF and I explored the pyramids, tombs, and temples of Egypt, we learned how the early ancient peoples had once lived as frenetic hunters, but when connected to the still waters of the Nile, found a way to stop running and chasing. Even more importantly, when they quieted from within, it opened up deep reflections, leading to unprecedented discoveries about the universe, the planet, the seasons, the spirits, and the documentation of calendars. Only by calming could they progress as humans, leading to thousands of years of advances for the multitude of generations to come.

Later in the expedition, my friend and I traveled on a boat (a Dahabiya) where we lived on the Nile for five nights. We originally braced for what had been predicted as a noisy and rugged ride, but unexpectedly discovered that the vessel was not only quiet, it was silent, and floated effortlessly down the entire river, moving without hardly feeling the movement. I can't honestly put into words what happened over those days. But there was something unforgettable about constantly *floating* for six days down still waters, past those endless, tall, thick, strong yet feathery sage-painted date palms (similar qualities to those trees I had noticed on that monumental bike ride) backed by the soft amber sands, leading to the wonderous temples beyond that settled my spirit in a way that didn't feel entirely possible before.

Later this year, I'm back to Africa, seeing elephants and rhinoceroses in their natural habitats, sitting with the Himba tribe, and supporting Mother's Shelters in isolated villages. While there I will micro-flight over, then sit at the very edge of Victoria Falls in Zambia and helicopter over the unique landscapes in Namibia where the tallest sand dunes in the world meet the ocean, drink champagne atop the mountains at sunset, and sleep under the stars in one of the most remote places on the planet. Then it's off to the Summer Olympics in Paris, see the Foo Fighters in Seattle to hear live *Times Like These* and party with my girl tribe in Nashville.

December 21, 2023, Park Plaza, Toronto, Turning 60

It was my turn to speak. I began with a quote from F. Scott Fitzgerald, *The Curious Case of Benjamin Button:*

"For what it's worth: It's never too late or, in my case, too early to be whoever you want to be. There's no time limit, stop whenever you want. You can change or stay the same, there are no rules to this thing. We can make the best or the worst of it. I hope you make the best of it. And I hope you see things that startle you. I hope you feel things you never felt before. I hope you meet people with a different point of view. I hope you live a life you're proud of. If you find that you're not, I hope you have the courage to start all over again" (The Curious Case of Benjamin Button Screenplay Quotes by Eric Roth, n.d.).

I stood on the large black-and-white squares which within the hour would be filled with nonstop, vibrant dancers twisting and twirling to my favorite tunes. I paused to catch my breath and peeked over my notes. The large golden-yellow globes that spattered light across the ceiling and bounced from the vibration of the room caught my eye. And then, I heard the roar of cheers. The clapping hands blurred as I scanned the crowd right to left and back again.

I continued.

"You see, that's just what I did.

Somehow, twenty years ago I found the strength and courage to:

- Recover my health.
- Rebuild my home.
- Rebuild my family.
- Rebuild my friendships.
- Rebuild my career."

It would be the event of the year. My sixtieth birthday, Gatsby Style.

All of my hard work, courage, faith, strength, and resilience had led me to that very night and beyond.

I had the time of my life, and honestly, everybody else did as well. It filled my heart. Even Gatsby would have approved.

I also know my grandmother was looking down on me that night, cooing and giggling as she always did. Loving me, just loving me.

My Gigi was giving me a nod for all the diligence I had shown, cultivating my own business, and now reaping my own harvest.

My parents were shaking my hand.

My daughter was looking up to me.

My friends were fully embracing me.

But most of all, I was *sizzling* inside. That same sizzle that came from deep hard conversations.

It filled my heart in the exact same way.

Yellow Paint

The yellow paint of my past had long been painted over. The apartment had been closed down for twenty years. It just wasn't needed anymore. The space had since been replaced by a yoga studio, which my daughter designed, with a lush carpet, beautiful rugs, candles and Buddhas, and filled with gifts from friends. That's okay. The yellow walls just weren't needed anymore, and in fact, hadn't been for a long time.

Turns out yellow paint wasn't really paint.

The yellow was in the golden globes bouncing from ceilings, literally glistening in my eyes, reflecting the light and energy back to me, and then back to everyone else dancing with me.

Turns out yellow paint wasn't just in those golden globes.

Yellow paint lived in bubbles and giggles, sidewalks and boats, grit and guts, pickles and love, tribes and commitment, backbones and babies, breezes and bikes.

Turns out yellow paint doesn't just save us.

Turns out yellow paint means just a little bit more.

If we notice, it doesn't just light up the darkness. It awakens our curiosity to go further.

It reveals a pathway previously not seen.

It makes an invitation.

It makes suggestions worth choosing.

It warms our healing.

And on that invitation in the journey, we find our way back home.

We see ourselves fully, for the first time.

Then, we turn up the music to dance.

My story is your story.
My Blackness is your darkness.
My yellow paint is your gift.
And so, I ask you this…

Did you get lost in the darkness?
Did you find your yellow?
Did you pick it up?
What messes did you clean up?
What power did you find?
Are you hunting or reflecting?
Are you bracing or floating?
Are you dancing like a fool?

We get one chance to live.
We get invitations to live again.
I had seven and then woke up

I, I'm a one-way motorway

I'm a road that drives away, then follows you back home

I, I'm a streetlight shining

I'm a wild light, blinding bright, burnin' off and on...

I, I'm a new day rising

I'm a brand-new sky to hang the stars upon tonight…

It's times like these you learn to live again…

(Foo Fighters - Times Like These, 2002, the year I dropped the cord...)

LISTEN ALONG

REFERENCES

5 Ways Narcissists Compensate for Their Inferiority. (2018). Psychology Today.
https://www.psychologytoday.com/ca/blog/communication-
success/201807/5-ways-narcissists-compensate-for-their-inferiority

2000 Books. (2018, April 16). Radical Acceptance - How to develop radical acceptance
as taught by meditation guru Tara Brach. YouTube.
https://www.youtube.com/watch?v=1Y-6IBN45k4

A quote by Oprah Winfrey. (n.d.). Www.goodreads.com.
https://www.goodreads.com/quotes/24752-i-ve-come-to-believe-that-each-
of-us-has-a

AC/DC – Hells Bells. (n.d.). Genius.com. https://genius.com/Ac-dc-hells-bells-lyrics

admin. (n.d.). *How Birth Order Affects Your Personality – Dr. Kevin Leman.*
https://birthorderguy.com/parenting/how-birth-order-affects-your-
personality/

Adrenal Fatigue. (n.d.). Www.endocrine.org. https://www.endocrine.org/patient-
engagement/endocrine-library/adrenal-fatigue

American Psychiatric Association. (2017, November). *Gender Dysphoria Diagnosis.*
Psychiatry.org.
https://www.psychiatry.org/psychiatrists/diversity/education/transgender-
and-gender-nonconforming-patients/gender-dysphoria-diagnosis

Amicable. (2022). Amicable. https://amicable.io/divorce-anxiety

Bellini, S. (2023). Making (and Keeping) Friends: A Model for Social Skills Instruction:
Articles: Indiana Resource Center for Autism: Indiana University Bloomington.
Indiana Resource Center for Autism.
https://www.iidc.indiana.edu/irca/articles/making-and-keeping-friends.html

Blue Zones Project. (2021, November 4). Dan Buettner. https://danbuettner.com/blue-
zones/blue-zones-projects/

Bob Seger & the Silver Bullet Band - Shame on the Moon Lyrics & Meanings | Song
Meanings. (2024). Song Meanings.
https://songmeanings.com/songs/view/3530822107858933430/

Brene Brown. (2012). Daring Greatly: How the Courage to Be Vulnerable Transforms
the Way We Live, Love, Parent, and Lead. Penguin Random House Audio
Publishing Group.

Brene Brown. (2017). Braving the wilderness: The quest for true belonging and the
courage to stand alone. Random House.

British Vogue. (2019, August 21). *Brené Brown on Vulnerability And Coping With Social
Media Cruelty*. British Vogue. https://www.vogue.co.uk/arts-and-
lifestyle/article/brene-brown-writes-for-vogue

Bruns, J. R., & Richards, R. A. (2010). *Tiger Woods syndrome: why men prowl and how to not
become the prey*. Health Communications, Inc.

Canada, (2024). *Changes to family laws*. Justice.gc.ca. https://www.justice.gc.ca/eng/fl-
df/cfl-mdf/index.html

Caudill, M., & Benson, H. (2016). *Managing pain before it manages you*. The Guilford Press.

Cherry, K. (2024). *Erikson's stages of development*. Very Well Mind.
https://www.verywellmind.com/erik-eriksons-stages-of-psychosocial-
development-2795740

Christina Perri - you are my sunshine. (n.d.). Www.youtube.com.
https://www.youtube.com/watch?v=uqvfbIuJd6Y

Cleveland Clinic. (2023, April 10). *What Are Natural Killer Cells (NK Cells)?* Cleveland
Clinic. https://my.clevelandclinic.org/health/body/24898-natural-killer-cells

Coloroso, B. (2010). *kids are worth it! Revised Edition*. Harper Collins.

Depression after divorce. (2023, June 14). Www.medicalnewstoday.com.
https://www.medicalnewstoday.com/articles/depression-after-divorce

Divorce Law in Canada (96-3e). (n.d.). Publications.gc.ca.
https://publications.gc.ca/Pilot/LoPBdP/CIR/963-e.htm

Dr. Alison Bested - Environmental Health Institute Canada. (2023, September 11).
ENVIRONMENTAL HEALTH INSTITUTE of CANADA (EHI-
CANADA) - Partnering towards Healthier People in Healthier Places.
https://www.ehicanada.com/dr-alison-bested/

Eminem - Lose Yourself Lyrics & Meanings | Song Meanings. (2002, September 22). Song
Meanings. https://songmeanings.com/songs/view/3530822107858481075/

Explore the Blue Zones in the 4-Part Netflix Docu-Series. (n.d.). Blue Zones. https://www.bluezones.com/documentary/

Fact Sheet: Vicarious Trauma. (2021). https://www.cdcr.ca.gov/bph/wp-content/uploads/sites/161/2021/10/Trauma-Fact-Sheets-October-2021.pdf

Fergie, Q-Tip & Listenbee – A Little Party Never Killed Nobody (All We Got). (2024). Genius. https://genius.com/Fergie-q-tip-and-listenbee-a-little-party-never-killed-nobody-all-we-got-lyrics

Fibromyalgia and Sleep: Sleep Disturbances & Coping. (2020, November 20). Sleep Foundation. https://www.sleepfoundation.org/physical-health/fibromyalgia-and-sleep

Flaherty, S. C., & Sadler, L. S. (2010). A Review of Attachment Theory in the Context of Adolescent Parenting. *Journal of Pediatric Health Care, 25*(2), 114–121. https://doi.org/10.1016/j.pedhc.2010.02.005

Foo Fighters – Times Like These. (n.d.). Genius.com. https://genius.com/Foo-fighters-times-like-these-lyrics

for, D. (2023, November 2). *DHEA for Women: Could DHEA Help Boost Your Mood, Focus, Libido, Fertility, and Energy?* Drjennarayachoti.com. https://drjennarayachoti.com/blog/dhea-for-women

Fresh Start Therapy & Consulting. (2017). Fresh Start Therapy & Consulting. https://ruxandralemay.com/men-physical-intimacy

Gill, T., & Hosker, T. (2021, February 10). *How ADHD May Be Impacting Your Child's Social Skills and What You Can Do to Help.* Foothills Academy. https://www.foothillsacademy.org/community/articles/adhd-social-skills

Girl on Fire. (2012, September 4). Genius. https://genius.com/Alicia-keys-girl-on-fire-lyrics

Grassini, S. (2022). A Systematic Review and Meta-Analysis of Nature Walk as an Intervention for Anxiety and Depression. *Journal of Clinical Medicine, 11*(6), 1731. https://doi.org/10.3390/jcm11061731

how brands do communication with female consumers. (2024, March). Mintel. https://www.mintel.com/consumer-market-news/she-power-is-influencing-the-world-how-brands-do-communications-with-female-consumers

Howe, N., Recchia, H., & Kinsley, C. (2023, March). *Peer Relations | Sibling Relations and Their Impact on Children's Development.* Encyclopedia on Early Childhood Development. https://www.child-encyclopedia.com/peer-relations/according-experts/sibling-relations-and-their-impact-childrens-development

Human Dignity Trust. (2022). *A history of LGBT criminalisation*. Human Dignity Trust. https://www.humandignitytrust.org/lgbt-the-law/a-history-of-criminalisation/

Interpersonal Effectiveness. (n.d.). DBT. https://dialecticalbehaviortherapy.com/interpersonal-effectiveness/

Jimmy Cliff - I Can See Clearly Now lyrics | Musixmatch. (2016). Musixmatch.com. https://www.musixmatch.com/lyrics/Jimmy-Cliff/I-Can-See-Clearly-Now

Kabat-Zinn, J. (2013). Full catastrophe living: Using the wisdom of your body and mind to face stress, pain, and illness. Bantam Books.

Kinsey Institute. (2009). *The Kinsey Scale*. Kinseyinstitute.org. https://kinseyinstitute.org/research/publications/kinsey-scale.php

Kinsey, A. C. (1948). *Sexual behavior in the human male*. W.B. Saunders.

Lee, C. I. (2023, April 24). *How Attachment Style Shows Up in Friendships*. LA Concierge Psychologist. https://laconciergepsychologist.com/blog/attachment-style-friendships/

Leman, K. (2015). The birth order book: why you are the way you are. Revell.

Leonard Cohen – Ain't No Cure for Love. (2024). Genius. https://genius.com/Leonard-cohen-aint-no-cure-for-love-lyrics

Lewis, K. (n.d.). *Parental Alienation Can Be Emotional Child Abuse*. https://www.ncsc.org/__data/assets/pdf_file/0014/42152/parental_alienation_Lewis.pdf

Lewis, R. (2023). *Erikson stages of psychosocial development in plain language*. Healthline. https://www.healthline.com/health/parenting/erikson-stages

Life Changes Stress Test. (n.d.). Behavioral Healthcare Providers. https://www.bhpcare.com/patient-information/self-management-tools/life-changes-stress-test/

MacKinnon, E. (2011, December 8). *Do Ocean Waves Really Travel in Sets of 7?* Livescience.com. https://www.livescience.com/33624-waves-ocean-sets-seven.html

Maya Angelou Quotes. (n.d.). Brainy Quote. https://www.brainyquote.com/quotes/maya_angelou_383371

Mayo Clinic. (2022, December 13). *Complicated Grief - Symptoms and Causes*. Mayo Clinic. https://www.mayoclinic.org/diseases-conditions/complicated-grief/symptoms-causes/syc-20360374

McLeod, S. (2024, January 24). *John Bowlby's attachment theory*. Simply Psychology. https://www.simplypsychology.org/bowlby.html

Mcleod, S. (2024, January 25). *Erik Erikson's Stages of Psychosocial Development*. Simply Psychology. https://www.simplypsychology.org/Erik-Erikson.html

Mittleman, J. (2023). Sexual Fluidity: Implications for Population Research. *Demography*, *60*(4), 1257–1282. https://doi.org/10.1215/00703370-10898916

Monte, T. (2016, October 12). *The 7-Year Cycles of Life*. Tom Monte. https://tommonte.com/the-7-year-cycles-of-life/

Myalgic encephalomyelitis/chronic fatigue syndrome (ME/CFS) - Diagnosis and treatment - Mayo Clinic. (2024). Mayoclinic.org. https://www.mayoclinic.org/diseases-conditions/chronic-fatigue-syndrome/diagnosis-treatment/drc-20360510I

Nast, C. (2022, August 9). *Serena Williams's Farewell to Tennis—In Her Own Words*. Vogue. https://www.vogue.com/article/serena-williams-retirement-in-her-own-words

Paulhus, D. L., Trapnell, P. D., & Chen, D. (1999). Birth Order Effects on Personality and Achievement Within Families. *Psychological Science*, *10*(6), 482–488. https://doi.org/10.1111/1467-9280.00193

PCL-R Demonstrates Inadequate Field Reliability and Validity. (2017). *Paloaltou.edu*. https://doi.org/1006098818/module_167992454520_PGP_-_Super_Nav_-_graphql

Randy Newman – You've Got a Friend in Me. (n.d.). Genius.com. https://genius.com/Randy-newman-youve-got-a-friend-in-me-lyrics

Real, T. (2003). I don't want to talk about it: overcoming the secret legacy of male depression. Fireside.

Rod Stewart - Sailing Lyrics & Meanings | Song Meanings. (2004, December 28). Song Meanings. https://songmeanings.com/songs/view/64122/

Saakvitne, K. W., & Pearlman, L. A. (1996). *Transforming the pain: a workbook on vicarious traumatization*. W.W. Norton & Company.

Stangor, C., & Walinga, J. (2014). *The Origins of Personality*. Opentextbc.ca; BC campus. https://opentextbc.ca/introductiontopsychology/chapter/11-2-the-origins-of-personality/

Statista Research Department. (2022, May 9). *Ukraine War Casualties 2022*. Statista; Statista. https://www.statista.com/statistics/1293492/ukraine-war-casualties/

The Curious Case of Benjamin Button Screenplay Quotes by Eric Roth. (n.d.). Www.goodreads.com. https://www.goodreads.com/work/quotes/56454126-the-curious-case-of-benjamin-button-screenplay

The Rolling Stones - Paint It Black Lyrics & Meanings | Song Meanings. (2013, February 27). Song Meanings. https://songmeanings.com/songs/view/41035/

The Tension of Opposites – Bram Levinson. (2022). Bramlevinson.com. https://bramlevinson.com/the-tension-of-opposites/

Ukraine civilian war casualties 2022. (n.d.). Statista. https://www.statista.com/statistics/1293492/ukraine-war-casualties

Vikström, L., Shah, S., & Janssens, A. (2020). Introduction: disability, partnership, and family across time and space. *The History of the Family, 25*(2), 177–201. https://doi.org/10.1080/1081602x.2020.1761427

Wallerstein, J. S., & Blakeslee, S. (2006). *The good marriage: how & why love lasts.* Grand Central Pub.

Wass, V. (2020). A crisis is an opportunity riding a dangerous wind. (Chinese proverb). *Education for Primary Care*, 31(6), 331–331. https://doi.org/10.1080/14739879.2020.1852607

What is Imago? - Harville and Helen. (2022, March 15). Harville and Helen. https://harvilleandhelen.com/initiatives/what-is-imago

Wikipedia Contributors. (2019, December 22). *Chelation therapy.* Wikipedia; Wikimedia Foundation. https://en.wikipedia.org/wiki/Chelation_therapy

APPENDICES

A/ How to Assess Your Own Invitations for Growth

Invitations for growth. Determined by key life experiences including, but not exclusive to major rejections, betrayals, unresolved endings, health crises, mental health crises, traumas, losses, etc. A good way to recognize experiences as invitations is by seeing if they took otherwise underdeveloped or fairly positive beliefs, you were holding about yourself, others, life and love and destroyed them. In turn, these changed beliefs cause and worsen aggressive, passive or passive aggression reactions to future stress.

Combined, these crises, the associated negative beliefs and the poor coping, place you at higher risk for future problems, usually more serious. That is why if you don't heal from the first invitation, the next ones will hit you harder. However, it is these *same* events that invite growth. It is where the pain is at its greatest that we are challenged to dig deep to uncover underlying opportunities to strengthen our beliefs, in ways that were not previously obvious to us. The growth not only prevents future major negative experiences; it raises us up to resilience, peak performance and joy.

Below are the major events described in this book, how they related to the significantly negative experiences of my life, the corresponding invitations that were offered, those that were not 'received', and the one that was. I invite you to consider yours!

Theme	Mine	Invitation Offered	Invitation Not Accepted/ Accepted	Yours
1. Rejections	Brothers' Rejections	**Invitation:** Others' rejections are not about Me. I am good enough as I am... Others don't get me for other reasons. (Birth Order, Age Difference, Gender) **Invited To:** Show up to Share and Connect with Others from Worthiness not Shame. *KG* Deeper Healing, (Chapter 10)	**Internalized:** Personalization I don't belong. I'm not good enough. Others will reject me. Life is lonely. **Led Me To:** Cling Control/ Dominate	Add Yours Here
2. Unresolved Losses Creating, Shame, Complicated Grief, Depression	Grandma's Death, the *lost* last 'Good-Bye'	**Invitation:** Shock, Fear and Disbelief Immobilized me and that is normal, especially as a teen, especially with past insufficient rewards for emotional expression. Fear is a Shared Experience. Regret without Shame. **Invited To:** Self-Compassion to reduce Shame, Accept	**Internalized:** Shame of self and Fear of Endings I am weak. Others will leave. Life is loss. Endings are unbearable. **Led Me To:** Feel less worthy due to increase shame and fear.	Add Yours Here

		Imperfection, Reframe the meaning of the Good-Bye (The Normalizing, Precipitating, Benefitting *KG* Shame Tool introduced in Chapter 4) Face fears. Find the 'bearable' in endings to reduce avoidance of endings.	Avoidance of Endings/ Stayed in Unhealthy Relationships to Avoid the Ending	
3. Betrayals	First Love Cheater (High School)	**Invitation:** Others Get in my Way because of their Broken Journeys, I Deserve Better **Invited To:** End Relationship when Multiple Lies are Revealed. Level Up Expectations in Future Relationships (*KG* Grounding Grief Tool introduced in Chapter 6) (Depersonalize others poor actions (KG Deeper Healing Chapter 10)	**Internalized:** Personalization I will Never Be Chosen. Others are Better Than Me Love hurts. **Led Me To:** Stay, Accept Manipulation Beg to be Loved Go on to date Authors	Add Yours Here

4. Major Endings	Best Chance at Marriage Lost (the 1989 Break Up)	**Invitation:** Understand why the conflict stage occurs in relationships and work it out before the relationship ends, or Ground the Grief - Discover how endings reflect Shared Contributions from Deeper Wounds and Missed Invitations in the Attractions/Frustrations of the relationship	**Internalized:** Personalization I am alone. Men leave me. Love isn't Attainable for Me. There's No Point to Love.	Add Yours Here
		Invited To: Be curious instead of angry. *KG* Couple CBT and Imago Program, (Chapter 6) *Or* Leave with Self Worth Intact. Develop Insight to have a more conscious Relationship Next Time *KG* Grounding Grief, Introduced in Chapter 6, CBT, (First Introduced in Chapter 2), Deeper Healing Programs (Chapter 10)	**Led Me To:** Medicate with Sex and Alcohol	

| 5. Traumas | Sexually Transmitted Infection | Invitation: Repair Shame and Improve Confidence, Find a Healthy Sense of Control without Passivity, Passive Aggression or Aggression. Work Through Rage
Invited To: Communicate Directly with Husband about the Blame and Shame
Or
Leave the Relationship with Confidence
KG Shame Tool (Chapter 4) Couple CBT, Imago Programs (Chapter 6) Grief Tool (introduced in Chapter 6) | Internalized: Shame I Hate Me I Hate Him No One Else Will Want Me This is The Best I can do. Make This Work.

Led Me To: Bury Deny Minimize Fake Displace Rage | Add Yours Here |
| 6. Catastrophic Health Crisis | Chronic Fatigue Syndrome | Invitation: Hear the Cues from the Body: to reduce Anxiety, Find Balance, Support and Mindfulness. Reframe Control Less is More
Invited To: Leave Marriage Leave Job | Internalized: Avoidance I'll Get Better Keep Pushing More is More

Led Me To: Ignore Cues, Work Harder, Ignore Gut | Add Yours Here |

		Seek Medical Attention for Symptoms Sooner Practice Mindfulness *KG* Self-Care (Chapter 9) CBT (Chapter 2) DBT, (Chapter 7) VT (Chapter 9), Deeper Healing Programs (Chapter 10) Grief Tool (introduced in Chapter 6) Surrender Without Defeat (Introduced in Chapter 9)	Feelings, Stay in Marriage, Stay in Job	
7. Catastrophic Loss, Loss of Control	Pregnancy Loss and Divorce	Invitation: Don't Give Up When All is Lost Use the Power behind Not Giving Up Finding Joy Use Hard Work and Unconditional Love from my Legacy to find Resilience Let Go of Shame to Face Endings Invited To: Work Hard Play Harder Learn to Live Again	Invitation Accepted! I am worthy I can have control without overcontrolling Others can be trusted. Love is possible. Life is incredible. Endings are bearable. Led Me To: Internal Calming Depersonalization Setting of healthy boundaries Taking educated Risks	Add Yours Here

		Opened the Invitation Toward: Improved Self-Care Maximizing Sleep, Eliminating Gluten, Pacing Corrected Negative Thoughts of Shame and Blame, Stinky Thoughts of Control and Perfectionism, 5minute daily CBT Tracks Emotional Regulation from Radical Acceptance, Surrender without Defeat, 2minute Meditations for Breathing, Self-Compassion, Self-Affirmation and Wise Gut Channelling Grounded Grief Repaired Shame Conscious Parenting Depersonalized with Legacy, Birth Order, Gender Roles, and Alternative Explanations to reduce shame, loss	Modeling direct conflict resolution without aggression Modeling vulnerability Using Steady Patience Separating Self if Relationship is Unhealthy Backbone Parenting Being the best version of me Ultimate Freedom Striving for Excellence	

		of control and unworthiness, Deeper Mindfulness of my Illness Rebuild Health, Home, Family, Friends, Business, Follow Wise Gut, Use You've Learned to Inspire Others. **Everything in This Book!** Acknowledging I am A Work in Progress		

B/ How Life Experiences at Different Developmental Stages Relate to Typical Adult Core Beliefs and Behaviors

Based on the 6 developmental stages discussed in this book, adapted from Erickson's Psychosocial Stages of Development (Lewis, 2023b).

Trust, Control, Autonomy, Worthiness, Identity and Intimacy.

Use this chart to:

- understand how positive and negative life experiences, at certain ages
- make impacts on the corresponding positive and negative development of teenage, young adult and adult core beliefs and behaviors
- of the healthy and wounded parts of self.

(Common examples of the beliefs and behaviors of the two parts of self are provided).

Over time, one of the parts of self, becomes predominant.

This a progressive model; success at a previous stage increases mastery at a subsequent stage. Lack of success, failure or disruption at a previous stage reduces mastery at a subsequent stage. Major crises and traumas cause fixation on/regression to an earlier stage of development and the wounded self takes over. Emotionally Focused Therapy draws on the components and resilience of the Healthy Self to repair the Wounded Self.

Area of Impact	Healthy Self	Wounded Self
1. Trust vs Mistrust (birth to 3 years)	Trust	Distrust
Major Life Experiences	Secure Attachments	• Anxious Avoidant Disorganized Attachments • Inconsistent Responses • Distance • Unreliable or Abusive Caretakers • Abandonment • Separations
Core Beliefs	"I can trust myself and I believe in the goodness of people." "People earn their trust with me by being consistent, reliable, and encouraging to me." "Life is Predictable" "Love is Consistent and Available".	**Aggressive Side of the Wounded Self:** "I can't depend on others." • "Others can't be trusted." • "Life is better when you don't rely on others." • "Love is too dangerous; I'll just get let down." **Passive Side of the Wounded Self:** • "I can't trust anyone." or "I trust everyone regardless of how they show up." • "Others never do what they say will." Or "Others don't mean to hurt me (even though they are) • "Life is scary." Or "Life is perfect." • "Love isn't possible." "Love is everywhere." **Passive/Aggressive Side of the Wounded Self:** • "I'm not sure if I can trust anyone or not." • "Others confuse me." • "Life confuses me." • "Love is a game."
Behavior	Secure Relationships Good boundaries based on a mutual level of direct	Rigid Avoidant Anxious Connections **Aggressive Side of the Wounded Self:** • High Conflict/Punish by directly disengaging.

	engagement with trust, confidence, and empathy.	Passive Side of the Wounded Self: Disengage to hide *Or* Enmeshment with Others • Losing self • Over agreeability and • Ignoring red flags Passive/Aggressive Side of the Wounded Self: • Test, Resent, Lie, Set Up
2. Control (2 years to 8 years)		
Major Life Experiences	Moderate Control Safety. Predictability. Age-Appropriate, Choice-Making Opportunities.	Over or Under Control Rigid Overbearing Expectations *Or* Chaos Poor Conflict Resolution Dysregulated Caretakers Multiple Moves
Core Beliefs	Moderate Control "I can't control everything, I accept what I can't, and I can empower myself and others in things that are important to me." "Others share opinions with me that I can take or leave." "Life is about choices." "Love is about finding our unique way of combining our preferences."	Over or Under Control Aggressive Side of the Wounded Self: • "I have to control everything otherwise the outcome will be wrong or chaotic." • "Others stand in my way." • "Life is better if you have the upper hand." • "Love is fine as long as I'm in charge" Passive Side of the Wounded Self: • "I can't control anything. • "I have no control" • "Others' needs are more important." • "Life is scary; there's too many risks." • "Love is scary too; too many chances to get hurt which I have no control over."

		Passive/Aggressive Side of the Wounded Self: • "I need more control, but it would be dangerous to advertise that." "I should just agree even if I don't. • "Others should just decide." • "Life is too unpredictable." • "Love is too risky."
Behavior	Moderate Control Display positive Leadership with flexibility and openness to team members' ideas. Negotiate and advocate for myself and others by constructively speaking up, deciding, and planning toward getting me closer to what I really want in life.	Over Powering or Powerless Aggressive Side of the Wounded Self: • Overworking/overdoing • Controlling • Demanding/Dominating • Perfecting • Obsessing • Burning out • Chronic pain and illness Passive Side of the Wounded Self: • Underachieving and passivity • Being conflict avoidant • Poor self-care and discipline • Procrastinate • Please Passive/Aggressive Side of the Wounded Self: • Eating disorder • Passive aggressive communication • Silent treatment • Backhanded comments • Agree but Resent • Sarcasm

3. Autonomy (6 to 12 years)		
Major Life Experiences	Interdependence Sharing. Co-operative. Interdependent and Appropriately Dependent and Independent. Determination is Valued and Modelled.	Over or Under Dependence Restriction by others. Over taking by others. *Or* Models of Over Selflessness.
Core Beliefs	Interdependence "Even when there are limited resources, we can each find a way to meet our mutual goals."	Over Independence or Dependence Aggressive Side of the Wounded Self: • "Every man for himself." • "Others need too much." • "Life is better on my own." • "Love isn't possible." Passive Side of the Wounded Self: • "Nobody cares what I need." • "What you need is most important." • "Life is better off alone." • "Love is determined by someone else." Passive/Aggressive Side of the Wounded Self: • "I don't know what I want, but I don't really want what you want either." • "I'll pitch in, but do what I want regardless" • "Life is better off alone." • "Love isn't possible."
Behavior	Interdependence Sharing Co-operating Negotiating	Over Independence or Dependence Aggressive Side of the Wounded Self: • Dominating • Selfish • Stubborn • Clinging Passive Side of the Wounded Self: • Having Trouble Receiving • Avoiding • Isolating

		• Overly Adaptive/Social Chameleon **Passive/Aggressive Side of the Wounded Self:** • Appear Interested, but delay procrastinate tasks
4. Worthiness (10 to 16 years)		
Major Life Experiences	Worthiness Positive and consistent acknowledgment, acceptance and validation. Unconditional Love.	Unworthiness Criticism and judgment/shame received or modelled. Being ostracized. Others taking little to no responsibility for their actions Others showing little empathy listening or acceptance. Failures. Rejection. Betrayal.
Core Beliefs	Worthiness "Doing my best is good enough." "Others are doing their best too."	Unworthiness **Aggressive Side of the Wounded Self:** • "I'm perfect." • "Something's wrong with everyone." • "Life goes better when others agree with me." • "Love serves me first." **Passive Side of the Wounded Self:** • "Something's wrong with me " • "I'm not good enough." • "Others just lie anyway." • "Life is too hard." • "Love is too hurtful. They'll just leave me anyway once they get to know me." **Passive Aggressive Side of the Wounded Self:** • "I'm not getting what I deserve." • "Others don't understand." • "Let's see if they can figure out what I need." • "I didn't think my partner would do what I needed."

Behavior	Worthiness	Unworthiness
	Good performance. Taking educated risks. Open communication. Flexibility and acceptance when mistakes are made without judgment.	**Aggressive Side of the Wounded Self:** • Arguing • Overworking • Narcissism • Seek Unhealthy Relationships **Passive Side of the Wounded Self:** • Internalizing feelings • Sabotaging • Hiding from social opportunities • Underperforming • Over accommodating **Passive/Aggressive Side of the Wounded Self:** • Cheating • Lying • Testing • Faking
5. Identity (13 to 18 years)		
Major Life Experiences	Clear Identity Freedom to explore who you want to be with encouragement and support.	Confusion Being shamed, judged, punished when exploring.
Core Beliefs	Clear Identity "I love who I am, and I am free and open to learning more about myself." "Others let me explore and experiment." "Life is fun." "Love creates space for me to be me."	Confusion **Aggressive Side of the Wounded Self:** • "I don't know who I am, but I will find out one way or another." • "Others know who they are., so I better figure myself out anyway I can." Or "Others are losers." • "Life is there to explore at any costs." • "Love is my playground." **Passive Side of The Wounded Self:** • "I don't know who I am, and I'm scared to find out."

| | | • "It's only a matter of time before people find out that I don't know what I'm doing."
• Others don't care to get to know me."
• "Life has too many choices."
• "Love just swallows you up."
Passive/Aggressive Side of The Wounded Self:
• "I'll try to figure out who I am without showing it." "I'll have to be someone I'm not."
• "Others won't get me."
• "Life is fake."
• "Love is lie."" |
| --- | --- | --- |
| Behavior | Clear Identity
Excelling, promoting self for success
Learning, and safely exploring.
Experimenting without severe risks. | Confusion
Aggressive Side of the Wounded Self:
• High risk lifestyle
Passive Side of the Wounded Self:
• Suffering with Imposter Syndrome
• Low risk living
• Under-performing
• Overcompensating
Passive/Aggressive Side of the Wounded Self:
• Fake internet identity/persona
• Hurtful impersonating
• Compulsive lying |
| 6. Intimacy
(18 to 40 years) | | |
| Major Life Experiences | Intimacy
Deep authentic connections.
Vulnerability is encouraged and rewarded.
Healthy Intimacy; close without intrusion or rejection. | Isolation
Superficial communication.
Betrayal or being punished for sharing. |

Core Beliefs	Intimacy	Isolation
	"I can be imperfect myself and accept others for who they are too." "Others care about me." "Life is meaningful." "Love lets me reveal myself. The vulnerability of that deeply fulfills me."	**Aggressive Side of the Wounded Self:** • "It's all About Me." • "Others are too emotional." • Life goes better my way." • "Love goes better when my partner agrees with me." **Passive Side of the Wounded Self:** • "I'm unlovable." • "Others won't love me for who I am." • "It's better to keep your feelings to yourself." • "Love hurts too much." **Passive/Aggressive Side of the Wounded Self:** • "I'm not getting my needs met. • "If they don't love me, I'll find someone else who will." • "If I have to tell my partner what I need, there's no point." • "Life is a game." • "Love means I never have to be alone."
Behavior	Intimacy	Isolation
	Vulnerable sharing and active listening of fears, needs and joys without being crushed or crushing.	**Aggressive Side of the Wounded Self:** • Oversharing • Lack of reciprocity • Over-argue • Judge others • Crushing **Passive Side of the Wounded Self:** • Under sharing • Superficial relationships • Isolating self • Avoiding • Cancelling social plans • Deflecting • Crushed by truth **Passive/Aggressive Side of the Wounded Self:** • Infidelity

		• Indirect communication • Testing

C/ The Cognitive Behavioral Therapy Template

CUES	**CHANGE YOUR LIFE** BRAIN- BODY- BEHAVIOR-
HONEYMOON	TIME AND SPACE AWAY!- Immediate Removal from Immediate Environment
ADJUST	Bring stress 6/10 PHYSICALLY DISCHARGE- *Or* VISUALLY SOOTHE- *Or* DISTRACTION- physical- positive person- mental task- cathartic task-
NEW THOUGHT	ONE SENTENCE FACT- present specific factual thought – police report, film script of blocking, chronology (neutral)
GOAL	WHAT DO I REALLY WANT? - Micro/ Macro- for myself, from myself
EMPOWER	SPEAKING – - 'I' MESSAGE TO SOMEONE - EDUCATE ON IMPACT "I feel ____ when you ____" - MAKE A REQUEST "What I need from you is____" ACTIVELY LISTEN TO PARTNER'S /FAMILY MEMBER'S 'I' MESSAGES *Or* DECIDING -DECISION MAKING *Or* PLANNING - FUTURE PLANNING

D/ Pathway from CBT Change Program to Dialoguing

Improves Communication for Families

Improves Communication and Intimacy for Couples

TRIGGER (C!) – Brain, Body and Behavioral Cues of a Trigger Occur

'H' – A code word, phrase or gesture is called to force a needed break

CBT   **CBT**

A   A

N   N

G   G

E   E

"I'm ready to talk, are you?"

DIALOUGUE; "I feel/felt_____ when you _____ (ed)...."

GLOSSARY

Birth Order Effect – The theory that the number, ages, place in the sibling line, twins, births and deaths of siblings plays a role in shaping our mental, social, and emotional health.

Cognitive Behavioral Therapy – The therapeutic approach that rests on the premise that what we think, determines how we feel, determines what we do. Correcting negative unrealistic thoughts supports healthier, more assertive actions.

Coloroso Parenting – A style of parenting developed by Barbara Coloroso who defined back bone parenting to help parents set boundaries while helping build good decision-making skills and self-esteem for their children.

Dialectical Behavioral Therapy – An evidence-based model of therapy that focuses on emotional regulation including: addressing physical needs and toxic relationships/habits, negative thought correction, mindfulness, distress tolerance and interpersonal scripting.

Emotionally-Focused Therapy – Focuses on understanding and shifting deeper emotions for therapeutic change through: reflection, awareness, expression, and correction.

Enmeshment – Blurred boundaries between people where there is overinvolvement due to an individual subconsciously using another to meet their deeper unmet needs. Individuality is undermined. There is loss of self and overdependence that impedes normal development.

Family Systems Theory – A theoretical therapy approach that focuses on the family members as parts and roles of an overall system and explains how different parts affect others toward maintaining balance, functioning, and homeostasis.

Fear of Engulfment – Fear of losing a sense of self through a violation of personal boundaries. Most commonly experienced by individuals whose boundaries were enmeshed with parents/sibling/early friendships growing up. As adults, these individuals unconsciously/consciously assume intimacy with another will replicate the same dynamic and usually avoid close relationship to manage the fear.

Grounding Grief – Emotional anchoring of shame and blame to facilitate emotional growth from the ending of a relationship. This reduces acting out the grief. This prevents complicated grief and subsequent depression. The ending is neutralized by identifying:
- the clues of failure,
- the corresponding invitations for growth,
- the frustrations with each other,
- the tipping point,
- how and why the invitations were not used,
- how the individuals' histories explained the attractions to each other,
- and, most importantly what the 'take-away' or power is now to move on, taking the underlying lesson of the unused invitation not possible in this relationship, into your life and into your next relationship.

Imago Therapy – A theory developed by Harville Hendrix that suggests we consciously or unconsciously attract partners who replicate the kind of love (good and bad) which we experienced as children to give us opportunities to grow.

Radical Acceptance – A key component of Dialectical Behavioral Therapy rests on the premise that emotional regulation is improved when worthiness embraces imperfection, accepts what is beyond our control and releases judgment.

Self-Care Therapy – The part of therapy that addresses basic needs of healthy eating, restorative sleeping, regular exercise, good work/life balance for positive interactions, and taking charge of treating medical needs, illness and injuries.

About Karen/KG Method

I knew from the age of fourteen that I yearned to have deep conversations about real issues that made a real difference. So, as a teenager, I contributed as much as I could to the communities in which I lived. In 1986, I became a clinical social worker, graduating from McMaster University with dual Honour degrees in Sociology and Social Work (BA, BSW).

After receiving my master's degree in social work at the University of Toronto in 1990, I worked in the field of interpersonal trauma, providing comprehensive individual, group, couple, and family therapy to victims, offenders and their families for over a decade. I opened my private practice in 1998, the year my daughter was born, and I never looked back. I knew I had a gift. I would help people make sense of their complicated lives that would invigorate them to make the changes they had been looking for a long time but didn't know how. I would guide them on a deeply passionate and accountable journey of mastering self-care strategies, and transforming reactive patterns into intentional choices. Together, we would cultivate compassion, acceptance, and strength in facing their struggles, grounding their grief into empowerment. From there, we would safely navigate the raw depths of shame and rage, uncovering a path to meaningful, lasting success and joy.

I have the best job in the world sitting next to brave humans who are in deep pain every day, supporting them toward making choices and decisions with purpose, worthiness, and true freedom. I also knew that what I knew was worth sharing beyond the therapy room.

So, I got behind my own *Yellow Paint* to write this book.

A graduate of McMaster University and the University of Toronto, Goslin began her career in children's mental health and intergenerational trauma before founding her private practice, KG & Associates, in 1998. Goslin adapts evidence-based treatment approaches, creating leading-edge programs and tools which combined, form the *KG Accountable Therapy* Method.

She has fiercely dedicated her professional career to ensuring those suffering with anxiety, depression, rage, shame, betrayal, addiction, chronic illness, grief and trauma, find clear pathways through their struggles. To be *informed* by increasingly more serious invitations from the pain. To make brave choices toward creating and sustaining their best lives.

Ultimately, Goslin's work creates safe, deep, honest spaces that allow her clients to move beyond exploring important connections, beyond making powerful reframes, toward making life-changing decisions. Convinced her *KG accountable therapy* method was powerful enough to take beyond the therapy room, she is now sharing the skills and insights she has gained through her own personal journey and professional work in *Yellow Paint: Learning to Live Again.*